DEAR READER,

I am very pleased to offer this, the second edition of *The Everything® Investing in Your 20s & 30s Book*. I've been involved with the financial market since 1987, and I wish this book had been available then, for it is truly written for people who want to not just learn about investments but to have a **hands-on, how-to guide** from which to build a base and grow their wealth.

Let's be frank: the financial markets are influenced more than ever by the **rapid spread of information**. The markets are evolving on an almost daily basis from constantly shifting politics, changes in trade relationships, and rising interest rates. Thus, prices tend to move rapidly, and investors without the right information and training on how to use that information could face big losses.

But if you have the **right information** and know how to use it, you can set yourself up for success throughout the rest of your life. Whether you want to learn about the basics of budgeting, mutual funds, stocks, bonds, and real estate, or more complex investing options such as cryptocurrencies, sector investing, college savings plans, and commodities, learning about investing now is essential to building wealth. I sincerely hope you enjoy this book and that it helps you to start your wealth-building on a great note.

Sincerely,
J. Duarte, MD
JoeDuarteintheMoneyOptions.com

WELCOME TO THE EVERYTHING® SERIES!

These handy, accessible books give you all you need to tackle a difficult project, gain a new hobby, comprehend a fascinating topic, prepare for an exam, or even brush up on something you learned back in school but have since forgotten.

You can choose to read an Everything® book from cover to cover or just pick out the information you want from our four useful boxes: Questions, Facts, Alerts, and Essentials. We give you everything you need to know on the subject, but throw in a lot of fun stuff along the way too.

QUESTION
Answers to common questions.

FACT
Important snippets of information.

ALERT
Urgent warnings.

ESSENTIAL
Quick handy tips.

We now have more than 600 Everything® books in print, spanning such wide-ranging categories as cooking, health, parenting, personal finance, wedding planning, word puzzles, and so much more. When you're done reading them all, you can finally say you know Everything®!

PUBLISHER Karen Cooper

MANAGING EDITOR Lisa Laing

COPY CHIEF Casey Ebert

ASSOCIATE PRODUCTION EDITOR Jo-Anne Duhamel

ACQUISITIONS EDITOR Zander Hatch

DEVELOPMENT EDITOR Zander Hatch

EVERYTHING® SERIES COVER DESIGNER Erin Alexander

THE EVERYTHING® GUIDE TO
INVESTING
IN YOUR
20s & 30s

YOUR STEP-BY-STEP GUIDE TO:
- Understanding Stocks, Bonds, and Mutual Funds
- Maximizing Your 401(k) • Setting Realistic Goals
- Recognizing the Risks and Rewards of Cryptocurrencies
- Minimizing Your Investment Tax Liability

CRYPTOCURRENCIES

SOCIAL MEDIA IPOs

SOCIALLY CONSCIOUS INVESTING

APPS/SECURITY

JOE DUARTE, MD

Adams Media

New York   London   Toronto   Sydney   New Delhi

Adams Media
An Imprint of Simon & Schuster, Inc.
57 Littlefield Street
Avon, Massachusetts 02322

An Everything® Series Book.
Everything® and everything.com® are registered trademarks of Simon & Schuster, Inc.

This Adams Media trade paperback edition May 2019

ADAMS MEDIA and colophon are trademarks of Simon & Schuster.

For information about special discounts for bulk purchases, please contact Simon & Schuster Special Sales at 1-866-506-1949 or business@simonandschuster.com.

The Simon & Schuster Speakers Bureau can bring authors to your live event. For more information or to book an event contact the Simon & Schuster Speakers Bureau at 1-866-248-3049 or visit our website at www.simonspeakers.com.

Interior design by Colleen Cunningham

Manufactured in the United States of America

7 2021

Library of Congress Cataloging-in-Publication Data
Names: Duarte, Joe, author.
Title: The everything® guide to investing in your 20s & 30s / Joe Duarte, MD.
Description: 2nd Edition. | Avon, Massachusetts: Adams Media, 2019.
Series: Everything®.
Includes bibliographical references and index.
Identifiers: LCCN 2018058753 | ISBN 9781507210307 (pb) | ISBN 9781507210314 (ebook)
Subjects: LCSH: Finance, Personal. | Investments. | Stocks. | BISAC: BUSINESS & ECONOMICS / Personal Finance / Investing. | BUSINESS & ECONOMICS / Personal Finance / Money Management. | BUSINESS & ECONOMICS / Personal Finance / Retirement Planning.
Classification: LCC HG179 .D823 2019 | DDC 332.67/8--dc23
LC record available at https://lccn.loc.gov/2018058753

ISBN 978-1-5072-1030-7
ISBN 978-1-5072-1031-4 (ebook)

CONTENTS

ACKNOWLEDGMENTS

For my family and my agent, Grace Freedson, as always. Special thanks to Frank and Jean Kollar for running JoeDuarteintheMoneyOptions.com. And to Mark Mathes, Steven Halpern, and everyone at MoneyShow.com, without whom the word wouldn't get out. Also a great deal of gratitude to Zander Hatch for the awesome edits. But most of all, a very special and heartfelt thanks to those who read my books. Thank you for letting me do what I love, over and over again. You're the music. I'm just the band.

INTRODUCTION

In the modern world of investing, you'll find more options than ever before. You can invest in stocks, bonds, real estate, mutual funds, ETFs, cryptocurrencies, IPOs, and dozens more. But what's the difference between all these options? Which ones are safe? Which ones are risky? Which ones offer the greatest return on investment? And how do you know which one is the best for you?

Here you'll find the answers to these questions and more. You'll learn all about investing for people like you: people in their twenties and thirties who wish to build wealth over their lifetime. It is not about getting rich quickly or how to become a professional trader. Instead, it's about following your road map to investing and putting in some hard, but rewarding, work.

In this book, you'll learn:

- How to evaluate and invest in all of these different options while developing, shaping, and adjusting your long-term plan
- How willing you are to take risks with your money
- How to manage that risk to make money
- All about choosing asset classes, such as stocks, bonds, real estate, and mutual funds, to create an asset allocation mix that makes sense for you

Most importantly, you will learn how to develop a plan through which you will build your wealth without guesswork and anguish. If you've never invested before, that's okay. No matter what, as long as you are in your twenties and thirties, time is on your side. If you start investing now, you will have ample opportunities to build the kind of financial future that you are looking for. Time to get started.

CHAPTER 1

Are You Ready to Become an Investor?

It's important to understand the big picture. Investing is the long-term process by which you build wealth, and has two basic components—saving and compounding. Saving is the act of putting money away for the purpose of investing. Compounding is what money does for you by earning interest, by the price appreciation of your investments, or both. Together these two processes grow your money. Once you understand these concepts, you are ready to get started.

Can You Afford to Invest?

You have to start somewhere. At the early stages of the investing process, important questions should be raised. Simply stated, investing without money is like quenching thirst without water. So a great place to start is by asking the question of whether you can afford to invest. Once you've answered this crucial question, other logical questions will follow.

How Will You Finance Your Investing?

The money you use for investing can come from anywhere—a savings account, an inheritance, or even a lottery win. For most people, investment money is money earned from a job or profession, even a side gig. If you've got some money already put aside, you're ahead of the game. The more you have, the better your starting point. One thing to keep in mind: never borrow money to invest until you gain experience and know your way around the markets well. That one act would start your investment plan at a deficit.

ESSENTIAL

Build your savings first. Billionaires build their fortunes by owning and managing their businesses. The stock market is a place where they preserve the purchasing power of their fortunes. For example, Warren Buffett, through his holding company Berkshire Hathaway, owns businesses such as Geico, multiple local real estate companies in key states such as Texas, and General Reinsurance Corporation. He uses the profits from his businesses to buy stock in other companies such as Coca-Cola and Apple. That way he diversifies his holdings, but also earns dividends and price appreciation from the stock market.

A simple way to figure out if you can afford to invest is to count how much money you have left at the end of the month after all your bills are paid. If it's $100, that's as good a place to start as any, and that is money that will be put to good use by saving it in a bank account or a money market mutual fund. A money market mutual fund is a special type of mutual fund that invests in short-term interest-paying bonds (maturity of less than ninety days) such as US government Treasury bills or what is known as commercial paper (similar short-term bonds issued by corporations). Think of a money market mutual fund as a holding tank for your money while you decide what to do with it. Any amount is good, but the more you have, the better off you will be in both the short and long run. So if it's less than $100, it means that you need to work a little harder at controlling your expenses or figure out how to make more money, such as exploring a side gig or working overtime. However, be careful that this doesn't interfere with family or other important aspects of your life. Still, even $100 is better than nothing.

ALERT

Pay off as much debt as possible before you start investing. Debt is a drag on your ability to save. Think of debt as a big sack of potatoes that you carry on your back everywhere you go. By paying debt down and eliminating it altogether, you are taking a big weight off of your financial shoulders. Being lighter makes you move faster.

No matter what, it makes good sense to have at least $1,000 saved before you make a move such as buying shares in a mutual fund that invests in stocks or bonds, a good entry-level place for investors. If it's possible, always go for more. So if it was easy to save $100 the first month, get greedy and go for $200 next month, so you can grow your nest egg more quickly and benefit more from compounding.

If you don't have extra money at the end of the month, there is no point in trying to invest yet. In that case, your first step should be to trim your expenses. If you're trying to make money without some kind of reliable backing, you're asking for trouble. So don't put your rent or food money into a mutual fund; you may find yourself without a place to live or going hungry.

Details Are Important

Successful investors are very specific about what they are going to do and how they are going to do it. For example, plan what you will set aside for investment, how often you will invest it, and how you will monitor your progress. As time passes and your investments grow, make changes if and when they are needed. Consider revisiting your goals and your expectations. A reliable plan in the early stages of investing is to set aside at least $100 per month until you get to $1,000. While you are saving money to invest, you should also be researching different mutual fund companies to find out which one makes more sense to you. Some of the more popular and reliable mutual fund companies are Fidelity Investments, Vanguard, and T. Rowe Price.

ESSENTIAL

The major reasons most small investors give up is that they don't have enough cash and that they risk too much too soon. That means that they don't have enough money around to get them through tough times or to recover from mistakes. Markets will always rise and fall, so in order to stay in the game, set aside as much as you can before you try to put it to work. Then keep adding as much as you can as often as possible. That's how you will make the most out of compounding.

Know Your Risk Profile

Knowing how much you are willing to risk in investments is a tricky business, as it depends on both your personality and your ability to be objective based on your circumstances. If you are willing to jump out of an airplane without a parachute, you might like to trade options and futures without doing your research or doing some paper trading without risking real money. Of course that's not wise, and I don't recommend it even if you are an ex-CIA agent used to taking outlandish risks. But by the same token, people who don't like to leave their house if there are clouds in the sky don't make good investors either.

ALERT

Trading options is risky, but it's a great way to invest if you're trying to build income. Consider this technique only after you've learned about stocks and are experienced in the investing world.

Still, it makes sense to know what your tendencies are. Once you know, you can explore the different kinds of investments and methods that may make sense for you. Regardless of your risk profile, as an investor there is no substitute for planning, study, risk understanding, and patience. What's the best way to figure out your risk profile? Ask yourself these three questions:

- How much can I afford to lose?
- How much do I need to reach my goals?
- How do I react to losing?

If you have only a few hundred dollars to your name, and you need them to get by, you should avoid high-risk investments and concentrate on saving money that you will invest in the future.

ESSENTIAL

Take your time before deciding and don't be afraid to reconsider a decision. If you are uncomfortable, consider taking other steps to remove your uncertainty. To decrease anxiety, trade on paper where you put imaginary money to work and follow the results without risking real cash. Invest in what you enjoy or are good at understanding. If stocks are not for you, consider real estate, bonds, or even something like investing in a franchise. There are many asset classes and investment opportunities, each one with its own set of risks and potential rewards. A good rule to follow is that if you don't understand it, you shouldn't invest in it.

Think things through. If your goal is to have a million dollars by the time you retire and you are only twenty-three years old, you're in good shape as time is on your side. In this case, everything depends on how much money you can save over time and how well that money can be invested in order to maximize the combined savings and compounding dynamic. If you get sick to your stomach and pull your hair out when your favorite football team loses a game, lower-risk investments may be the way to go for you, especially when markets become volatile in response to an unexpected event that is well beyond your control.

Setting Realistic Goals and Timetables

Your timetable starts when you decide to start investing. Your first step is to decide when you will open your account and how much you will put in it. If you have money set aside, you're ahead of the game. If you have less than $1,000, your best bet is to put that money in the bank or in a money market mutual fund and continue adding to the account until you have enough to start investing. Avoid putting that money in a CD (certificate of deposit) or another type of account that won't allow you to add to it or that will limit how often you can put money in or take it out.

Put It in Writing

Wishing for something won't help you get it, but writing your goals on paper, reading them frequently, and reviewing and refining them will get you places. The more specific you are, the better off you'll be. Note the goal, the time frame to reach the goal, the amount of money you'll need, how much you have now, and what you are willing to do to get to your goals.

If your long-term goal is to retire early, write down the age of retirement, where you'd like to live, and how much money you think you'll need. Write it in such detail that you can see yourself doing it. "I want to retire when I'm fifty. I want to move to Cape Cod and live in a house by the shore with a great view of the sea. I plan to do a little consulting work on the side and run along the beach with my dog every day." Experience this fully every time you look at your sheet of paper or your smartphone. If you have shorter-term goals, like owning a home or visiting a specific foreign country, include those as well and divide your savings and investing capital between them.

Break the process down into stages. Set monthly, quarterly, and yearly goals. Write down exactly how much you'll put into your IRA or 401(k) every month. Decide how much you'll pay in debt every month and to whom and how much money you will dedicate to each area. This process will require a great deal of time and planning, and it's likely to require adjustments along the way.

Review and Refine Your Plan

Keep a set of lists with clear and concise objectives and revise them frequently, sometimes every day. The time interval between checkups and changes is up to you. The key is to get in the habit of making your financial situation something you monitor and adjust as frequently as it makes sense, especially when your situation and your needs change. Most of all, keep track of how much progress you're making. Do what makes you comfortable, but check at least on a monthly basis.

Moreover, consider getting help as needed. For example, is your spouse or significant other participating in the plan? Does that person understand the goals? If it's not going the way you planned, take a step back and review the situation on your own perhaps and then together once you've given it some thought. Give yourself credit for what you've accomplished and review where things didn't go as you planned. If your goals change, it's not a setback, just a reboot. Go through the same process of planning for your next goal.

Simply talking things over with friends or relatives may be helpful. If what you're doing isn't working, it may be time to get a second opinion. Successful people are usually willing to lend a helping hand to those in need. By raising the issue with someone who's been there, you may discover that your problem isn't as big as you think. The answer may be something as simple as getting a recommendation for a good advisor who is willing to be your consultant, or the name of a good investment club.

Find some good online resources for retirement planning and personal finance, like MarketWatch.com's personal finance and retirement sections. The personal finance section offers great ideas for budgeting, saving money on credit cards, how to get bargain trips, and great general tips on how to save money. The retirement section is terrific for getting organized and staying updated on changes in mutual funds, IRA rules, and what to do with your 401(k) plan.

Discount brokers are great resources for baseline savings and investing information. The key is to continue to build capital. So even if you're stuck, continue to put money in that savings account or money market mutual fund as you figure out your next move. Just that simple step will keep your future investment fund growing.

How Much Will You Need to Get Started?

Theoretically, you can start with a nickel. But in the real world, the more you have when you start investing, the better off you'll be. What's even more important is gauging how much you'll need to save and invest over time and to adjust this accordingly as your financial situation changes. A rule of thumb used by some mutual fund companies is that you should save eight times your annual ending salary, the money that you have after taxes and expenses, in order to retire. It's not likely that a young person can do that right away, so it can be done in a stepwise fashion.

For example, if you start at age twenty-five and you save one time your ending salary by the time you're thirty-five, the next goal should be to save three times your ending salary by the time you're forty-five, five times by the time you're fifty-five, and so on. Remember, this is just a formula. Life isn't always this neat, but you do have a benchmark. You can modify this formula by starting to save earlier, adjusting the amounts more frequently, or changing your retirement age goal. You can also try to put more money away every chance you get as long as you stick to the goal amount. Become a savings machine. If you have a 401(k) plan as your main retirement source, max that out and start a separate IRA to add more money to your retirement.

> **ALERT**
>
> Searching through the free content on a mutual fund or bank website can give you a fair amount of useful information. Just be aware of the fact that their goal is to get you to invest your money with them. Make sure that you use the information that is sensible without necessarily buying into a sales pitch.

Always Think Liquid

You've got some savings; you've got a plan; and you're looking for ways to get things moving. One of the most useful things to do when investing is to consider the flexibility or liquidity of any investing vehicle. Liquidity is the ease of moving the money around—cash in hand is the most liquid of assets. Liquidity certainly comes in handy if something changes, such as a sudden short-term price drop in the stock market that gives you an opportunity to buy shares at lower prices. Let's say that you get a side gig that pays quickly or you get a bonus or a raise at work. Suddenly you have extra money. That extra money could take you to your $1,000 initial investment target, letting you start your investing plan sooner than you might have intended. If your savings is locked up in an illiquid CD that won't let you move the money around for six months or a year, you'll be stuck and will have to wait until the CD matures before you can get started on your longer-term investment plan.

Bank Accounts versus Money Market Mutual Funds

Bank accounts and money market mutual funds are the most liquid savings and investing vehicles. And although they are similar, they are not the same. You set up a bank account with a bank and you open the money market mutual fund with a brokerage or mutual fund company. Savings accounts pay interest rates. Checking accounts sometimes pay interest. Money market mutual funds pay interest rates and have check writing privileges, but they often require as much as between $1,000 to $2,500 minimum balance, and some may limit the number of checks that you can write from the account. Therefore, a good rule is to have a bank account for savings, a checking account for paying bills, and a separate money market mutual fund as the central holding area for investment capital.

ESSENTIAL

Build investment capital by putting money in your money market fund before you put it to work. By delaying transferring money directly into a stock or bond fund, you are providing a cushion against potential losses and building up your cash reserves. This money may come in handy in the future, especially if the markets fall, giving you an opportunity to buy shares in your stock or bond fund at a cheaper price. You may be able to set up your money market fund to automatically transfer money from your bank account. Bottom line: if you put $500 into your money market every month, only invest a portion that you are comfortable with, such as $250, in your stock or balanced mutual fund.

Open a money market mutual fund account as your initial investment decision. This account will serve as your central investment account. From there you can switch money to mutual funds, stocks, and other investments with a phone call or a click of your mouse.

FACT

You can set up a brokerage account or a mutual fund account or both. The difference is that with a brokerage account you can buy stocks, bonds, and mutual funds, while a mutual fund account only allows switching between the mutual funds in the fund family that houses the account. At the same time, if you are not interested in stocks or bonds, a mutual fund account will work just fine for you.

Next, you'll decide how much money you'll set aside for investing and how often you will add to your investments. A good method is to add at least a constant or nearly constant amount every month. If your goal is $100 every month, but you only have $50 this month, add the $50. Try to add $150 next month. No matter what, just keep adding to your account.

> **ALERT**
>
> Separate savings from investments. Once you have enough money to invest, split your funds between a bank savings account and a mutual fund/brokerage money market account. You need to have some money in the bank for emergencies so that you don't have to tap your investment account unless it is absolutely necessary.

Even if you check your balances every week or month, give your accounts a thorough checkup every three months. If you're not where you thought you should be, ask yourself why and do your best to make it right. You can adjust your timetable to conform to your circumstances. Things happen, so if you lose your job or a health emergency pops up, things may get difficult for a while. Stay patient and do your best to stay on track. But if you get a promotion and a raise, give your investment account a raise, too, and modify your addition schedule.

When you reach a milestone, as in when you get to your first $10,000, see what you can do to get to $20,000 faster than what it took to get to $10,000. Then do it again when you get to $30,000. Always give yourself room for error, but always make changes and look for ways to make your returns better. Investing is a fluid process. And those who keep up with what they are doing in a systematic fashion do better.

Know Before You Invest

Once you've opened your investment account, keep that money in the money market mutual fund as long as it takes for you to decide what to do with it.

Shares in a money market mutual fund do not fluctuate in price. Although you are buying shares, each share is worth $1. That won't change unless very difficult financial circumstances develop. It's only happened once in the history of investing, during the 2008 financial crisis. Take your time and try out some strategies on paper before committing to real-time investing. You can buy shares in a growth mutual fund on paper and follow the share price over a few weeks. Correlate how the fund does in relation to the stock market. If conditions remain the same and the fund does well over the period, pull the trigger and keep an eye on things.

FACT

The Federal Deposit Insurance Corporation (FDIC) does not insure money market mutual fund accounts. Money in these accounts is "at risk" of loss. The good news is that even though it can happen, the odds of losing money in a money market account are almost zero.

Once you've done some research, it may make sense for you to invest in a well-managed mutual fund that invests in stocks, bonds, or both (a balanced approach). If you know someone who had good results with a particular mutual fund, research it for yourself. Here's where talking to your mom, your dad, or an uncle or friend of the family with some money may come in handy.

ALERT

A mutual fund prospectus tells the story of what to expect when you buy shares of the fund. Not only will it describe the fund's investment philosophy, its current holdings and allocation, and its overall approach to investing, but you will also get a snapshot of past performance. And while history isn't everything, knowing how a fund performs during a bad market is essential if you are trying to decide whether to hold shares for several years, especially during bear markets.

Don't bank on their advice too much, though. Get the prospectus and see for yourself. Monitor the share price. Compare the fund's performance to the stock market and see how it has behaved during similar periods of economic activity and interest rates in the past. Explore both how well the fund has done over time, and how well it's done recently. Start following its price on a weekly or daily basis for a few weeks. Always compare your funds, or your stocks, to the appropriate benchmark and to the general market. When you read a mutual fund prospectus it will always tell you which major stock index it is trying to emulate or beat. Most diversified growth or growth and income mutual funds will use the Standard & Poor's 500 Index (S&P 500) as a benchmark.

ESSENTIAL

When investing in individual stocks, "kick the tires" before you buy. That means going to the supermarket and seeing if anyone is buying products made by that company, seeing how many cars are parked in the parking lot of a certain company which retails specific products, and listening for which companies get a lot of press in financial circles. Use this as the starting point for your research; then follow it by reviewing earnings and research reports, asking questions, and getting a long-term view of the company from a stock chart. You can find excellent stock charts on the web at StockCharts.com.

Once you get better at investing and start to invest in individual stocks, it's a similar dynamic to investing in a mutual fund, with a bit more detail. With a mutual fund you're investing in a management style, expertise, and investment strategy. With an individual company's stock you're investing in the potential for profits of one entity. Yet, it's not that different. Get as much information as possible on the company. Ask people about their experience with the stock. Research the company and its products. Know its fiscal strategies, its management style, and review its future plans. For example: if you go to a coffee shop on a regular basis, it's always crowded, and it's part of a major chain like Starbucks, research the company. See how it's doing. And consider investing in it.

The Basics of Market Analysis

Individual investors have a responsibility to their future and their families. Investing is not a game. It's a serious activity that should be taken up only by those who wish to take it seriously. It's almost a second occupation, and you should be prepared to make a serious commitment.

The Global Economic Dynamic Is Changing

After the 1980s, national economies became synchronized and turned into a global economy. Commerce between companies, individuals, and countries functioned to a great degree as a single entity. But after the 2016 US presidential election, the global economy is no longer as synchronized. As a result of the renegotiation of trade pacts between nations (especially between the US and its North American trading partners) and the placement of sanctions between nations, the potential for long-term trade disputes is something that will be around for a while. Certainly, this has changed the playing field to some degree, but it has not changed everything.

For example, electronic payments and the instantaneous flow of information through cell phones and the Internet still make for very fast responses to news and the subsequent directions of money flows. And even with the changes to the global marketplace, there are still four basic investment markets to monitor or at least to learn about: stocks, bonds, commodities, and real estate. A fifth potential market is that of cryptocurrencies, which deserves its own section in Chapter 15. Each individual market responds to variables in its own country's economy, as well as to various external influences, such as changes in interest rates, trade relationships, or political changes in major economic regions around the world such as the United States, China, or Europe.

It's also not uncommon, even after 2016, to see US stocks react to important economic data from China or Germany, such as changes in Gross Domestic Product or other key economic variables. This is because, despite changes in policies and relationships, US and major foreign companies still sell products all over the world, and economic growth or contraction in the other economies of the world can affect the future profits of US and major global companies.

Central Banks and Markets

Central banks are government banks that function to monitor and respond to the economies of their country by raising or lowering interest rates. And because interest rates are the most important influencers of economic activity, knowing about central banks and how they can affect your pocketbook is extremely important. In general, weakening economies lead central banks to lower interest rates. Economies that show so much strength that inflation is starting to rise lead to higher interest rates.

The most powerful influence on global financial markets is the direction of interest rates because the trend of interest rates will influence the amount of risk you should consider taking in any market or business endeavor. This is because interest rate trends influence how easy or difficult it is to borrow money. The US Federal Reserve (also known as the Fed) is considered the world's most influential central bank. The bond market moves in response to the actions of the Federal Reserve and other central banks, and the other markets, stocks, commodities, and real estate eventually follow.

As a general rule, lower interest rates are good for stocks and bonds, because stock and bond prices tend to rise in response to lower interest rates. Commodities, such as gold, oil, wheat, corn, and coffee, and gasoline prices respond less to interest rates and are more influenced by supply and demand as well as the general state of the world's political climate and how these factors affect trade policy. Real estate responds to both interest rates and supply and demand for land and housing. However, after the 2007–2008 subprime mortgage crisis and the presence of zero interest rates for nearly a decade, the housing market became much more sensitive to interest rates than in the past. It is likely that this will remain in place perhaps for the foreseeable future.

Even though interest rates rule the roost, each one of these markets has its own set of dynamics and should be known and understood both as an individual place to invest as well as how it's behaving in response to the others, to interest rates, to inflation, and to the global political situation at any time.

Political Influences

Politics often lead to market volatility. Wars, trade disputes, and military agreements between nations can affect all four markets because the global markets are still financially interconnected despite the changes in crucial policies after the 2016 US presidential election. Indeed, it is still possible for any investor to invest in just about anything, anywhere, at any time, through direct investments, such as stocks and bonds, or through mutual funds.

Keep in mind that events in Moscow, Rio, Buenos Aires, Pyongyang, Baghdad, or Beijing can and will affect your personal investments. The world of the twenty-first century is still connected. News still travels fast. Money still moves at the touch of a button or a signal from a robot trader. All markets are still interconnected and still tend to move in the same general direction over time. Therefore risk can go from a very low level to a place of extreme danger in a few minutes at any time. Thus all investors should become "experts" in their chosen investment fields to the extent that they can be aware of the risk of losses.

Evaluate and Adjust Your Approach

Don't be in a hurry. Because you are young, you can afford to take a step back and consider your options. This chapter has been about creating your road map for making decisions, getting basic information, and taking your first steps to start your investing career. You should have the tools now to know if you're ready to become an investor and how to get started.

Remember, there is an orderly method for getting started with investing, with a beginning, middle, and endpoint. All along the way, the three basic steps are asking questions, letting the answers lead to the next step, and getting used to the notion that frequent evaluation is the way to keep things going in the right direction.

Writing your plan down, keeping it handy, and reading it on a regular basis reinforces your goals, letting your subconscious mind do its job, which is to process information and eventually help you to make better decisions. By paying attention to the markets on a regular basis you will improve your understanding of how they work, and by checking how your investments respond to the action in the markets you will get a good feel as to what works and what doesn't.

The "Ready to Invest" Test

Before investing, make sure you've got these areas covered:

1. Have steady income
2. Have money left over after meeting your obligations
3. Consider the effect of possible upcoming personal changes such as marriage, children, illness, or divorce before investing
4. Build savings before establishing an investment capital fund
5. Use a money market mutual fund as your platform for investing
6. Know your risk profile
7. Do your homework and work everything out on paper before investing in anything in real time
8. Invest in mutual funds before investing in individual stocks

CHAPTER 2

Steps to Grow Your Nest Egg

Every investor needs a source of investment capital. This is often called the nest egg, and it is the lifeblood of your investment plan. This chapter is about starting, growing, and using your nest egg for investing. More than a holding tank, the nest egg is both a launching and a landing pad. Money will come into it, earn interest, and be deployed to individual investments based on the overall plan and your asset allocation.

Give Your Finances a Physical

Optimize your nest egg by first taking an honest inventory of your finances. Make two lists: "Sources of Income" and "Expenses." Be as specific as possible in both of them. First, make a list of your sources of income:

- Wages from your job(s)
- Bonuses
- Child support or alimony
- Rental income
- Interest income
- Dividend income
- Capital gains income
- Other income

Next, list your expenses. This list may be larger than the income list. Be brutally honest with yourself and include every possible expense that you can think of on this list. You can always pare it down later. Here are some sample expense categories:

- Savings
- Mortgage or rent
- Utilities
- Car payment
- Other
- Public transportation
- Credit card payments
- Student loans
- Any other loan payments
- Home maintenance
- Child care
- Child support or alimony
- Insurance: car, health, home, other(s)
- Out-of-pocket medical expenses
- Health insurance if self-employed
- Computer expenses

- Cell phone
- Entertainment/recreation
- Food: dining out/groceries
- Clothing and shoes
- Gifts and donations
- Hobbies
- Interest expense
- Household/personal care products
- Federal, state, and local income tax
- Social security tax
- Property tax
- Retirement contributions
- Investments
- Pet expenses

This is a great exercise as you'll be surprised at how much you spend and where you spend it. The purpose of this checkup is to help you find expenses that can be cut or savings that can be increased to create a sound budget and free up money for investments. Consider what you spend on subscriptions (online and off), and holiday, birthday, and anniversary gifts. Do you really need some of those things? Given the amount of free information on the Internet, you may not need some of those magazine or website subscriptions. Maybe you need to cut back on how much you spend on gifts for others and online shopping for yourself as well.

ESSENTIAL

Use as many sources of data as possible to do your financial physical exam. Include credit card statements, loan statements, receipts, and your checkbook. By including as many expenses as possible, you will get the most complete picture of where your money goes and you'll give yourself the best chance of success when you start preparing your budget.

Savings and investments are included as expenses in order to judge how much of your money is already committed to this portion of your finances. Pay close attention to how much you are already putting into savings, your 401(k) plan, or an IRA. If you have zeros or minimal amounts next to these bullets, then you definitely have your work cut out for you. But don't be discouraged. Every negative situation is just an opportunity for improvement. Consider making a reduction in one of your "luxury" areas, such as buying $100 worth of expensive coffee and chocolates every month and taking that money and putting it in your 401(k) or IRA. You don't have to torture yourself, but maybe doing something like this every other month or once a quarter will work for you.

The Great Analysis

Once you've made your list, evaluate its strengths and weaknesses. Ask yourself if you're putting your money in the best possible places and, if you're not doing so, consider the best use for it. Be fearless and honest. Keep what makes sense and dump what doesn't work.

For example, if you're spending a lot of money on private tennis lessons, but you're not getting to the pro tour, that's a sign that your tennis lesson money might be better spent on paying off some credit card debt, saving for retirement, or both. You can still play tennis and still stay in shape but maybe you should scale back on the private lessons and go to group workouts that cost less. Even one or two changes along these lines can make a big difference and the mere fact that you've spotted a pluggable hole in your finances is huge.

It's a good idea to update the list you've made on a monthly basis and to see where there is progress and what needs work. Other areas that can easily be trimmed include entertainment expenses, such as movies. Matinees are cheaper than paying full price, and *Netflix* or video rentals may make sense. You don't need to see every movie in IMAX. And if you go to the theater, small popcorns and small drinks are likely better for your wallet (and your health) than the more expensive larger ones. You don't have to go to the movies every week. Also, books tend to be cheaper—free at the library—and are often more fun than movies. Be creative, and be true to yourself and your plan. Once you've analyzed your income and expenses, you can start to make a budget.

Artful Budgeting

It has been said that medicine is part art and part science. In many ways so is budgeting. There is no absolute way to budget, as much depends on the factors that affect each individual's life, income, spending habits, and overall circumstances. The one constant in all budgeting is the goal: to trim expenses as much as possible in order to pay off debt and leave money for saving, investing, or other financial objectives, such as taking vacations, sending the kids to a special camp in the summer, or upgrading a home.

How Much Money Do You Have?

A good budget starts with knowing how much money you have available each month. That figure is the result of the physical exam you gave your finances, after subtracting expenses from income. It's a good idea to do this calculation based on figures for at least three to six months as you can start seeing some trends. Once you analyze a few months' worth of data, you should develop a pretty good idea of where your money is going and how you can redirect it to better use.

Where Is Your Money Going?

You may discover that your finances are dying a slow death of losses via small expenses such as grocery shopping, cups of coffee, cigarettes, beer, wine, and going out for food with friends. There is nothing wrong with living a little, but if you're not careful, these little things can add up and make the pain of the big expenses, like rent or mortgage, car payments, and loans, much worse.

Two packs of cigarettes per week cost somewhere around $40–$100 per month depending on where you live and what brand you smoke. That's $480–$1,200 per year. A daily $2 latte is $14 per week, $56 per month, and $672 per year. Tennis lessons can run $70–$100 per hour or more per week. That's $3,640 to $5,200 per year. That's a total of somewhere between $4,800–$7,100 per year on stuff that you can reduce or cut out. You get the picture. The "little" things can add up in a hurry and by finding things you can do without or that you can replace with cheaper alternatives, you can make a big difference in your spending.

Realistic Targeting of Expenses

Once you have a good idea where you are spending your money, you can start making some decisions about where to make adjustments. Divide your expenses into sections. Look at the big expenses first, then look at the medium expenses, and finally look at the smaller costs. The numbers will be different for everyone. The "bigs" may be those expenses that total above $300 per month and are likely to include rent or mortgage costs, car payments, and maybe some credit cards. The "mediums" may contain insurances and student loans—these would be the $50–$300 group—while the "smalls" should be those expenses below $50. The "smalls" will likely be the largest section and will include your bills for dry cleaners, babysitters, groceries, movies, and other things that we often spend money on just because they happen to be convenient.

FACT

Consider switching to a zero interest rate credit card. You will pay a "fee" up front, but you will usually have a year to pay off the card balance at a lower interest rate. This will free up money that can be used to pay other expenses, to put toward savings and investment, or both.

Separate the three groups of expenses and add them up as individual categories. By putting numbers together with expenses, and then grouping them, you will get a better idea as to the effect each group is having on your finances and how to attack them. Some areas will be difficult to reduce or replace. For example, mortgages, rents, student loans, and car payments are likely to remain fixed costs. But there are plenty of other expenses that have the potential to be adjusted. That means that your biggest chances for spending cuts are likely to come from the "smalls." But that doesn't mean that you shouldn't spend time exploring the "bigs" and the "mediums." Here are two examples of how to look at your groups, ranging from big to small:

In the "big" column, a $2,000 credit card balance at 13% interest per year, on which you're only making minimum payments every month while you continue to charge, could turn into a $3,500 balance in five years, assuming that the interest rate stayed the same. If interest rates rise, you would pay more. Consider targeting the credit card debt as your first success in order to free up money for saving and investing. If you pay that credit card off and instead save $3,500, it could grow to nearly $4,500 in five years at 5% compounded interest.

ALERT

Here's a tax tip which can help you save money and improve your budget. If you own a home-based business, your coffee and grocery expenses may be at least partially tax deductible. Every little bit helps.

In the "small" column is grocery shopping. A larger-than-expected "surprise" here may be from buying prepared foods, which cost more. Start buying fresh food and cook it yourself more often. Snacks are also expensive and can be cut back. Sodas, flavored water, and coffee drinks add up too. Consider going to the grocery store more often and buying only what you need each time, instead of making one big monthly trip where you might buy more than you really need of any one item. One trick to help control your grocery spending is to pay cash and never spend more than what you have in your pocket. Sometimes that might mean putting something back on the shelf. Never have more than $50 in your pocket when you go grocery shopping and you won't overspend. Set concrete spending targets on your choices, and pinpoint the things that won't hurt as much as others. If nightly dining out is standing out as a big expense, cut the five nights of dinner out per week to one or two and use the nights out as treats for making a good decision.

Intangible Benefits

Think outside the box as there may be more benefits besides freeing up some money when you make some spending cuts. In turn, those "extra" benefits may have a positive impact on your budget. By cooking your own food you are more likely to be eating fresh, less processed food. There are clear health benefits to be gained from this, which may translate into lower medical expenses.

If you spend $30 per month on public transportation, it may make sense to walk more. Do you really need to hail that cab? If you take the subway, consider walking one stop farther before taking the train. Walking is good exercise, and the ticket may cost less if you buy it three blocks farther along. If you can walk to work, it may be worth it to take that thirty-minute walk and the thirty-minute walk home every day.

FACT

It pays to shop and read the label. A 31-ounce jar of store-brand salted peanuts costs $5.99, while the 32-ounce jar of a popular brand costs $7.99. Two dollars is a lot of money to pay for an ounce of peanuts. If the store peanuts are just as good as or close to the national brand in flavor and consistency, this is an easy choice. It makes sense to compare similar products and to try different strategies.

Look for free stuff when you treat yourself. If you buy Starbucks coffee by the bag at the grocery store, there is a coupon for a free cup of coffee at the bottom. That can add up to twenty or more free cups of coffee per year if you're a regular customer. You can order your coffee online and possibly get free shipping. By doing this, you save about $1–$2 per bag compared to the grocery store.

Shop around for your cell phone plan. You may find significant savings as often as twice per year when the plans do updates or service upgrades. Sometimes they'll throw in a free phone. A $20 per month savings will bring you $240 per year.

See the Difference

The next step is to compare how much money you will actually spend after your analysis and your targeted cuts. Whatever is left is your free cash flow—what you will put in your bank account or your money market mutual fund in order to build your savings and investing capital fund. Track this figure over three months and see where things stand. Get greedy when you can and add in more every chance you get.

> **ALERT**
>
> You need a name for the money you will use to invest. Consider calling it your "investing capital fund." It's a good descriptive term, but it's also a sign that you are starting to get in the right mindset and you are becoming a more serious investor.

If you've made good decisions based on your financial checkup and your analysis of the data, and have begun to artfully budget, you should start seeing some of your debt shrink, and you should be noticing that what's left in your pocket has grown each month. Even if it's a small amount, such as $50, it's progress. As you pay more things off, like credit cards, if you control your expenses and you adjust your objectives, your free cash flow should start to grow along with your investing capital fund.

Personal Finance Software and Apps

There are many different ways you can track your personal finances. You can spend money on software like Quicken, or you can use an Excel spreadsheet. If you're trying to save money, the spreadsheet may be the way to go. If you want to plan for the future, or centralize your finances, software often lets you do your budget, do your taxes online, as well as write checks and pay bills. You may want to do a spreadsheet at first and then move up to the software as you get better. The important thing is to get organized and to give yourself the ability to track your budget and to gauge your successes and failures so that you can make changes as needed.

Start with the simple entries and add details as you progress. Balancing your checkbook and paying bills is a good beginning. It will get you comfortable with the software and help you to develop a routine. The data you enter into the software will also become the basis for your budgeting.

ALERT

Your bank or investment firm may have free financial and budgeting software available on its website. This may be all you need to get started before you spend money on other software or apps.

Personal finance software that you pay for or that your bank or other trusted institution provides free of charge is likely to be more reliable and helps you get better organized, as it has built-in templates that can save you time and effort as you plug in data. It also has graphing and trending functions, which let you see your progress over time.

You can buy Quicken at www.quicken.com. Another popular software for budgeting is Mint, found at www.mint.com; for Moneydance, hit www.money dance.com. All three software packages can also be found on *Amazon*. The basic version of each software package costs between $30 and $40 after rebates.

Get Some Apps

Smartphones are absolutely fantastic for keeping tabs on your stocks and gathering information. Indeed, for smartphone and mobile fans, there are plenty of apps to help you get started with investing.

Mint is a highly popular and useful free app that is easy to use for anyone. Once you input your personal financial data, the app displays a summary of all your information—saving and investment accounts, credit cards, and bills—and frequently updates so you can analyze your current situation at one glance. This makes it incredibly easy for you to make a budget, assess your savings, or make decisions about your investments. The app also updates your credit score and analyzes your financial data to make suggestions that may make sense for you, such as CD rates that pay well or the credit cards with low interest rates.

ALERT

Be skeptical of free online software from sources that you can't verify, especially if they ask you to provide your name, social security number, and other personal data. These programs can be identity theft scams or data brokers in disguise. Either way you lose. A good example of a scam of sorts involved the popular Robin Hood brokerage app, which allows stock trading with no commission. In September 2018, the Securities and Exchange Commission, which oversees most of the financial world, accused the company of allegedly selling data about stock trades placed on its platform to high-frequency traders on Wall Street. Computer programs would then take the data and place trades ahead of the customers in order to make money off of the transaction even before it took place on behalf of the Robin Hood customers. Nothing on Wall Street is truly free. Read the fine print and be cautious of free stuff.

MoneyBook is a basic app that also tracks your expenses and helps your budgeting. It has a much simpler look and is easier to begin with than Mint. So if you're a little unsure of how to get started with investing apps, this may be a good place to get started and organized. But simplicity isn't free as it does have a subscription price. On the bright side, it is a very easy to use and visually appealing app.

Toshl Finance is another great expense tracking and budgeting app. It has three functions: expense tracker, budget keeper, and bill organizer. With Toshl, you can keep it simple or get very specific. For example, you can create subcategories of budgets and expenses. This will help you keep highly accurate records of where your money goes and how you can make needed changes. The bill organizer even reminds you when your bills are due. And if you decide to take a vacation overseas, you can track your travel budget and use the currency converting tool.

A great place to review financial apps and figure out which ones are best for you is CNET.com. This is a highly reliable technology review site which describes and rates apps, software, and hardware similar to *Consumer Reports*. If you can't find what you're looking for in the headlines, you can search for your topic. It really helps make finding the right app a breeze.

Develop a Progress Checklist

Update your budget on a monthly basis, as early as possible after you have all the data. By starting early, you have a chance to make adjustments and gain ground on your objectives at a faster pace. Include data from your checkbook, bank and credit card statements, as well as receipts. Make the changes in your spreadsheet or your budgeting software and consider graphing the categories over time. A picture really is worth a thousand words.

Adjust the List As Needed

Making a budget and an investment plan is a fluid process. You may miss your targets in some areas and exceed them in others. If you miss the numbers altogether, don't be discouraged. That just means that you have to reexamine what you're doing and make more adjustments. You may have too much detail and may need to combine some categories or rethink your priorities. There is no absolute way to do this, especially if your circumstances change. Small changes can add up, so look for easy places where you can cut spending without causing yourself too much pain.

Anytime there is a significant change in your life, it will affect your budget. Getting married, changing jobs, changes in salaries, having a child, having to take care of a loved one, and many other inevitable events can affect how you spend your money and will have to be adjusted for.

Leaks and Consequences

When adjusting your list, spend some time looking for leaks, those little expenses that can add up without you noticing, but can cause a good deal of damage to your budget. Spending leaks come mostly from impulse buying of things that you thought you needed at the time. Much of the time this kind of buying is influenced by advertising and is best avoided as it can ruin your budget. If you fall prey to this kind of situation on a regular basis, it will make reaching your goal more difficult.

The best way to plug the leaks is to only buy what you need and to be prepared. Make your grocery list beforehand and stick to it while trying to use only cash and limiting the amount in your wallet. You've got to stay disciplined. If you buy things online, go to the item you need and don't fall for the "people who bought this also bought" ploy. If you're buying a book that costs $20 and there is an offer for buying a second book for $15, it's best to avoid the second book. Even though spending $35 for two books may sound good, in real terms, you spent $15 on impulse. That's $15 that could have gone elsewhere, like your investment capital fund. If you fall for this kind of thing on a regular basis, it will add up. Be strong.

Don't Quit

Making a budget and sticking to it can be discouraging, but it helps if you channel your inner Scrooge. It's natural, when your goal is to invest, to want to jump right to it. But the hard truth is that you need capital, first to save and second to invest. And unless you win the lottery, the most likely source for it is your income and what you do with it. That means that you need patience, planning, and motivation.

Try to make the budget as simple as possible. If you have a family, make it a team effort. Reward yourself for hitting a milestone, such as when you hit your stated goal for investing at the end of the month or when you pay off a credit card. There is a good feeling when you've made progress, and success tends to bring more success.

Remember that your budget is a means to an end. It's a useful tool. Don't lose sight of the goal, which is to have enough money left over at the end of the month to start an investing plan.

CHAPTER 3

A Quick and Dirty Overview of the Twenty-First-Century Economy and Investment Vehicles

The economy is a complicated structure with a nearly infinite number of moving parts. Still, as an investor, you will have to gain a fair knowledge of how economies generally work. You won't need a PhD in Economics, and you won't need to develop your own economic models. But it will be helpful for you to have a good grasp on the big picture regarding economic activity at any one point in time and how it will affect interest rates and the return on your money, whether it's invested in stocks, bonds, mutual funds, real estate, commodities, or a combination of asset classes.

How Economic Activity Affects Everything

Think of the economy as a money generating machine and its accompanying distribution system. No matter where you live or invest, things are made, grown, harvested, distributed, and eventually bought and sold by someone at some point. The economy is essentially the sum of all of those activities and transactions, and how the money that travels through each transactional point is deployed.

Whether you are investing via stocks, bonds, or mutual funds anywhere in the world, the basic behavior of all economies is generally similar. Whether your money is invested in China or the US, a strong economy expands. It generates jobs. Jobs lead to paychecks. Paychecks lead to purchases. Purchases lead to business expansion, more jobs, more paychecks, and so on. A weak economy contracts, leading to job losses and, in general, the reverse of what you see during good times.

ESSENTIAL

Economies are cyclical, which means that general trends can reverse at any time. Usually changes in interest rates and government policies are involved in changes in the overall economic trend.

Still, no matter who's in charge or what they are doing with interest rates or policy, economic activity can go too far up or down with significant consequences. For example, if an economy expands too rapidly, it usually leads to inflation. That's when there is too much money available and not enough goods for purchase. That leads to increased demand and higher prices. The flip side is a recession, a period during which the economy contracts. This tends to be a time when there is too large a supply of goods. It is also a period where money, at least money in circulation that can be used to buy things, expand businesses, create jobs, and so on, is scarce. Prices for goods and services often drop, or remain fairly stable, during a recession. When a recession goes on for longer than a few years and job losses mount, it's often called a depression. A depression is a grim period of history where there is a great deal of suffering. The hallmark of a depression is the inability of people to find work and the widespread loss of property in the face of rising poverty.

FACT

In the Great Depression there was widespread unemployment, with the peak unemployment rate reaching 25% in 1933. In comparison, during the Great Recession (between 2007–2009), the unemployment rate peaked at 10% in October 2009.

Economic Forecasting Is Inexact

Economic forecasting is very difficult, which is why economists are often referred to as "dismal scientists." This inexactness, or apparent unwillingness of the economy to follow the "rules" in a precise fashion, is easy to understand because at the very root of how economies function is human behavior. Human behavior is predictably unpredictable and economists, whose jobs are difficult under the best of times, often use computer models which can sometimes fail due to inadequate assumptions based on past performance of economic trends. For example, during the acceleration of the US economy after 2016, economists continued to predict low GDP growth for months when in fact GDP was growing at a much faster rate.

Moreover, while the Fed and private sector economies wait for data to make decisions, the real economy and the markets respond rapidly and decisively to events. Events such as changes in interest rates and other economic data can affect the markets more quickly than economists can react due to the rapid dispersal and amplification of news via social media. This creates financial market volatility, which trickles to the performance of retirement funds and cash management accounts, and influences financial decisions such as buying a new home or car. Therefore, economic trends which in the past might have taken years to develop can now become evident within weeks or months.

Indeed, behaviorally speaking, when people feel good about life they spend money, fueling economic activity. When things aren't going so well, they spend less and economies tend to slow. The hardest part of economics is pinpointing the exact transition points from one trend to the other. That's why it's best to keep your economic analysis in general terms while appreciating that it's nearly impossible to base your investments solely on economic forecasting. Staying practical and staying in touch with the markets and the economy is the best approach.

Above all, remain patient and don't fight the general market price trend. The economy is the hardest to gauge when the trend is changing. Markets can either anticipate or respond to a change in the economy and change direction accordingly. Thus, depending on the majority opinion of the market's participants and the prevailing economic data, a rising market will eventually become a falling market and a falling market will eventually find a bottom before rising back up.

FACT

A bull market is when stock prices generally rise for extended periods of time, usually months to years. A bear market is the opposite. Generally, bull markets last longer than bear markets.

The key to understanding the fundamentals of the economy is to appreciate the fact that events develop in an unpredictable fashion and that economic trends take time to develop and change. For instance, job losses when economies soften often start slowly and may remain undetected for some time. Meanwhile, investment trends, such as rising stock prices, often overshoot the general trend of the data. But at some point, when the market realizes that the economy has changed, the price trend may change suddenly. The point is that the timing of economic cycles and markets is imprecise. It might take several months before a key change in the economy is noticeable, thus the reaction in stock prices may be sudden as the unknown becomes apparent. The same applies to every market.

Interest Rates Should Interest You

Interest rates are set by the Federal Reserve in the United States and by other individual central banks around the world. Each central bank sets the rates for its own particular country or region and traditionally the trend for all interest rates was very similar. However, after 2016, this is not as reliable given the changes in trade policy after the US presidential election. This is because, starting in 2008, the Federal Reserve lowered interest rates aggressively in order to reverse the deep recession caused by the subprime mortgage crisis. As a result, investors and the general public became used to zero interest rates over nearly a decade.

This was a very abnormal period in financial history which created a distorted view of the economy and of the risks involved in investing. Thus, when the Federal Reserve began to raise interest rates in 2016 and volatility slowly returned to the markets, many investors were surprised by their losses during periods when the market turned lower. The reaction in real estate was even more dramatic as mortgage rates began to rise and a booming housing market lost a great deal of momentum. As interest rates rise, all markets become more volatile, and due to the speed with which information spreads, market and economic trends can change rapidly.

Congress mandates the US Federal Reserve to "fight inflation" and to "maintain full employment." Economists, mathematicians, and professionals at the Federal Reserve study the economy and create reports which are used by the decision makers at the central bank to make decisions as to how to adjust interest rates.

Although there is no set formula for when the Federal Reserve makes a decision to raise or lower interest rates, the central bank generally changes interest rates when the rate-setting committee, known as the Federal Open Market Committee (FOMC), agrees that the economy has slowed to the point where lower rates are needed or when there is a danger of inflation and it needs to raise rates. The FOMC usually meets six to eight times per year to review data and make interest rate decisions.

Interest Rates Make the World Go Round

Interest rates, set by the Federal Reserve and other central banks, have a ripple effect through the economy, the markets, and your daily life. When the Fed changes any of its key interest rates, markets respond by adjusting asset prices. This can lead to changes in the rates charged for car loans, student loans, credit cards, and mortgages. The interest rates you pay when you buy on credit depend on the decisions made by the Federal Reserve.

ESSENTIAL

The FOMC reports its decision on interest rates after every meeting, and the chair holds a press conference after the decision is released. This decision and the press conference receive heavy press coverage and usually influence stock and bond prices. Catch the action on CNBC.com. For more information and details on the Fed, go to www.federalreserve.gov.

The Federal Reserve has two important rates that you may hear mentioned in the news. The federal funds rate tells banks what interest rates to charge one another for short-term overnight loans, which they use to balance their books. The discount rate is the rate that the Fed charges banks to borrow from the central bank. Changes in either or both of these rates usually lead to important moves in the stock and bond markets, with ripple effects to the economy.

How Interest Rates Affect Stocks and Bonds

As a beginning investor, the most important thing to understand is that the Federal Reserve and the major central banks in China, Japan, and the European Union have the power, by making changes to interest rates, to affect the value of your investment portfolio.

FACT

The price of a stock often rises in expectation of good things such as future earnings and falls when the company actually reports the excellent earnings. This is often referred to as "buying on the rumor and selling on the news."

Interest rates are a big influence on stock prices, even more so than the state of the economic cycle. Generally, stocks tend to do well when interest rates are low or falling, whether the economy is very strong or just getting by. This is because interest rates are determined using projections for market factors in the future. If interest rates are low or stable, stocks usually follow along, as investors buy in order to participate in the trend toward rising earnings and profits of companies. But if the projections say that interest rates should rise soon, stock prices might begin to fall even if the market is doing well overall. As a stock investor, your job is to invest in stocks, not in the economy. Thus, a big key to success for stock investors is to know the trend of interest rates, their relationship to the economy, and the effect that relationship is having on market prices.

Bonds, on the other hand, tend to do well when the economy is not doing so well. That's because inflation reduces the net return on bonds. The interest earned by bonds remains fixed, and fixed returns can't compete with rising inflation. If a bond pays an interest rate of 5% and inflation is running at 2%, the net interest rate is 3%. If a bond pays 3% and inflation is rising faster, say at 4%, the return has been reduced to -1%.

Savings Accounts Don't Mind Higher Interest Rates

Rising interest rates aren't necessarily a bad thing. If you have a fair amount of money in a savings account or a money market mutual fund, the interest you earn on those savings will be higher as rates increase. Generally, money market mutual funds and savings accounts are low-risk investments, and earning a higher return with lower risk is a positive. If you have $1,000 in a money market mutual fund that is earning 3% per year, your return would be $30 per year. At 6% it would be $60 per year.

Mixed Blessings in Real Estate

Real estate also responds to interest rates. Lower interest rates lead to lower mortgage rates, which usually attract buyers. Higher interest rates do the opposite. Supply and demand for homes, especially new homes, also respond to interest rates. Builders borrow money to finance their business. As a result, lower interest rates tend to spur home building while higher interest rates tend to do the opposite. If you are a rental property owner, higher interest rates may be a good thing, as fewer people tend to buy homes and may decide to rent.

FACT

The average investment portfolio has both stock and bond investments. The purpose of allocating the money to different asset classes is to protect the investor against changes in the economy. The goal is to have the stock part of the portfolio rise in value during a strong economy and for the bond portion of the portfolio to decrease any potential losses from the stock portfolio if the economy and the stock market turn lower.

Important Numbers and Reports to Watch

There are a large number of economic reports released on a daily basis. Taken as a whole, cities, counties, and states release reports on a regular basis. The stock, bond, and commodity markets usually focus on the national reports released by key agencies of the federal government. There are five essential reports that no investor should be without knowledge of.

The Employment Situation Report

This is the granddaddy of them all. Also known as the Jobs Report, this key set of data is released by the Bureau of Labor Statistics the first Friday of every month and usually leads to some kind of significant move in both the stock and bond markets. It is especially important near elections or during heated political periods as all political parties, including minor parties such as the Green Party or Libertarians, often make use of the data reported to further their political agendas.

ESSENTIAL

You can keep up with the schedule for report releases by visiting *The Wall Street Journal*'s "Markets" section; you'll find it under the "Calendars & Economy" header.

The two big components of this report are the number of new jobs created and the unemployment rate. More new jobs signal a growing economy. The unemployment rate is a fuzzier number with some statistical nuances that tend to be negligible for most investors. Generally, a low unemployment rate is a positive.

Consumer Price Index (CPI)

Every month, the US Department of Labor's Bureau of Labor Statistics reports on inflation at the consumer level, or what you pay when you buy things. The Federal Reserve uses CPI as a data point for making changes in interest rates. If the CPI number starts to move above where the Fed thinks it should be, it may signal that higher interest rates may be on their way in the future. A lower-than-expected CPI may signal a slowing economy. And a falling CPI may be a signal that the Federal Reserve will decide to lower interest rates. The stock and bond markets pay very close attention to this number if it is above or below expectations.

Gross Domestic Product (GDP)

The Gross Domestic Product is a report released by the US Department of Commerce's Bureau of Economic Analysis on a quarterly basis, with revisions often following the initial report. GDP is a big-picture item that reports on the sum of all the goods and services produced in the United States. It's a snapshot of how much the economy grew or contracted on a quarterly and yearly basis expressed as a percentage. Generally speaking, a figure of 4% or above is considered a sign of a strong economy while 2% or below is seen as steady or slowing depending on the trajectory of the trend in the numbers. Generally speaking, GDP between 2% and 3.99% is considered sustainable, although that may change in the future. Two consecutive quarters or more of negative growth is the definition of a recession.

GDP is not always as big a market mover as the Jobs Report, unless there is a surprise. For example, if the markets were expecting 3% growth, but the actual figure is 5.2% growth, that means that the economy is growing at a much faster rate than expected. Stocks, bonds, and maybe even the Federal Reserve would respond to this type of number. The type of response would depend on where the market cycle is at the time. For example, if the economy had just emerged from a recession, the 5.2% figure would be considered a pleasant surprise and stocks would likely rally in a big way while bonds would likely sell off. If that type of number has been released after a secular bull market, it would be interpreted as a sign that the economy was overheating, which would have a negative effect on all markets as everyone would expect a round of interest rate increases from the Federal Reserve. The potential for an unexpected number and an equally unexpected response is a perfect example of the inexact nature of economic forecasting and of the predictably unpredictable behavior of markets.

Institute for Supply Management (ISM) Report

The Institute for Supply Management's *Report On Business* is a highly anticipated private sector report that often moves the market. Investors usually focus on the Purchasing Managers' Index (PMI). If this index is above fifty, it's a sign of growth in the manufacturing economy. A number below fifty suggests a slowing economy. The PMI has ten components which are placed into the formula that gives the overall PMI number. The ISM index components are: new orders, production, employment, supplier deliveries, inventories, customers' inventories, prices, backlog of orders, exports, and imports.

The Beige Book

This report is a summary of the information gathered by the Federal Reserve about the economy for the previous six weeks. It's based on interviews and research done by the Fed staff in each of the central bank's twelve district banks. The full text can be found at the Fed's website upon release. CNBC, Bloomberg, and FOX Business News all spend a good deal of time reporting on the information in each installment. It's an interesting read if you have the time as it often provides detailed quotes and observations regarding current economic conditions, and how they may affect future plans by business owners.

Stocks, Bonds, and Mutual Funds

Think of stocks, bonds, and mutual funds as three different ways to participate in the fortunes of a company, or in the case of a bond, in the fortunes of a company, government, or government entity. The difference between a bond and a stock is that bonds are IOUs while stocks are pieces of a company. A mutual fund is an investment company that invests in stocks, bonds, commodities, or a combination of several asset classes.

What Is a Stock?

Shares of stock are pieces of a company that give the holder the opportunity to participate in the fortunes of the enterprise, good or bad. Stocks rise and fall in price and may also pay dividends. It can be tough to determine what exactly causes a specific stock's price to rise or fall but in general, the price of a stock rises and falls based on these general factors: sales of the company's products, the decisions made by management, interest rates, and external economic forces. Only the stock of public companies trades on exchanges or through some kind of over-the-counter arrangement as in the shares of penny stocks.

Only investors with a good knowledge of the financial markets and a good-sized portfolio of at least $50,000–$100,000 minimum should consider investing in individual stocks. The reason for this is that individual stock prices tend to fluctuate more than mutual funds over time.

ALERT

A bad earnings report could ruin a small portfolio of stocks. If you own three hundred shares of XYZ stock and it misses its earnings expectations, XYZ could lose a large portion of its value in a hurry. If XYZ is 20% or more of your total portfolio, you could take a big cut.

What Is a Bond?

Companies or governments borrow money by selling bonds. While governments fund programs via bond sales, companies often sell bonds in order to expand plants, develop new products, buy back their own stock, or buy back bonds that pay higher interest rates in exchange for bonds that pay lower interest rates. By selling bonds to investors, companies avoid or decrease upsetting their earnings streams, and are thus able to continue normal operations.

FACT

Bonds have two parts: the price and the yield. The price is what you would pay for the bond if you bought it. The yield is the interest rate that it pays. A bond quote involves both price and yield.

Governments sell bonds in order to pay off debt and to continue to fund their current and future obligations. The US government runs on money it gains by selling US Treasury bonds, which are considered the highest-rated bonds in the world. Government agencies also sell bonds in order to keep enough capital around to keep granting student loans and to fund other programs without depending solely on taxpayers to directly foot the bill.

Why should anyone care about bond yields? Bond yields, especially the yield on the 10-year Treasury note (TNX), are benchmarks for mortgages, car loans, home equity loans, and many other interest rates. It's good to know when bond yields fall, as it could be an opportunity to look into refinancing a mortgage or other loan.

ESSENTIAL

News reports, especially regarding Treasury bonds, focus on the yield or interest rate. When a news reporter says that bonds "are rallying," it means that interest rates are falling.

What Is a Mutual Fund?

A mutual fund is an investment company that invests in assets on behalf of its clients. Investors buy shares in the mutual fund, not in individual assets or companies. Mutual funds have managers. Some mutual funds have a sole manager. Others are managed by committees of individuals and buy and sell assets based on the votes of the committee. Mutual fund managers are licensed by their states, and their actions are governed by the rules of the Securities and Exchange Commission. Fund managers are highly educated, often in finance as well as other fields of study. They have to pass rigorous examinations and are required, like all investment advisors, to attend continuing education classes and seminars. Companies that sell mutual fund shares to the public are highly regulated by the federal government.

ESSENTIAL

Consider buying your first mutual fund shares from a larger fund company that has been around for a long time. These companies tend to have better online and phone support and often sponsor seminars and classes for beginning investors.

Mutual funds offer a document called a prospectus, which lists the kinds of assets they invest in, the rules they follow, how they analyze the markets, their past performance, and most importantly, what they owned at the time the prospectus was filed.

Fundamental and Technical Market Analysis

There are two ways to analyze markets: technical and fundamental. The latter is the most common method used by investors, but it is not always the best when used on its own. Fundamental analysis is all about facts and data. All earnings and economic reports, as well as news and events that affect prices, are considered fundamental analysis. A mutual fund prospectus, an opinion piece that you read on a financial website, and even a look around a retail store of a company that interests you, are considered fundamental analysis.

Fundamental analysis is essential as it will build a knowledge base about your investments, which in the long haul is an excellent thing. The disadvantage is that company fundamentals don't always immediately correlate with the price of a stock or the direction of any market. And that's where technical analysis can help you make better decisions regarding the timing of when to buy or to sell.

General Fundamentals of the Financial Markets

Fundamental data (the fundamentals) is the information that affects market behavior and direction: news items, economic releases, and events in general. Each market—stocks, bonds, and commodities—has its own set of fundamentals. And while all markets have their own rhythm, because of the rapid spread of news via the Internet, all stocks, bonds, currencies, and commodity markets around the world are linked to one another in terms of price. So regardless of trade policy or geopolitics, what happens in one market can, and often does, have repercussions in other markets.

If a positive US Jobs Report leads to a rally in US stocks, investors may see similar moves in Asian and European markets on the next trading day. If you own a mutual fund that owns Japanese stocks, there is a good chance that it, too, will have a good response.

What happens in stocks, bonds, and commodities can also affect the currency markets. At the same time, events that affect the US dollar, the euro, and other world currencies can have positive or negative effects on stocks, bonds, and other financial markets around the world.

Fundamentals of the Stock Market

The stock market is where stocks of companies trade. In the United States it is composed of three major indexes: the Dow Jones Industrial Average (INDU), the Standard & Poor's 500 (SPX), and the NASDAQ Composite Index (NASDAQ). There are other well-known indexes, including the Dow Jones Transportation Average (DJT), the Dow Jones Utility Average (DJU), and others which detail prices in individual sectors of the overall stock market. For example, there are specific indexes used to gauge the prices in biotechnology and financial stocks.

An index is a group of stocks whose prices are worked through a formula to provide the value of the index at any one time. The Dow Jones Industrial Average has thirty stocks, and the price of the index at any time is what an investor would pay for one share of the index. So, if the Dow's most recent quote is 16,000, that's how much one share of the index would cost. The

Standard & Poor's 500 (S&P 500) has five hundred stocks. The NASDAQ Composite Index houses over four thousand stocks.

Company earnings, interest rates, and company mergers influence stock prices. External events, such as wars, changes in commodity prices, and trends in the bond market, also influence stock prices.

Fundamentals of the Bond Market

The bond market is much bigger than the stock market in terms of how much money exchanges hands there at any given time. It also has a much greater influence on the global economy than do stocks. While stocks often respond to economic trends, the bond market directly influences major economic trends. That's because bonds are all about interest rates, and credit depends on the general direction of interest rates. Generally speaking, rising interest rates slow economic growth while falling interest rates tend to stimulate growth.

ALERT

It is said that bond traders love bad news. Remember that bonds hate inflation. Inflation happens when economies grow too rapidly. A slowing economy is the best time to own bonds.

Technical Analysis

Technical analysis is a topic worthy of its own book. The bottom line is that it's based on reading and analyzing price charts. Beginning investors should know the basics. A picture, especially combined with good knowledge of the fundamentals, is really worth a thousand words. Here are the basic concepts that you can complement with an excellent tutorial that you can find at StockCharts.com, where a search for the ChartSchool will get you started on the right path.

Price charts have three basic components: prices, moving averages, and other key points that let you get a good grip on whether this is a good time to enter or exit either the market or any individual stock, bond, ETF (exchange-traded fund), or mutual fund. Price charts can seem confusing at first. But by learning each individual section, anyone can know enough about them to get a good feel for whether the chart is flashing good or bad news, which is the most important aspect of technical analysis, to add a timing component to the fundamentals of any asset.

ESSENTIAL

Becoming proficient in technical analysis is extremely useful if you choose to engage in short-term trading.

If you're new to the study of price charts, this section gives you a tour of the essential information you'll need to glean useful information from them. Investors who focus solely or primarily on charts are known as chartists or technicians.

The First Look

Charts are divided into time periods. The most common periods cover the price action over one year with each period of the chart covering the price action for a day of trading. The first look at the chart is often revealing. Just by looking at the general direction, up or down, of prices, you get an idea as to what the action has been over any period of time you choose.

Moving Averages

Price charts are full of lines that are known as moving averages. Commonly used moving averages are the twenty-day, the fifty-day, and the two hundred–day moving average. Each moving average plots the average on prices for the number of days, ending on the last day plotted. Moving averages smooth out price action. A rising moving average is a positive factor for any financial instrument as it tells you that prices have trended higher for the past twenty, fifty, or two hundred days.

> **FACT**
>
> The two hundred–day moving average is often referred to as the line that divides bull and bear markets. Generally speaking, when prices remain above the average, the market is considered to be in a bull phase. When prices remain below the average, the market is considered to be in a bear phase.

Support and Resistance

Prices have important starting and stopping points. These are generally known as support and resistance. Support areas are where buyers tend to come in and buy. Resistance points are areas where sellers get the upper hand. Generally speaking, markets that find support are usually worth considering or buying into. Markets that find it difficult to move above resistance are usually worth avoiding or considering selling in.

> **FACT**
>
> After the 2008 subprime mortgage crash, Wall Street increased its use of computer trading algorithm-based strategies for stock trading. An important side effect of this change is that technical analysis is now more useful than ever, since the machines leave clues in the market's technicals, as they are known in market jargon. These clues can be easy to decipher if you know what to look for.

Volume

These charts also have vertical bars at the bottom that count the trading volume for the stock pictured on the chart. This is the number of shares that traded for the particular stock on that day. Good charts have different colors for volume on up days and on down days. For example, prices on up days may be white or green while prices on down days may be red.

Generally high volume, up or down, especially over time, is a signal that the market is continuing to head in the direction of the volume. At some point volume reaches extreme levels, which can be a signal that the trend is about to reverse.

Investors that combine both fundamental and technical analysis have a more complete picture of where they are putting their money. Perhaps the best use of technical analysis is that it can be very helpful in choosing when to enter or exit any market. If you learn the few basic concepts of chart analysis, you will have a nice base to start from and will be able to make more informed decisions about your investments.

Robot Tricks

Every market cycle has its own particular wrinkles, and because technical analysis is a visual pursuit, it will help you spot key market phenomena. Many robot trading programs or algorithms are based purely on technical analysis and use moving averages and other forms of support and resistance levels as triggers for making trades. Around 2009, people began to catch on to the fact that the robots almost always bought stocks at key support levels. It became a well-recognized trading technique to wait for prices to fall to a key moving average, perhaps the fifty-day or the two hundred–day lines. This frequent occurrence, the buying of stocks when they traded near expected support levels, became known as "buying the dip." Thus, if you didn't use technical analysis during this period of time, you would have likely missed many opportunities to buy before prices resumed their upward climb.

ALERT

Prices often consolidate just above or below the twenty-, fifty-, and two hundred-day moving averages. Therefore, it pays to be patient before buying or selling when prices approach these lines.

CHAPTER 4

A Close Look at Stocks

Stocks are a good place to start when you're a young investor because these are the investment vehicles that, over time, offer the most potential for portfolio growth. However, because stock prices can be volatile, they should not be viewed as automatic wealth-building vehicles but only as part of a diversified portfolio. As you learn more, you should also consider what kind of a stock investor you may become: a trader with a shorter time frame in mind, a buy-and-hold investor, or somewhere in between.

The Exchanges

A stock exchange is still a place where buyers and sellers meet to transfer shares to one another but the stock exchanges of the present are totally different animals than those of even the early 2000s. The best-known stock exchanges are still the New York Stock Exchange (NYSE), also known as the Big Board, and the NASDAQ, but that's about all that remains similar to the past. Even now the NYSE is almost fully automated. Although the NYSE still has floor brokers, known as specialists, who match orders from buyers and sellers, these positions are becoming relics and are likely to be fully replaced by machines at some point in the future. The NASDAQ is fully electronic, with market makers and their huge electronic platforms matching buyers and sellers.

ALERT

A good rule of thumb is to have a planned exit point for any stock you buy before you actually hit the trade button.

There are other major stock exchanges around the world, such as the London Stock Exchange and the Frankfurt Stock Exchange. There are also myriad other exchanges with weird names like Arca, electronic "trading floors" that are nothing but server farms in places like Hoboken, New Jersey. In these places, Wall Street's big banks and high-frequency trading houses fight for commissions and deploy their trading algorithms.

If you trade stocks, you need to be well versed in sophisticated analysis and tools if you want a decent chance of success. That's because most trades are now conducted electronically and you are mostly trading against high-frequency trading (HFT) computers or traders who are using sophisticated software programs. However, online brokers now provide sophisticated trading programs for active traders that let you get a better handle on your odds of success through various analytical tools. These are your best bet because they are often free of charge if you trade enough for the commission costs to cover the cost of the program. Each broker has its own requirements for no-cost trading. Some brokers may charge a fee for access to their trading program to investors who don't qualify. You can also subscribe to online high-end charting and trading platforms, which in many cases allow you to route your own orders as opposed to those offered by your broker.

> **FACT**
>
> To learn more about high-frequency trading, check out Michael Lewis's book *Flash Boys: A Wall Street Revolt*.

Who Polices the Store?

The stock market, just like all large-money enterprises, is a risky place where fraud is not uncommon. The exchanges and industry associations such as the NASD (the National Association of Securities Dealers) do a fair amount of self-policing, as do state-run securities boards. The big cop is the Securities and Exchange Commission (the SEC). The SEC has two main functions. First, its job is to enforce federal securities laws, investigate possible violations, and recommend solutions. Second, it must protect investors, especially small investors, from scams and from unscrupulous brokers. Still, bad things happen to good people, so you should be very aware of the risks before you start trying to trade your account in individual stocks.

The SEC's website, www.sec.gov, provides free investment information through its EDGAR (Electronic Data Gathering, Analysis, and Retrieval) database. You can find the latest public company reports, such as 10-Q and 10-K forms, that offer a look into the inside workings of companies. These forms often tell you about a company's upcoming plans, expectations, and more importantly, its concerns and potential difficulties.

What Stocks Really Are

Stocks are pieces of companies. When a company "goes public," the owners transfer shares of the company to the public in an initial public offering (IPO). After the IPO, stocks trade on exchanges. By owning stock, an investor shares in the fortunes of the company, good or bad. Shares of common stock grant the shareholders rights, including the right to influence company policy and direction through votes at the annual shareholder meetings.

For example, in 2014 Alphabet (Google's parent company) split its shares into two classes. Those shares with the GOOGL symbol retained all rights. A second set of shares with the GOOG symbol does not have shareholder voting rights. Sometimes, but not always, nonvoting shares can have a higher dividend payout than voting shares.

Stock Indexes

An index is a group of stocks whose values are pooled together using a mathematical formula. As each stock in the index trades, its most recent price is processed through the formula, leading to the value that is reported during the stock market trading day and when stocks stop trading at the close. An example of indexing is the frequent value quoting of the Dow Jones Industrial Average, the most commonly quoted stock index in the world. A Dow quote of 16,000 means that it would cost $16,000 to buy one share of the index at that place in time.

Types of Stock Indexes

There are dozens of indexes that quantify the value of groups of stocks, but they can all be divided into two major categories: diversified and sector-specific. Diversified indexes house several types of stocks, while sector-specific indexes measure the value of stocks in the same sector of the economy.

The Dow Jones Industrial Average (also referred to simply as the Dow) is composed of thirty large global blue chips, or high-quality corporations in different industries. Members of the Dow Jones Industrial Average include software giant Microsoft and oil giant ExxonMobil. The Standard & Poor's 500 Index (S&P 500) contains five hundred large companies. It's considered the market benchmark because it has more stocks than the Dow; thus, it offers a wider view of the market and how the market is reflecting economic activity.

The NASDAQ Composite Index (NASDAQ) has over four thousand stocks. It's traditionally weighted toward technology companies, but is considered a diversified index as it also has biotech, banking, and energy stocks.

FACT

The stock of a company may be included in several sector indexes simultaneously. For example, shares of Apple are found in five separate indexes, including the NASDAQ-100 Index and the S&P 500 Information Technology Index.

Sector-specific indexes include the Semiconductor Sector Index (SOX), the Biotechnology Index (BTK), and the Bank Index (BKX). Each of these sector indexes contains only stocks from that particular sector of the economy. For example, SOX includes Intel and companies that are involved in the semiconductor chip sector. You can find companies such as Amgen in BTK. And banks such as JPMorgan Chase and Bank of America are in the Bank Index.

ALERT

Get to know both sector-specific and diversified indexes as you gain investment knowledge. The action in any sector of the market may have a significant effect on the whole market and your portfolio, including your mutual funds.

Types of Stocks

There are two broad categories of stocks: growth stocks and income stocks. Growth stocks such as Amazon grow their sales, revenues, and eventually earnings at rapid rates and offer investors the opportunity for capital appreciation. These stocks can make you money when you buy low and sell high, and tend to be companies either in their early stages of being publicly traded or well-established companies who deliver products and services which are in high demand. As the company matures, growth tends to slow and the stocks start paying dividends, which produce income. Profits from the company's profitable operations produce dividends. Income stocks, such as oil and bank stocks, are primarily owned for their dividend payouts.

FACT

Dividends are portions of a company's profits that are passed on to shareholders. They are usually, but not always, paid out on a quarterly basis. Some companies pay both a quarterly dividend and extra dividends throughout the year depending on circumstances. A great place for information, such as lists of stocks that pay high dividends or information on specific dividend-paying stocks, is www.dividend.com.

Inside Growth Stocks

Growth stocks are pieces of companies whose sales, revenues, and profits grow at a faster rate than whatever the current norm is in a market. For example, if the S&P 500 has a sales growth rate of 10% per year, a dynamic growth stock could be growing its sales at a 20% clip or even faster. This makes the stock of these companies very attractive, often for extended periods of time. Perhaps the best example of a long-standing growth company is Amazon. Growth stocks usually pay no dividends and pour every resource possible into the company in order to continue their growth.

The Income Producers

Income stocks are also known as yield stocks and tend to be those of older, established companies that pay out a high percentage of their earnings to shareholders through dividends. The most common yield stocks are those of electric utility companies. Blue chip oil stocks, like ExxonMobil, and tobacco giant Altria Group, are also reliable dividend payers. Altria's dividend has remained very popular over time, attracting buyers to the stock. It's a good idea to own both growth stocks and dividend-paying stocks in any diversified portfolio.

ESSENTIAL

Investors who are just getting started should consider a mix of growth and income stocks in their portfolio.

A special kind of dividend-paying stock is the preferred stock. This type of stock pays a higher yield than the common stock of a company and has a lifespan defined by its redemption date. It also pays a guaranteed fixed dividend that gets paid no matter what the company's earnings do.

ALERT

Beware of dividend-paying stocks with an extraordinarily high yield, or dividend rate. If either a common or a preferred stock has an uncommonly high dividend yield, especially compared to similar companies in its sector, or the overall market as measured by the S&P 500, there is usually a reason to be careful. High dividends are often a sign that the stock price has fallen significantly and that the company has not cut its dividend—usually a sign that the company is in trouble. A good rule of thumb is to check the dividend yield of the S&P 500 online and use it for comparison. For example, if the S&P 500 yield is 2% and XYZ common is paying 8%, you should do some more research before chasing that high dividend.

Preferred stocks are always part of a separate class of shares, distinct from common shares, the class of stock with which most people are familiar. The share class of a stock, either common or preferred, is determined by the company when the stock is issued to the public. For example, if XYZ has both common and preferred shares, XYZ common has the symbol XYZ when it trades. Its preferred stocks trade with the symbol XYZ.A, XYZ.B, and so on, depending on how many classes of preferred stocks there may be. Preferred-stock holders have no vote at the annual company meeting and do not have any of the rights of holders of common shares. That means that if you don't like what a company is doing, when it comes time to vote for change, you are out of the loop. That's the price for getting a higher dividend.

General Characteristics of Growth versus Income

Growth stocks can be very risky. They tend to be the section of the market where day traders and momentum traders make their living. These stocks can move, up or down, in a big way in a short period of time. By the same token, you can also reap a larger reward by taking the risks of owning some growth stocks. One way to cut risks is to own a growth stock mutual fund that owns large numbers of growth stocks and can cushion the risk of one or two stocks that happen to have a big move to the downside on any given day.

ALERT

Fast-moving growth stocks are also known as momentum stocks. Momentum stocks tend to rally over long periods of time and make huge gains over the period. Eventually they all come crashing down. Beware, not even these go-go stocks go up forever.

Sizing Up Individual Stocks

There are three capitalization categories in the stock market: small, midsize, and large (also known as small-cap, mid-cap, and large-cap). Capitalization is the value of the company in dollars in the public market. To calculate any stock's market capitalization you multiply the current price of the stock by the number of outstanding shares.

Small-cap companies are companies whose market capitalization is less than $3 billion. Mid-cap companies are between $3 billion and $6 billion. Anything above $6 billion is considered large-cap. Blue chip stocks are those with very large market values, such as Apple, Microsoft, and Google. The definitions of market capitalization size tend to shift based on whether the market is trading at a very high or low level. For example, if the market has been declining for a long time, the definition of a small-cap stock might differ from what it would be if the market happened to be trading near its all-time highs. In a declining market, small-cap may be defined as stocks with market caps at $1 billion or less, while large-cap may refer to stocks that are valued over $3 billion. The take-home message is that there are several tiers of stocks and that each tier has its own characteristics.

ALERT

Stock quotes at *Yahoo! Finance* automatically provide stock market capitalization values, so that's a good resource to check out.

Small-Cap Stocks

Smaller stocks tend to be faster growers, but they may be small for a good reason, such as their products are very niche-specific or because they are a development-stage company and don't have any products in the market. Many speculative biotechnology stocks are in the small-cap sector. As a class, small stocks tend to be riskier than large-cap stocks. They usually don't pay dividends. By the same token, a small company, which is able to expand its sales, earnings, and scope, may become a mid-cap, a large-cap, or a blue chip stock at some point in the future. As with growth stocks, owning a well-managed, well-established small-cap stock mutual fund can help to reduce the risk of owning these individual companies. The benchmark index for small-cap stocks is the Russell 2000 Index (RUT) of small-cap stocks.

Mid-Cap Stocks: The Sweet Spot in the Market

Because they are usually well-established companies that have a track record, have stable earnings, often pay dividends, and tend to grow at reasonable rates, mid-cap stocks are often referred to as the sweet spot of the market. Don't let that fool you, though. As with any area of the market, mid-cap stocks can be risky; therefore, doing your homework before investing is essential. The benchmark index for mid-cap stocks is the Standard & Poor's MidCap 400 Index (MID). As with other areas and sectors of the market, a mid-cap stock mutual fund is worth considering.

Blue Chip and Large-Cap Stocks

Blue chip stocks are the names everyone recognizes when they think of the stock market. These are companies like Walmart, Procter & Gamble, and Pfizer. The Dow Jones Industrial Average houses thirty of the bluest of blue chip stocks in the world. But the S&P 500 also has its share of blue chip stocks, as well as being the home of the 500 largest stocks in the US stock market. Blue chip stocks are usually near the top of their industry, deliver reasonably predictable earnings on a quarterly basis, and are often the backbone of conservative stock portfolios. Large numbers of mutual funds and institutional investors own blue chip stocks.

Cyclical, Defensive, and Value Stocks

Three other categories of stocks that you should be aware of are cyclical, defensive, and value stocks. These categories include small-cap, mid-cap, large-cap, and blue chip stocks that behave in similar ways to one another.

Cyclical stocks are companies whose price action tends to change with the business cycle. These include the steel, chemical, construction, heavy machinery, and mining companies. Generally, when the economy is expanding, these stocks tend to move higher. A great example of a cyclical stock is

Dow Chemical (NYSE: DOW). These stocks can be difficult to buy and hold for short periods of time, but can be important parts of long-term holdings because they often pay very good dividends.

Defensive stocks tend to be relatively stable and often, but not always, have very small price fluctuations. This category includes utility and health-care stocks. They are not immune from long-term down trends in the market, but they tend to hold their value better during down periods than most growth and momentum stocks.

Value stocks are those that are cheap relative to the overall value of the market. These are usually stocks of companies that are doing quite well but are being ignored by the market, which tends to focus on momentum stocks a fair amount of the time. Value investors tend to be very patient and often have to wait for long periods of time before the market recognizes their stock. Value stocks tend to be companies that sell at less than two times their book value. For example, in September 2018, JPMorgan Chase (NYSE: JPM) was selling at just 1.71 times its book value. This was a classic value scenario.

Important Market Sectors

The S&P 500 is divided into eleven sectors. Each sector is given a weighting in the index, which is the amount of influence it has on the overall price of the index.

For example, in September 2018, these were the approximate weightings:

- Information Technology: 21%
- Health Care: 15%
- Financials: 13%
- Consumer Discretionary: 10%
- Telecom Services: 10%
- Industrials: 9%
- Consumer Staples: 7%
- Energy: 5%
- Utilities: 4%
- Real Estate: 3%
- Materials: 3%

You can see that the areas where people spend big money. Information Technology, Health Care, Financials, Consumer Discretionary, and Telecom Services add up to nearly 70% of the index. If you were to construct your own S&P 500–inspired stock portfolio, this is the model that you would use. This weighting changes over time depending on the economy and the general state of the markets.

Penny Stocks

Penny stocks are the danger zone of the stock market. They are almost always a sure way to quickly lose money. Despite a few success stories, the odds of getting lucky in this area of the market are almost zero. When you hear about how Apple and Microsoft were once penny stocks, consider that Google, Facebook, and Twitter were not penny stocks when they went public.

Penny stocks are stocks with a price generally below $5 per share. And there is usually a good reason for it, such as the company losing money, doesn't have any viable products, has fallen on hard times, or is under investigation. If you must invest in penny stocks, do your homework. Research the company, its products, and its management team. Consider their business sector and their competition. If they actually do have the new holy grail, and no one but you has figured it out, you may actually defy the odds and hit that one-in-a-million home run. But don't bet the house on it.

CHAPTER 5

Choosing Stocks to Buy

The ideal stock is one that moves steadily higher over a long period of time, pays a good dividend, and has all the characteristics of a great company. Because you are putting real money into a financial instrument whose price rises and falls, often several times within a few minutes, evaluating and owning stocks is complex and requires patience. Moreover, to be a successful stock investor, you need careful thought and a well-put-together plan that lets you pick winners consistently and lets you know when it's time to sell.

Five Points That Make a Great Company

There are five characteristics of a great company:

1. Great products
2. Superb management
3. Excellent customer service
4. Adaptability to current trends and changes in current customer needs
5. Accountability to shareholders

In other words, a great company has great products, great corporate ethics, excellent management, and is able to communicate its successes as well as its failures in a timely and honest fashion. A terrible company is usually marked by shifty management, inconsistent returns, and a lack of direction.

Analyzing Ruth's Hospitality Group

Ruth's Hospitality Group, an operator of upscale steak houses with a casual feel, is a perfect example of a great company because, even though it is a small-cap stock, it excels in the way it runs its business. Just because a company is not a household name doesn't mean it's not a great business to invest in. A great company is able to execute its business plan during good times and bad, which Ruth's has done over the years and for which it was rewarded by the market. For example, from 2014 to 2018, the company grew its net income from $16 million to over $40 million while consistently beating market expectations. An even better measure of Ruth's success was the company's stock price over the period, which rose from $10 a share to $30 at its peak. And it did all that by excelling at each of the five characteristics of a great company.

Great Products

Ruth's Hospitality Group has a great niche in the steak house market: a place where customers can have an upscale steak dinner in a relaxed but elegant atmosphere. As a result, it attracts a broad customer base of all age groups, ranging from businesspeople to families. It offers a broad cross section of high-quality steaks and seafood complemented by gourmet side dishes, fine wines, top-shelf liquor, and a top-notch dessert menu. Most recently, it has adapted to changing demographics while keeping its current customer base well served by expanding its offerings into a bar-bistro model, which targets the after-work, single-diner, and younger crowds.

FACT

Ruth's Hospitality Group has humble roots and is a classic success story. The company was founded in New Orleans in 1965 by a single mother, Ruth Fertel, who had no restaurant management experience but was full of the entrepreneurial spirit. She bought the Chris Steak House by mortgaging her house and fought for her successes with grit and determination. When the original restaurant burned down, she moved to a new location and added her own name to the banner, and that's how the name of their signature restaurant, Ruth's Chris Steak House, came about.

Management

While some companies are headed by big-name CEOs, Ruth's has a very down-to-earth management team which focuses on running the business, not in shameless self-promotion. You can see this approach quite well in the transcripts of the company's earnings calls, during which management's approach is to speak softly and articulately about not just the current quarter but their future strategy for growing the business. It's during these calls that you get the feel for the company's slow and steady balanced approach to growth via expansion into well-thought-out locations and through acquisitions of specific real estate in prime locations. The company is evenly split between corporate-owned locations and franchises, a thoughtful approach which keeps management focused on the company's future plans without diluting management's efforts by making them run a far-flung empire.

Customer Service

The company's customer service is superior to that of many of its competitors, and is central to the brand's success, as the hosts and waitstaff are professional, well informed about the menu offerings, and courteous. Of course you should expect that at all upscale restaurants, but the difference at Ruth's is the personal touch that the waitstaff brings to the meal when they discuss their favorite meals and offer menu tips. The best part of the experience is the timing of reservations and the dining room atmosphere, which is very relaxed and calm. Whereas some high-end steak houses have crowded lobbies and dining rooms, Ruth's lobbies are quiet and comfortable, as Ruth's manages their reservation flow to keep the number of people in the lobby manageable and the dining room flow comfortable for the customers without the loud, noisy mess you often find at other high-price restaurants. This seemingly insignificant act shows the attention to detail which brings customers back. Finally, unlike some of its competition, Ruth's balances its sales growth by not overpricing the food. Instead, it focuses on increasing traffic to its restaurants while expanding the size of the chain prudently in order to keep the earnings growth stable.

Adaptability and Innovation

Companies have to remain relevant in order to maintain and grow revenues and earnings. Ruth's adapts to current trends by varying its menu options, but also by its ongoing store renovation, remodeling, and relocation strategy. Ruth's strives to have enough locations to be convenient to its customers but not to have a restaurant on every corner and overcrowd the market like a fast-food company. They do so in an ongoing fashion by revamping eight to ten restaurants per year, either by relocation or renovation. They also make each dining room unique in its décor and atmosphere, which keeps the same great dining experience visually fresh. Their individualized décor also helps each individual Ruth's avoid the feel of a chain restaurant while keeping the same excellent standards across the entire company.

ESSENTIAL

Consistency in service, presentation, and quality are keys to greatness, and so is the trademark ingredient in Ruth's steaks—clarified butter before serving. So whether you're eating at locations in Dallas, New Orleans, or Wailea, you can expect the same excellent experience, great food, and great service.

Accountability to Shareholders

Aside from having great steaks and running a profitable company that is tuned in to customer needs, a great company has to take care of its shareholders. You don't want to buy stock in a company that does not have the shareholders' best interests in mind. That's where listening in on company earnings calls, reading earnings call transcripts, and keeping up with media and analyst coverage of the company pays off. Ruth's press releases and earnings calls are usually frank and truthful and contain useful information. Ruth's rarely sugarcoats its future expectations and tends to admit when it's made a strategic mistake while offering solutions.

Buy What You Know and Know What You Buy

As simple as this concept sounds, it's a great place to start when you are looking to jump-start your stock picking. You use health products on a regular basis. You travel; you buy groceries; you stay at hotels; you eat at steak houses or casual dining restaurants; you use a bank—even an online bank; you can see what other people are eating or driving; and you have credit cards. You also know that even though a product is popular, it may be a fleeting phenomenon, which is why your personal knowledge of a concept or a product is a great place to start, but not the only factor that you should use in deciding whether to buy a stock.

Once you've picked a product and decided on a company, consider these factors:

- Does this company meet the criteria for a great company?
- What are the current sales growth and earnings growth rates?
- How is the valuation?
- How is this stock behaving compared to the market?
- Does this company pay dividends and is the dividend growing?

Is This a Great Company?

This is an easy one. Let's say that you just bought a new cell phone from a startup company called XYZ that is trying to expand its market share. You like the phone and you start seeing other people buying it. That's the signal to dig more into this company as you apply the "Five Point" approach. Check for the presence of each of the five key characteristics:

- Great products
- Superb management
- Excellent customer service
- Adaptability and innovation
- Accountability to shareholders

See what the answers are. If the company earns the five points that describe a great company, then it's time to do more homework.

Checking Sales and Momentum

XYZ's sales presumably come from selling cell phones and accessories. A good rule of thumb for growth companies is that they should have at least three or more quarters of sequential sales growth. Great growth companies deliver more than 20% growth, and the exceptional ones accelerate their growth at a sustainable and consistent pace. Those are the companies that hit the home runs. Sales momentum is the one metric where the five characteristics of a great company come together. If sales rates are stale or decreasing, but you still see more XYZ phones around, it may be worth it to keep an eye on the company and see what it does over the next couple of quarters. You may be catching it at a period when the sales growth has not been reported. In this case, owning a very small number of shares, especially if the stock is rising in price without any news, could make sense.

ALERT

A perfect example of how sales growth and management's ability to deliver can affect stocks is the Tesla phenomenon. During the early twenty-first century, the green dynamic kept Tesla's brand in the forefront of electric car technology. Unfortunately, the company lost focus and sales became unpredictable, as did vehicle quality. When you add CEO Elon Musk's unusual behavior into the mix and his *Twitter* outbursts about company developments (which were not always reliable), you can see why the stock began to have a difficult time. If you're at the top of the heap, you've got to continue to deliver or your stock will run into hard times. And when the Securities and Exchange Commission sued Musk in 2018, it was a sign that perhaps the stock had seen its best levels for a while.

Earnings and Revenue Growth

Revenue, also known in investment language as the top line, is the amount of money that a company collects on its sales. Revenue growth signals that a company is selling larger quantities of its products, that it is able to collect on what it sells at a more efficient rate, and that its customers pay their bills, all signs of a well-managed company. Earnings are also known as the bottom line or what's left over after a company pays its expenses, including servicing its debt. Don't confuse earnings with cash flow, which is what's left before paying the bills.

Ideally, earnings and revenues grow simultaneously. If revenues are growing faster than earnings, the company may have a lot of debt and may not deliver earnings or earnings growth for some time. This is acceptable for young companies but not for established companies. Great companies consistently show a strong top- and bottom-line growth rate. Ten percent or above is excellent and is sustainable, while 20% is well above average and signals a company with even better potential. When revenues and earnings start to falter, it could be a sign that harder times are ahead, and evaluating whether you want to hold on to the stock makes sense.

Valuation

Valuation refers to whether a stock is cheap or expensive. There are many ways to express valuation, but price/earnings ratio and price-to-book are simple, accurate, and easy to find as part of stock quote information at stock market websites such as *MarketWatch* and *Bloomberg*.

Price/earnings (P/E) ratio describes how much you are paying for every dollar of earnings when you buy a share of stock. To calculate a P/E ratio, you divide the price of the stock by the most recent earnings per share. A price/earnings ratio of 10 is considered "normal" while a P/E ratio above 20 is generally considered expensive. It's best to understand P/E ratios as a measure not just of how expensive a stock is, but of what investors are willing to pay for a stock and what they are getting in return.

For example, it's not uncommon to see P/E ratios in the high teens or much higher for growth stocks that are delivering consistent returns. For example, in September 2018, Amazon, the premier growth stock of its era, had a P/E ratio of 179. This was clearly an expensive stock, but investors were paying up based on the company's astronomical growth rates—21% year-over-year earnings and nearly 100% on its earnings—and its increasing dominance of the retail sector. At the same time, Snap Inc. had a P/E ratio of -10, a sign that the company was losing money. Amazon shares were trading at $1,978 while Snap shares were at only $8.98. On the value end, tobacco company Altria Group had a P/E ratio of 16 with a share price of $62. Investors were willing to pay for Amazon's growth rate, while the main reason to own Altria at the time was the $3.20 yearly dividend—a 4.7% yield. Snap was best avoided at this time.

Price-to-book refers to the relationship between the price of the stock and the book value, which is the value of all of the company's assets. Amazon's price-to-book ratio was a lofty 27.5 while Altria's was 7.28. You can see the wide difference in valuation between a fully energized growth stock and a reliable value stock.

ESSENTIAL

When researching stock valuations, look at what you're paying for. When reviewing growth stocks, compare Amazon, a monster company with an expensive stock, outrageous growth rates, and market dominance, to a struggling company such as Snap. Then ask yourself if it makes sense to buy Amazon or Snap. In the case of Altria, the major reason to own the stock is the lofty dividend.

Also consider that price-to-book value can be misleading. Some company shares sell below book value and may not be cheap. In fact, they may be failing enterprises with sinking earnings and revenues on the verge of bankruptcy. In this case, it's the assets, such as buildings and other things that the company may own, that give it any value at all. Thus, valuation is only a small part of the overall analytical survey that you should perform.

Relative Strength

Relative strength (RS) measures a stock's performance in comparison to the market. The most common comparison is between an individual stock and the S&P 500. The higher the number, the better, as it means that your stock's price is rising faster than that of the whole index. When this happens, relative strength is considered positive. A back-of-the-napkin method of calculating this metric is as follows: if XYZ stock is trading at 50 and the S&P 500 is trading at 1,800, divide 50 by 1,800. XYZ's relative strength is 0.028. You can graph this on a daily or weekly basis if you're a stickler for details and spreadsheets. Investors.com displays the daily RS for all the stocks it lists in its daily stock quotes.

As with any other aspect of stock analysis, you should put relative strength in the proper perspective. If you own a bank stock that pays a steady dividend and the stock is rising at half the rate of the S&P 500, you are not necessarily in a bad position. Your stock is rising and you are getting dividends. On the other hand, if you own a growth stock and its relative strength is fading, it's likely a sign that you may have to consider selling it.

FACT

Valuation measures are useful tools but the ultimate truth when you own a stock is the price. When price starts to falter even in the absence of news, it is likely a sign that something is lurking in the future and that the smart money is selling before the news becomes public.

Dividends

Dividends are important, but they are not everything. Think of them as getting rent for being patient with a stock that is not moving very much. By the same token, avoid stocks that are either falling or not holding their value.

If a dividend isn't enough to keep stockholders in the stock, something must be going on behind the scenes. When the stock of an individual company falls, it's usually because someone with a lot of money knows something you don't. Always look at dividends within the context of how a company is doing, how it's running its business, and how it's managing its future.

To judge the quality of a dividend, compare it to the following benchmarks:

- The yield of the US 90-day Treasury bill
- The yield of the 10-year US Treasury note
- The dividend yield of the S&P 500
- The dividend yield of other stocks in its sector

Altria Group (NYSE: MO), the tobacco stock, has been a historical leader in dividends to its stockholders. In September 2018, the company's dividend yield was nearly 5%. In comparison, the US 90-day T-bill was paying 2.1%, the 10-year US Treasury note was paying nearly 3.1%, and the S&P 500's dividend yield was 1.9%. In this case, from purely a dividend-paying standpoint, Altria was the best bet. From a purely safety standpoint, the 90-day T-bill was your best bet because there is no risk of default and almost no price fluctuation in T-bills. Therefore, as with all aspects of investing, it's all about managing the risk/benefit ratio and your own risk profile.

Know Where You Are in the Market Cycle

The most difficult part of investing in stocks is knowing when it's best to buy, hold, or sell. If you are not in tune with this reality, you could lose large sums of money, sometimes in a hurry.

Bull versus Bear Market

The trend is indeed your friend. The official definition of a bull and a bear market is a price gain or loss of 20%. However, most traders simply refer to a period of time when stock prices are rising as a bull market and a period of time when stock prices are falling as a bear market, without too much concern for the exact percentage. In a bull market, the odds of picking stock winners is significantly higher than of doing so in a bear market, where the predominant direction of prices is down.

Being a Contrarian: Know When to Buck the Trend

A contrarian is an investor who can spot the time when it makes sense to go against the predominant price trend. For example, contrarians tend to buy near market bottoms and sell near market tops, whether in stocks, bonds or other assets. That's because they know that, generally speaking, a bull market starts when most people are expecting that stocks will never rise again. This is especially true during recessions, when the economy is declining and companies are making less money. Thus, their stock prices fall as investors realize that profits and earnings will fall due to the weak economy.

During these weak economic periods, the Federal Reserve lowers interest rates aggressively and eventually stock prices start to rise because lower interest rates decrease the return of savings accounts and other interest-paying instruments. At some point, the economy eventually improves, at least enough for stock prices to justify their gains, and more investors come in, fueling higher prices.

ALERT

Bull markets are hard-charging periods when stock prices rise on a frequent basis, the economy is usually steady or growing, and the outlook for profits is positive. During bear markets, everything is negative and the general price action takes a bite out of your portfolio and puts fear into the markets. Prices are falling, the economy is weak, and the profit outlook is uncertain.

Bear markets can last for long periods of time, often years, and can result from too much speculation in stocks, when the Federal Reserve raises interest rates, or both. In 2007 and 2008, stocks rolled over after the housing bubble burst. Prices fell throughout the year with almost no respite until finally bottoming out in 2009. This bear market was triggered by the Great Recession, and it began when too many people who bought homes on credit stopped making their mortgage payments. The banking system froze and the selling in stocks followed.

From October 2007 to March 2009, the S&P 500 lost nearly 57% of its value. In March 2009 when the market finally bottomed, as the Federal Reserve made it clear that interest rates would remain near zero for a very long time, stocks began a rally that gained over 300% before crashing in October 2018 as the Federal Reserve told the market interest rates were going much higher. Before you invest, make sure that the market is giving you good odds of being successful in your stock picks. Here is a three-point checklist that will keep you safe when analyzing the market:

1. Know whether stocks have been rising for a short or a long period of time. The longer the time that prices have been rising, the higher the odds of a significant decline.

2. Know what the Federal Reserve plans to do with interest rates in the short and long term. Lower interest rates favor stocks. Higher interest rates eventually lead to lower stock prices. The longer the life of the bull market, the higher the odds of a major decline. Between 2015 and 2018, the Federal Reserve raised interest rates from 0% to 2.25% and showed no interest in slowing down. As a result, by the third week of October 2018, the stock market was nearly in freefall when huge price swings in the Dow Jones Industrial Average were happening on a nearly daily basis.

3. Understand that even though you may buy the stock of a solid company, if the market reverses its trend and falls into a bear market or a significant correction in prices, your stock will likely fall along with the majority of stocks.

Technical Analysis: The Art of Reading Price Charts

Technical analysis of markets is the art of studying price charts and using your conclusions to make decisions about buying, selling, or holding assets such as stocks, bonds, or commodities. Price charts are based on the general principle that patterns tend to repeat over time and similar events tend to precede or follow similar price behavior. This can be true at important market bottoms (such as March 2009) and significant market tops (such as October 2018) as well as at some time in the future. Technical analysis works best when it is used along with fundamental analysis. There are entire and very thorough books dedicated to technical analysis that you can find through various booksellers.

And there are some great websites that are worth getting familiar with. One is *StockCharts*, which offers a great deal of free content and lets you customize charts in a way that is easy for you to understand. It also has great basic information and offers tutorials, which will help you learn how to read and analyze price charts and get comfortable with chart analysis. JoeDuarteintheMoneyOptions.com also features many price charts to illustrate trading decisions for subscribers.

CHAPTER 6

Buying Stocks and Monitoring Progress

This chapter is all about making the transition from paper investor to real-life stock picker. It starts with methods that offer you support as you move toward the point where you can fly on your own. After reading this section, you can decide which way to go based on your own risk tolerance and personality.

Investment Clubs

A nice transition from paper investing to real-life investing can be made through investment clubs. You and some friends pool your money and form a partnership. You can meet weekly or monthly and talk about stocks you own and monitor any existing holdings before voting on what to do next. It's even better if you keep in touch via texts, chats, social media, and emails, as you discover new ideas and make decisions whenever something changes. You can keep it informal or move toward a more organized approach. There is a non-profit organization called BetterInvesting that shows you how to set up and manage your investment club, for a subscriber's fee. BetterInvesting gets you going and offers instructional blogs and educational articles that continue the education process.

ESSENTIAL

The advantage of an investment club is that you can share the work and the reward while spreading the risk of any potential losses and learning from the experience of more than one person. When things don't go so well, an investment club is also a good place to cry in your pretzels.

Dividend Reinvestment Plans (DRIPs)

If you are not up to trading stocks just yet, you can look into a dividend reinvestment plan where you buy shares of common stock directly from the company. Usually you have to own at least one share of stock in the company through a broker before you can join the DRIP. There may be a handling fee to the company for keeping your shares, but there is no broker commission. This works well for buying shares of stock with low costs and is tailor-made for companies that pay dividends. You build up your position over time by buying shares at regular intervals and reinvesting the dividends. Reinvested dividends buy shares, or partial shares, of stock. If your stock sells for $100 and your dividend is $25, it would buy you one-fourth of a share.

DRIP investing isn't for everyone but is worth considering. You can explore DRIP investing at the DRIP Investment Resource Center (www .dripinvesting.org).

Who Will Do the Investing?

Once you've decided that you are going to be investing in stocks, ask yourself who will make your buy and sell decisions, and will you use a full commission or a discount broker to build and manage your portfolio?

Traditional Full-Service Brokers

A traditional full-service broker is a fast-fading breed: a professional in an office with a book of clients who uses research produced by the company they work for to pick stocks, which they then recommend to their clients. They may have a large number of clients and may or may not do much in the way of making judgments about you as an individual investor. Traditional brokers pass licensure exams and are registered investment advisors. They charge fairly large commissions and may also charge retainer fees for managing your portfolio. Traditional brokers get paid whether you make or lose money. Depending on your contractual agreement with your broker, they may have full discretion or partial discretion to trade your account.

ALERT

Beware of a full-service broker or advisor who only markets financial instruments sold by their company. These products, such as mutual funds and annuities, can have hefty fees and can often charge you even larger fees if you change your mind and want to exit them before a certain period of time.

Full-service brokers and advisors tend to market their services toward wealthy clients, so finding one who is conscientious about small accounts can be a difficult task. For most young investors, a full-service broker's job can be taken care of by a good knowledge base, a few good apps, and a discount broker with a good platform.

Discount Brokers

Discount brokers usually have branch offices as well as an online presence but most of the business is done by you online. The very large discount brokers such as Fidelity Investments, Charles Schwab, and Scottrade have excellent and comfortable branch offices where you can conduct business if you have to. The branch offices have computer terminals for research and trading, product brochures, and representatives to assist you. The representatives can answer questions, help you fill out forms, make exchanges between mutual funds, process withdrawals and deposits from your accounts, and set up appointments with investment advisors. Discount brokers also offer managed accounts and financial planning options for additional costs. The advantage is that you can do most of these things online and via your phone apps once you open an account.

Online discount brokers offer the following advantages:

- **Control.** You can make decisions on your own schedule based on your own experience and research. You can also trade or invest when you are ready instead of waiting for your broker to call you back.
- **Convenience.** With an online brokerage account you have access to your financial information at the speed of light from anywhere on your computer, laptop, or mobile phone apps. You can even make portfolio decisions while you are on vacation. If the market goes against you or your stock hits a sell point, you can do it in seconds from anywhere. If you need to interact with someone, discount brokers offer toll-free phone access, online chats, and branch offices.
- **Efficiency and Economy of Scale.** Full-service brokers are expensive, but because of intense competition, online brokers are much cheaper

than full-service traditional brokers. Online discount brokers usually charge less than $5 for executing your trades.

The DIY Investor

If you decide to go about investing by yourself, you will have to put some work into it but it's worth every penny. It does take time as you have to do your own research, make your own decisions, and take responsibility for your gains and losses. So you'll have to become a multitalented analyst. Moreover, aside from buying stock in companies that you find attractive, you have to figure out the market's prevalent trend and look for strong sectors by applying your analysis system, including the "Five Points" that make a great company.

DIY investors usually fare better with online brokers. Commissions are lower and most offer excellent support systems, including access to charts and to fundamental company information.

Consider a Consultant Advisor

It may make sense to get a second opinion when faced with a difficult decision. In those cases, it's good to find an advisor who may charge an hourly fee for providing an opinion on your portfolio. This may be a financial planner, your CPA, a registered investment advisor, or even a broker who consults with individuals who like to make their own investment decisions. Aunts, uncles, dads, moms, brothers, and sisters may know some stuff, too, and they may be cheaper.

Your Buy List

Once you've set up your account, it's time to put together your buy list. Here is where you put together what you know and what you've learned so far. First, consider whether you are in a bull or bear market. If stocks are generally moving higher, it's the former. If the economy is in bad shape, it's very likely that stocks are by and large falling. Either way, there is no harm in putting together a buy list and keeping tabs of the stocks on the list. Spend time each day studying their price charts and become familiar with their daily price swings.

Know Your Symbols

Stocks trade via their symbols. The New York Stock Exchange usually tags stocks with three-letter names, while the NASDAQ traditionally uses four letters. There are exceptions. Facebook (NASDAQ: FB) is only two letters on the NASDAQ, while Twitter (NYSE: TWTR) is an example of a four-letter symbol on the New York Stock Exchange. Online financial websites include the name of the stock and the symbol when they mention the company in articles. The references are linked to charts and news items.

Use the Stock Tables

Traditional stock tables, such as those found in print newspapers and online stock information sites such as *Yahoo! Finance*, list both the name and the symbol. Stock tables also include useful information, such as the high and low price over the past fifty-two weeks, the price/earnings ratio, dividends paid, dividend yield, the recent closing price, and the net change from the previous day's trading.

Putting Your List Together

You can start with as many stocks as you like and then pare your list down to the best of the bunch. Include the stocks of the companies whose products you use. Most consumer product companies pay reliable dividends. Consult the daily "New Highs" list that you can find on financial websites such as that of *The Wall Street Journal* and Investors.com. These are usually high growth stocks. Include some value, growth, and income stocks in your list and pick a few of each to include. Buy small numbers of shares, initially. You can add larger numbers later.

Don't have more stocks in your portfolio than you can keep up with. For a beginning investor, owning any more than ten stocks at any one time is probably too many. A good way to progress in your ability to pick stocks and to manage a diversified portfolio is by learning the steps through participating in your investment club and via paper trading. Once you get the hang of it you can start venturing out on your own with real money.

Think about Your Time Frame and Risk Tolerance

For most people, investing is a long-term process where they are looking for profits months or years after they buy a stock. That means that they are willing to be patient and will allow larger price fluctuations before making large changes to their portfolio. Long-term investors often see a price drop as an opportunity to buy more shares at a cheaper price, as long as they are comfortable with the long-term prospects of the company.

If you are nervous and impatient, you definitely want to study short-term trading techniques and become familiar with charting and technical analysis in fairly good detail before you start buying and selling stocks. Before you delve into short-term trading, consider that you can lose a great deal of money rapidly even if you are experienced.

Know Your Exit Point Before You Buy

Whether you are a patient long-term investor or a rapid-fire day trader, it's best to know your exit point before you buy a stock. There are two ways of doing this. Long-term investors often set targets, both in terms of price and time. You may decide that you will need the money in XYZ shares five years from the day you buy it, and you manage the position according to that strategy.

If you buy a stock and your goal is to make a certain amount of money, it becomes more difficult to achieve your exit point. You must remain vigilant. If you follow this price targeting strategy, you may buy a stock at $50 and set a target to sell it at $60. That price may be reached in three months or two years. If the stock hits the sell point in a short period of time, you can sell some of your shares since they hit your exit point, and let the rest of the position remain open and continue to move higher.

If you choose to let the partial open position ride, you can set another target and repeat the strategy. If you choose the second scenario, you should remember that your original target price was $60. If the stock rallies for a short period after it hits $60 and then rolls over and moves lower, you should stick to your target and sell it at $60 on the way back down. Short-term trading involves cutting losses at a certain percentage if a stock goes the wrong way. This is known as a sell stop. You can set sell stops either in terms of price points or in terms of percentages after you buy shares.

Executing Stock Trades

When you're ready to start trading, your number one concern is how to execute your trades. If you use a full-service broker, you would do that with a phone call. If you use an online discount broker, then you'll be using your mouse or your phone app. When you call your broker, you wait until your order is confirmed. When you trade online, you just follow the menu instructions, point and click, and your confirmation is on the screen almost immediately. Become familiar with the several types of buy and sell orders, and consider which one fits your strategy best before you actually trade. As a beginning investor, you may be best served by using market orders and considering the use of a sell stop. As you gain more experience you can consider more specific order types. You can also set price alarms that alert you when your stock has reached the price where you want to enter or exit.

Market Orders

This is the most common order used by individual investors. It means you want to buy or sell stocks at the current market price, or the going rate. Your order will be executed at the prevailing price when it hits the trading floor or the market maker. You will see two prices quoted, bid (the buy price) and ask (the sell price). The difference between the two prices is the spread. An example of Apple shares' bid price may be 522.57, while the ask price may be 522.90. The spread is 0.33.

Most trades are electronically executed by intermediaries: market makers, mostly through robot algorithms, and floor traders, are the intermediaries in the transaction. They pocket a piece of the spread as commission. High-frequency traders are always there ahead of you and will also affect the price you pay for any stock, usually to their advantage. It sounds unfair, but that's life in the stock market. Stock prices are digital, and the price you pay for a stock may be different than the bid and ask, due to the interaction of all the middle men and the often rapid flow of orders.

Less liquid stocks, which are stocks that trade less frequently, may have wider spreads. The closer the spread, the better your price is likely to be, even with all the intermediary flim-flam. Low-volume stocks can be difficult to buy but are usually more difficult to sell at a price that is favorable, especially if you have a small number of shares.

Limit Orders

You use limit orders when you don't want to buy a stock for more or sell a stock for less than a predetermined price; they can be placed as day orders or good until canceled (GTC) orders. GTC orders have a better chance of being filled since day orders expire at the end of the trading day in which you place them.

A limit order lets you attempt to buy or sell a stock at a specific price. For example, if Apple is trading near $225 and you want to buy one hundred shares only when the price falls to $220, you place a limit order for one hundred shares of Apple at $220 per share. Your order may not get filled, as the stock may not fall to $220. It may also get filled at the first available lower price if the stock falls through $220. What you know is that your order will not get filled above $220.

If you bought one hundred shares of Apple at $220 and it climbs to $250, you might want to sell it at $255. By placing a limit sell order for one hundred shares at $255, you know that your order will fill at least at $255 if and when the stock hits the price point. It may sell for a higher price, but it won't sell for less than $255.

Stop Orders

Stop orders to sell, also known as stop loss orders, are used to limit losses. If you bought Microsoft at $100 but don't want to take a big loss if the stock starts to flounder, you can set a stop loss, in dollar amounts or in percentage amounts, below the price. For example, your stop order may be to sell one hundred shares of Microsoft at $95. This limits your potential loss if the stock drops to $95 or below. Once your stock hits the stop point, it becomes a market order.

You can use stop orders to buy when you expect a stock to trade higher. If Microsoft is trading at $85 but is gathering steam, you may want to put in a stop order to buy one hundred shares at $85. When the price hits $85, your order becomes a market order and may be filled above or below your stop price depending on market conditions.

Managing Your Money

At first, think in terms of dollar amounts, instead of number of shares. If you buy one hundred shares of a $10 stock, it will cost you $1,000 plus commission. If you buy ten shares of a $100 stock, it will also cost you $1,000 plus commission. If you have $10,000 and you want to own ten different company stocks, think about how you will divide the money among the ten stocks, and consider commission costs as well. If your commission is $4.95, and you buy ten different lots of stock of varying share size, your commission will be $4.95 × 10 = $49.50 to buy and an equal amount if you were to sell them all at once.

Even if you're well-off and experienced, it's always a good idea to count every penny when you invest. But when you're just starting out, you should work out your costs on paper before you actually make a trade. This will train you for the future, as you may progress into more complex, shorter-term trading strategies where money management is even more crucial.

Keeping Up with Your Stocks

Develop a monitoring routine based on your personality and your schedule. Checking your portfolio may be as easy as logging on to your online account or your brokerage app periodically to see how things are going. The key is to be consistent and to be consciously involved. If you decide to check your portfolio every night, then do it every night. If you decide to check your portfolio once in the morning, once at lunch, and a third time an hour before the market closes on a daily basis, then that's your routine. The key is to figure out what works for you and then to be consistent.

Making Your Money Work for You Now

A great way to focus your efforts is to consider using your trading profits in your non-retirement account to offset some of your expenses. For example, if you reach the point where you can make $400 to $500 extra dollars per month via your stock trades, you can consider using that money for your car payment, a part of your mortgage or student loans, or as your contribution for your IRA. Don't put too much pressure on yourself to achieve this level of trading at the beginning, but it's something that you can add to your list of goals for the future.

ESSENTIAL

A good way to monitor your stocks frequently throughout the day is to use the CNBC app. You can set up several watchlists with up to twenty-five stocks in each. Group them by sector or class, such as health care, tech, and energy. You can even have a separate watchlist for ETFs.

When evaluating your portfolio's performance ask these questions:

- Are your investments keeping up with the market trend? This is especially important in rising markets where you want to see your stocks, ETFs, and mutual funds rise along with the trend.
- Are your investments keeping up with your plan and your goals? Do this especially when you make your monthly or quarterly check. Compare your portfolio to both your goals and the market trend.
- Is it time to make changes? Have your goals changed? Is your portfolio not meeting your expectations? Should you talk to an advisor or change your strategy? These are all important aspects of portfolio management that should be part of your arsenal.

The Buyer's Checklist

Here is a brief recap of successful investing habits:

- Start slowly via an investment club or a dividend reinvestment plan and paper trade.
- Decide on one of the broker styles.
- Write down your goals and develop a research routine.
- Put together a buy list.
- Decide how you will sell a stock before you buy it.
- Understand the different kinds of orders to buy and sell your stocks.
- Develop a portfolio management and monitoring routine.
- Review and adjust your method as needed based on goals and results.

CHAPTER 7

Bonds: The Glue That Holds Financial Markets Together

Talk of bonds is boring at parties, but as an investor you should know that bonds are the glue that holds the markets together. Think of it this way: without bonds, the global economy would be a totally different place, one of much slower growth and fewer prospects. In this chapter you'll learn why bonds are important and how they make sense for your portfolio.

What Is a Bond?

A bond is a loan packaged as a marketable security. When investors buy bonds, they are loaning money to a company, a municipality, or a sovereign government with the expectation that the money will be paid back at a predetermined date in the future along with interest. Bonds usually pay interest to the bond-holder, either in installments or as one lump sum when the bond matures. Most pay interest semiannually or annually. You can buy bonds directly as new issues from the issuer, or you can buy them through traders, dealers, or brokers in the secondary market. The market sets bond prices as supply and demand changes.

The major reason investors buy bonds is usually the interest portion of the bond. In exchange for the loan, the issuer agrees to pay the investor interest at regular intervals as well as return the original investment at maturity. Bonds are usually sold in discrete increments (multiples of $1,000). This is the par value or face value. Bond maturities are divided into short-, intermediate-, and long-term periods. Short-term bonds mature in less than five years. Intermediate-term bonds mature in five to ten years, while bonds with maturities above ten years are considered long-term. Bonds with maturities beyond twenty to thirty years are rare but do exist. Generally, bonds with the longer maturities pay the highest interest rates due to the higher risk potential. Bond prices and yields (the current effective interest rate) fluctuate based on any current market forces and trends. Rising bond prices lead to lower yields.

ESSENTIAL

Bond prices can move in the opposite direction of stock prices, especially US Treasury bonds, which are often seen as "safe" at times of market volatility or geopolitical tensions. This makes bonds an essential part of a diversified portfolio as rising bond prices can cushion any potential losses in stocks.

Bonds have a date of final maturity. That's when your initial investment, the principal, is returned. A callable bond is a special kind of bond that can be redeemed before the final maturity. If a bond is called, you get your money before the final maturity date. You still get your whole principal if the bond is called. You just don't collect the interest for as long as you expected, so you get less than you expected when you bought the bond. However, callable bonds often pay a higher interest rate, which makes them worth the risk of the early termination. The issuer has to inform investors whether a bond is callable before the sale in the prospectus.

Why Do Bonds Rule the World?

While stocks get all the press and publicity, it's the hardworking bonds that pay the bills. Bonds allow the issuers to finance projects and manage expenses sooner than if they had waited until they saved enough money to do so. So next time you see a big highway project, or a new factory being built, think about bonds as providing much if not all of the financial support for the task.

Comparing Bonds versus Stocks

A stock is a piece of a company. Stock investors, as partial owners, participate in the fortunes of the company. A bondholder is a lender. Lenders get paid unless the company goes bankrupt. This is why bonds are also known as fixed income investments. As a bondholder you know how much you will earn unless you sell the bond before maturity. For example, if you buy a one-year maturity $1,000 bond that pays 5%, you will receive $50 of interest in that year and you will receive your $1,000 back at maturity.

Corporate versus Treasury Bonds

A US Treasury bond is considered the safest bond in the world. That's because, even though the US government pays its bills with borrowed money, it will always pay its bills unless the world turns against it and stops buying US bonds. While this is possible, it's highly unlikely. That's why whenever there is major trouble in the world, such as a major war or an economic crisis, investors flock to US Treasury bonds. As they buy these bonds, prices rise and market interest rates drop.

Corporate bonds differ because they usually pay higher interest rates than Treasury bonds while offering higher risk of default. While the US government has theoretically come close to a default on its bonds, especially during government shutdowns, it has never defaulted. Corporations, on the other hand, have defaulted on their bonds. However, this is not very common, except during difficult economic periods such as the 2007–2009 economic recession.

FACT

The US government auctions off bonds regularly. Some auctions are known as refunding auctions. Refundings raise money for a specific purpose: for the government to raise money via the sale of new bonds to pay its interest debt to investors on their existing bonds.

What Makes Bonds Risky?

Bond risks are different than stock risks. The biggest risk for bonds is the possibility that you won't get paid and the issuer defaults. Inflation, the general state of the economy, credit risk, central bank interest rate risk, and income risk are the others.

Credit Risk: Risk of Default

Defaults are somewhat rare but not impossible. When a company or government goes bankrupt, bondholders are first in line to collect on whatever is left after the legal haggling is done. But it often turns out that if there is anything to collect, it's a lot less than what you were expecting. When a government or a corporation defaults, it sets off a flurry of legal activity which can take years to resolve. During that period, there is no certainty that investors will ever recoup any of their investment. The defaulting party would need to obtain new lines of financing and restructure the terms of the debt by extending the bond's life, reducing the interest rate it will pay, or both before the bondholders could be paid.

Inflation and Economic Risk

Inflation is the bitter enemy of fixed income investments. If you depend solely on the income from bonds, you lose money when prices of goods and services rise, since your income can't grow as fast as inflation. This occurs even if your interest rate is higher than the rate of inflation. For example, if your bond pays 5% and inflation is growing at 3%, your net return is 2%. If inflation rises to 4%, your net return now is only 1%. This is why bonds are good investments during periods of slow or falling economic growth. The exception is when inflation is rising during periods of slow economic growth, known as stagflation. If the economy is growing rapidly, it may be accompanied by inflation. In this case, bond prices will fall and the purchasing power of bond-generated income will follow.

Interest Rate and Price Risk

Interest and price risk is very important if you want to sell a bond before its maturity. If you bought a bond at $1,000 par with a yield of 5% and the price falls to $900, the market interest rate will rise, maybe to 5.03%, but your bond would be worth less than when you bought it. Thus, if you sold your bond under these circumstances you may lose some of your principal. If you have held the bond for a long enough period of time where it has paid interest, you may be able to sell it at a lower price and break even or lose some money. The flip side is that if the price of the bond rises, you may be able to sell it at a higher price. To make sense of this, just calculate how much interest you would gain by the time the bond matures and add this figure to the current market price of the bond. If your goal is to hold the bond until maturity, your price and rate risk is usually minimal, unless the bond defaults.

Managing Income Risk

In order to diminish the potential losses from inflation, from having to sell a bond before maturity or having a bond called, you should have the right mix of bonds in the portfolio. For example, an ultra-safe, low-maintenance bond portfolio may exclusively use US Treasury bonds, or mutual funds that invest in

US Treasury bonds in a mixture of 50% intermediate-term bonds, 30% short-term bonds, and the remaining 20% in inflation-protected bonds called TIPS.

A second approach is to use a technique called laddering, where you buy bonds of different maturities and stagger them so that your income stream remains stable. As one bond matures, you roll over the proceeds into the next bond. The key step in laddering a portfolio is to know the current inflation rate and to structure the portfolio so that the overall interest rate that it provides remains above the inflation rate. An excellent tutorial on bond laddering can be found on the Fidelity Investments website.

Corporate Credit Check: Know the Bond Ratings

The financial analysts at Standard & Poor's, Moody's, and other agencies review and rate corporate and municipal bonds. The ratings summarize the bonds' credit worthiness—the ability of the issuer to pay. Ratings are a report card on the issuer, in principle similar to your credit rating. Rating analysts look at the issuer's past payment record, the financial situation of the company, and the degree of risk associated with the bond. Issuers with the highest bond ratings are the most likely to make good on their debt. Sadly, the highest-rated bonds are the ones that are likely to pay the lowest interest rates.

The Bond Ratings Alphabet

The highest-rated bonds are rated AAA. The market considers AAA, AA, A, or BBB bonds rated by S&P as good quality. The equivalent good quality ratings issued by Moody's are Aaa, Aa, A, and Baa ratings. Bonds rated BB or Ba are considered lower quality and higher risk. Bonds with ratings below B are known as junk bonds. These pay significantly higher interest rates, but have a higher risk of default. Sometimes taking the risks offered by junk bonds pays off. But, in this sector of the bond universe, default is more common than in others.

Ratings Variability and the Tough Decisions

Bond ratings can change over time depending on the fortunes of the issuer. If a company offers BBB-rated bonds but its operations improve, their bond ratings may change to A or higher. This may increase the appeal of their bonds. If a company develops problems, their bond rating may fall below BBB or Baa. That's when you may have to make a decision to sell. Much depends on what your plans are for the income produced by the bond and your risk tolerance. The key is not to wait too long. If the company goes into bankruptcy, you could lose all your money.

Prices and Yields

Bond prices and yields fluctuate based on market circumstances and supply and demand pressures. If you want to sell a bond, you can find yesterday's price in the bond tables of *The Wall Street Journal*, *Barron's*, or *USA TODAY*. In today's real-time markets, those prices are strictly historical. Yet, they do give you an idea as to what your bond might be worth and can get you started as you look for a fair price. Price tables will differ with each paper or website. No one table can list every single bond, given the fact that there are millions of bonds available in the market at any one time. Your broker will have access to bond listings too. Here is the basic information that you will need and that you will find in most bond listings:

Coupon: 3.125%. This is the yield that the bond carried when issued.

Maturity date: 4/30/25. This is the date on which the bond matures.

Bid: 106.875. This means that a buyer is offering to buy the bond for a price of $1,068.75 on a $1,000 bond. This bond has already delivered a profit of $68.75 (6.875%) to the bondholder on a par value of $1,000.

Ask: 106.93. This means that a seller is willing to sell the bond for $1,069.30.

ALERT

Bond prices can be volatile. Because all markets are connected through the actions of the global economies and the coordinated action of central banks, bonds can be just as volatile for active traders as stocks. To avoid volatility, consider only buying bonds that you plan to hold until maturity. That means gravitating toward the highest-quality government bonds.

Buying and Selling Bonds

For a beginner, buying and selling bonds is difficult, but not impossible. Take your time, research the market, paper trade, and go live only when you feel comfortable. You may have to consider going through a full-service bond broker or work out the kinks of your online discount broker's bond quote and trading platform for a good while before you make your first real trade.

You can also buy US Treasury bonds directly from the government by visiting *TreasuryDirect*. Here you can buy Treasury bonds and US Savings bonds once you open your account. You can buy savings bonds through your bank as well. The great thing about savings bonds is that you can buy them for as low a price as $25 and pay no state or income taxes on the interest. Savings bonds can be bought without paying commission.

CHAPTER 8

Types of Bonds

To be successful as a bond investor, it helps to know how to structure the bonds in your portfolio to deliver the maximum return. That's what this chapter is about: providing details about different types of bonds; their risk and reward potential; and how they can fit into a well-diversified portfolio of stocks, bonds, and other investments.

Categories of Bonds

Bonds are versatile assets and can be used for income, capital gains, and as a hedge to risk from other broad portfolio components such as stocks or commodities. You can buy US government, corporate, municipal, or foreign bonds. Each category has its own risk/reward profile, as well as peculiar tax implications.

Bond investors are looking for steady income from periodic interest payments or to protect and build up their capital stores. Generally, but not always, bonds are more predictable than stocks. You know when you will receive your interest payments and when your principal will be returned. Thus, for investors primarily looking for income, the best approach may be to own bonds that pay interest semiannually and that have a fixed interest rate until maturity.

If you have a specific need for capital at a certain date in the future, zero-coupon bonds may be for you. You buy these bonds at a deep discount below the par value of the bond. At maturity you receive the interest that has been compounded over the life of the bond and the purchase price in a lump sum.

In other words, as with all investments, before you start a bond portfolio, it makes sense to have a good understanding of what your financial needs will be, a sense of your time frame, and a plan.

FACT

The global bond market is estimated to be worth $100 trillion, and $700 billion worth of bonds are traded on a daily basis. Compare that to the global stock market, which is estimated to be worth $64 trillion with daily trading volume coming in at $200 billion.

US Treasury Securities

The US Treasury bond market is the biggest securities market in the world, with an average turnover of over $500 billion per day. That makes it a very liquid market, and one in which you can raise cash rapidly if you need to. US

Treasuries are considered the safest securities in the world and are thought of by many investors as cash equivalents. That means that if you are a risk-averse investor, especially one who does not like the volatility of the stock market, and you don't mind holding on to a security for long periods of time, US Treasuries may be your investment of choice. Perhaps the best attribute of US Treasuries is that once you buy them, the interest rate that you will receive from that bond, until maturity, is locked in. That means that your return on investment is highly predictable. There are three kinds of Treasuries:

Treasury bills (T-bills) are short-term securities. Their maturities range from four weeks to one year. You can buy T-bills in $100 increments. T-bills are sold at a discount from face value. The discount is based on the interest rate paid by the bill.

Treasury notes (T-notes) are intermediate-term securities with maturities at two, five, and ten years. As with T-bills, you can buy T-notes in $100 increments. T-notes pay interest every six months until they mature. The 10-year US Treasury note yield (TNX) is considered the benchmark for most mortgages and longer-term loans. It is also the most widely quoted bond yield in the financial press.

Treasury bonds (T-bonds) are long-term securities issued by the US government. The most commonly traded T-bond is the thirty-year bond. The US Treasury also offers a twenty-year bond. Long-term Treasuries can be purchased at $100 increments and, like T-notes, pay interest every six months until maturity.

ALERT

While it is true that US Treasury securities are considered to be "safe" investments, this notion of "safety" is most applicable to bonds that are held until maturity. Treasury bonds' prices fluctuate, often in wide price ranges, in response to economic reports and geopolitical events. Thus, when you buy US Treasuries, plan accordingly.

Municipal Bonds

These are bonds sold by cities, states, counties, and even school districts. They are also known as munis and are very popular investments because of their tax-free advantages. Municipalities sell munis in order to finance projects, such as building or repairing roads, bridges, schools, parks, and sports arenas. Munis are popular because they are usually exempt from federal, and often state, taxes.

ALERT

Not all municipal bonds are tax-free at all levels of taxation. Check the bond prospectus and check your state and city tax laws.

Municipal bonds are often rated by rating analysts from Standard & Poor's and Moody's via similar ratings to those used for corporate bonds. Ratings range from AAA (S&P) or Aaa (Moody's) for the highest grades to BBB or Baa and below. When considering municipal bonds, look to own BBB-rated bonds or above. As in the case of corporate bonds, the lower the rating for a municipal bond, the higher the yield and the risk of default. With municipal bonds you can buy bond insurance in order to protect against losses.

The minimum investment for municipal bonds is $5,000, and they are then offered in multiples of $5,000. The general trends for interest rates, risk ratings, and other external factors, such as the local economy for the municipality selling the bond, affect the interest rate that any muni pays investors. Prices are listed in bond tables, which are similar to those for Treasury bonds. You may sell your municipal bond at a higher price than what you paid for it, but you will have to pay capital gains taxes.

If these bonds make sense for your portfolio, get to know the different types:

- **Revenue bonds.** These are bonds issued to finance specific products such as bridges, toll roads, or airports. Interest paid to investors comes from the revenues generated by the project.
- **Moral obligation bonds.** These are special circumstance revenue bonds issued by a state when it can't actually meet the bond obligation through its normal revenue stream, essentially taxes and licensing fees. In these cases, the state forms a special obligation fund that can be used to pay the bond obligation. The kicker is that the state has no legal obligation to pay bondholders from that special obligation fund, just a moral obligation. What makes this bond worth considering is that the state is actually putting its good reputation on the line, so the moral obligation is often considered more powerful in the markets than the legal obligation.
- **General obligation bonds.** These bonds, also known as GOs, are backed by municipal taxes and require voter approval. The principal is backed by the full faith and credit of the issuer.
- **Taxable municipal bonds.** If paying taxes on a municipal bond sounds ridiculous, consider that these bonds, despite the taxes, can offer higher yields than comparable corporate bonds, and are generally considered to have lower risks associated with them. Common uses for this kind of muni include financing of underfunded pension plans or building a local sports arena.
- **Private activity bonds** are used for financing both public and private activities.
- **Put bonds** allow the investor to redeem them at par value on a specific date (or dates) prior to the stated maturity. In exchange, put bonds offer lower yields than comparable municipals because of this built-in flexibility. This early out feature allows you to cash in your bond and exchange it for a higher-yielding bond if you have the opportunity to do so.

- **Floating and variable rate municipal bonds** are good to own if you expect that interest will rise at some point in the future, as the bond will adjust. Because of this feature, the price of these bonds may be more volatile.

Municipal bond prices can fluctuate fairly frequently; thus, it may make sense to develop a good relationship with a muni broker and to check prices with your broker on a routine basis, as well as in your local newspaper, and online if you use a discount broker.

ALERT

After the 2008 financial crisis, many municipalities were in financial trouble and many remain in danger of insolvency. Pensions in cities with poor management and unrealistic expectations on the return of pension investments are in particular danger. Consider the problems in Dallas with the police pension as well as the state of Connecticut and its budget deficit. Review the issues seen in these places and use them as a model for what you don't want in a muni bond issuer.

Corporate Bonds

A corporate bond, also known as a corporate, like all bonds, is a loan agreement between a corporation and investors. And while stockholders own shares of stocks, which are pieces of a company, by contrast, corporate bondholders are moneylenders to the company that issues the bond. Bondholders lend money to companies for a specific amount of time and a specified rate of interest. Corporate bonds tend to be riskier investments than Treasury or municipal bonds but, when properly chosen, have historically outperformed other bonds.

Corporates pay a higher interest rate because the issuing companies generally have a higher risk of default than governments and municipalities, although after the Great Recession, countries are not risk-free either. Greece and several US cities went bankrupt after the 2007–2008 financial crisis. In 2018, countries such as Argentina, Brazil, and Italy struggled with their debt, as did US retailers such as Sears. Corporate bondholders in companies such as Sears were in danger of their bonds defaulting as the situation unfolded.

ALERT

Corporate bonds are not insured and should be avoided if you are not a risk-taker. If you're more moderate in your risk acceptability, consider owning a mutual fund that invests in corporate bonds to reduce but not eliminate your risk.

Sinking-Fund Provision

A sinking-fund provision allows a company to redeem a certain number of bonds per year by using its earnings. Bonds with sinking-fund provision features must state that this is a part of the deal. The company, depending on its current circumstances, chooses bonds to be retired via this maneuver. Thus, your bond may or may not get chosen. If your bond gets chosen, you may lose money.

The bottom line is that corporate bonds have their positive and negative sides. Higher yields also mean higher risk. The possibility of a company bankruptcy, or of a quirky callable feature of the bond, makes it mandatory that you read everything very carefully before investing.

Corporate Bond Checklist

Here are points to consider with corporate bonds:

- Corporate bonds are issued in multiples of either $1,000 or $5,000. They are rated by S&P and Moody's using the AAA- or Aaa-based system described earlier in this chapter.
- Income and capital gains associated with corporate bonds are fully taxable at federal and state levels.

- Interest is paid annually or semiannually.
- If your goal is to invest in highly rated, high-quality corporate bonds from blue chip companies, and you hold the bond until maturity, your risk of default is low but not guaranteed.

Bond Calls

When a bond is called, it means that the issuer is redeeming the bond before maturity. The most common reason is that by calling in the bond and reissuing it at a lower interest rate, the issuer will save money. Only bonds that have a callable provision can be called early, whether they are government, municipal, or corporate bonds. The callable provision describes the details and conditions that allow the early redemption. For example, a fifteen-year bond may be called as early as eight years into its lifespan. If you reinvest in a bond issued by an entity which called your original bond, usually issued at a lower interest rate, your return will be different than that of the original bond.

Zero-Coupon Bonds

Companies, governments, government agencies, and municipalities can issue zero-coupon bonds. Zeros do not make periodic interest rate payments. Instead, you buy them at a deep discount and receive a higher-rate lump sum (both interest and principal) when the bond reaches maturity. The only reasons to own zeros are because they allow you to plan for that lump sum at maturity and are ideal for retirement planning. The downside is that even though you don't receive interest payments, you must report the amount of appreciation of the bond every year for tax purposes.

Here is how they work. If you buy a ten-year $10,000 zero municipal bond, you may pay $5,000. In ten years you would receive $10,000. The longer the time to maturity, the deeper the purchase price is discounted and the greater the return based on compounding of the interest that is not being paid.

High-Yield Bonds

High-yield bonds, also known as junk bonds, can provide a higher return, but often offer a higher risk of default or of a rapid fall in price. That's because the companies that issue these bonds have lower credit ratings than other companies; thus, their bonds get lower ratings from the ratings agencies. In order to attract investors, they have to pay a higher interest rate.

> **FACT**
>
> Wall Street likes to use "comfort" words. By calling a junk bond a high-yield bond, the issuers are hoping that you are not going to be frightened away. Don't be fooled. Junk is junk, and you should be wary of these bonds unless you are a well-diversified, well-financed, experienced investor.

The usual reason for the low credit rating is that the issuing company is at some stage of restructuring or involved in a merger where the bonds are part of the financing for the merger. In some cases, the bondholder may suffer from factors that affect the price of the company's stock. In these situations, not only may the bond lose value quickly, but it may also lose its liquidity and be very difficult to sell.

At other times, a company that issues junk bonds in its early growth stages improves its operations and its credit, and can issue higher-grade bonds in the future. This could be a situation where the company calls the lower-grade bonds in order to issue higher-grade bonds that pay lower interest rates. As a result, you may receive the high rate for a shorter period than you may expect.

No matter what you decide, understand that high-yield bonds are known as junk bonds for a reason, and that reason is that a fair amount of the time, they are just that: junk.

Mortgage-Backed Securities

Mortgage-backed securities (MBS) are bonds backed by mortgage payments. And until 2007, they were considered among the safest areas of the bond market. That's because it was widely believed that Americans would always pay their mortgages and that home prices would continue to rise. But this former safe haven in the bond market turned into a disaster area in 2007 and 2008 as the subprime mortgage became synonymous with the near collapse of the global economy. In fact, the take-home message for beginning investors should be to avoid this sector altogether.

The major reason for avoiding, aside from its high risk, is that it's a complex sector that often involves interest rates that are collected in derivative instruments known as collateralized mortgage obligations (CMOs), where more than one mortgage is pooled together in order to collect the capital to make the interest rate.

Consider that when you buy a corporate, municipal, or Treasury bond, you have to deal with only one issuer. In these cases, you only have to look to one payer—the US Treasury, a city, or a corporation—to make good on its promise to pay. Now, compare this to the path of a typical MBS. A bank sells the mortgage to the homeowner. Then the bank sells the mortgage to a servicing firm. Then, in order for investors to receive their interest payments, the homeowner must make his mortgage payment to the servicing firm that holds the mortgage. The servicing firm collects the money from individuals, then allocates the money to each particular pool or CMO, and then from that pool, it pays the interest to investors. That is clearly a situation in which there are too many steps in the chain of custody of the money. And the more steps, the more there is a chance for something to go wrong, which is what happened in

2007 and why the whole industry collapsed when the crucial step in the chain, the mortgage holder, stopped making payments.

FACT

As the real estate boom of the early 2000s slowed, in order to continue their earning streams, mortgage lenders sold mortgages to very high-risk clients, including people whose income and future prospects, under normal circumstances, would not qualify them for certain loans. As a result, and as common sense would suggest, those buyers stopped making their house payments and the boom became a bust, leading to the infamous Great Recession from 2007 to 2009.

If you have an interest in these kinds of bonds, consider investing in a mutual fund that holds the highest-rated MBS loans, those guaranteed by the Government National Mortgage Association (GNMA). Otherwise, look elsewhere.

The Bond Investor Checklist

Diversification is the key to success in bond investing. When you own a variety of bonds in a laddered portfolio, you can limit the volatility of your bond holdings. Your bond ladder should have an average maturity that coincides with your financial goals and your time range. Bonds are not without risk. Before buying bonds, also consider the following:

- Tax implications. Consider whether tax-free municipal bonds make sense in your portfolio. Review the potential risks of hidden taxes with your CPA, including that of triggering the AMT (alternative minimum tax) rules. And look into the potential consequences of owning zero-coupon bonds before you invest in them.
- Consider the inflation effect of your bond holdings. If your overall portfolio is well insulated from inflation, you may be able to avoid

taking extra risks with your bond portfolio in searching for a higher return.

- Practice safety first. A high-quality portfolio may not give the best return in dollar terms. But the peace of mind and the stability of such a portfolio are well worth the potential losses that can result from too much risk.
- Remember that your bond portfolio has multiple purposes. Aside from providing income, its function is to provide stability to the overall investment portfolio when stocks become volatile.
- Junk is junk, and mortgages sometimes go unpaid. Don't chase high-yield bonds just to make more money in the short term. Avoid most junk bonds, and if you must own mortgage-backed securities, consider a GNMA mutual fund.

CHAPTER 9

The Mutual Fund:
The Beginner's Best Friend

If there were ever a financial instrument ideally suited to a beginning investor, it would be the mutual fund. Created in Europe in the mid-1800s, mutual funds hit the American shores when Harvard University created the first American pooled fund. Initially ridiculed, mutual funds now house trillions of dollars of money and are major contributors to market activity as well as shareholder financial reward. This chapter is all about mutual funds and how they can be a significant part of your portfolio, both when you start and throughout your time as an investor.

What Is a Mutual Fund?

A mutual fund is a registered investment company that sells shares to investors and invests the pooled assets of all shareholders in the markets on their behalf. A mutual fund share's price is the net asset value (NAV) and is the result of the mutual fund's total assets divided by the number of outstanding shares. Thus, a mutual fund with $10 million in total assets and one million shares outstanding has a NAV of $10.

Always useful, mutual funds are especially excellent investment vehicles for investors just getting started. They allow you to participate in the markets, and provide a certain comfort level. Many investors that start their endeavors by using mutual funds move on to stocks, options, and futures. You may be one of them. The key is to take your time and transition to investments with higher risk and higher work requirement when you're ready.

FACT

Mutual funds are managed by professionals whose job it is to invest the funds' assets on behalf of their shareholders.

If you are considering becoming a mutual fund investor, you are not alone, and since there are nearly 10,000 funds available in the US, you'll have a whole lot of choices. Nearly 50% of all funds invest solely in stocks while some 20% invest in bonds and some 5% are money market mutual funds. The rest are funds which combine assets such as both stocks and bonds.

And because of the competition from exchange-traded mutual funds, the mutual fund industry has retooled itself recently. Many funds have begun to cut fees and have created more targeted funds where the goal is for the investor to have a specific amount of money by a certain date. These funds, called target date funds, can be useful as part of a diversified portfolio, including retirement accounts. For example, if you plan to retire in fifteen years, you could choose a fund that is targeted to wind down in fifteen years. The fund's asset allocation begins aggressively, with a higher percentage of growth stocks in its early stages, but becomes more conservative as the target date approaches by increasing cash and bond allocations. When the target date is reached, the fund is designed to be 100% in cash.

Why Mutual Fund Investing Is a Good Thing for Investors

Mutual funds offer investors two things: diversification and convenience. Diversification allows you to spread out your risk while convenience makes it easier for you to invest. Both are good reasons why you should consider investing in mutual funds.

Diversification

Because the fund manager picks stocks and constantly adjusts the portfolio, you don't have to. That means that your risk is spread beyond a handful of stocks. If a mutual fund can diversify into bonds and other asset classes as market conditions change, this can also add another layer of diversification and can protect you from excessive volatility in one asset class such as stocks. The net effect is that mutual funds can cut your costs, balance your risk, and let you participate in bull markets.

Built-In Convenience

Mutual funds are convenient as they decrease the amount of research work you have to do in order to invest in a general market trend. For example, instead of having a portfolio with fifty stocks, you can own more than one mutual fund. This helps balance the potential risk that can come with an aggressive growth stock fund by also owning shares in a conservative Treasury bond fund, especially if you are using funds from the same fund family, which lets you handle all your transactions online or by a phone call. You can also monitor hot sectors in the market and trade in and out of sector-specific funds that are acting well at any time. If international funds are acting well, you may want to own some shares there as well. A fund that specializes in real estate and a precious metals and commodity fund may also be worth considering. But be careful. You can also overdo your fund diversification, regardless of how convenient it is to make trades. Owning more than five to seven mutual funds at any one time is likely to increase your risk as well as possibly duplicating some of your holdings.

Know Before You Invest

Before investing, be aware that mutual funds are not guaranteed to make money. And unless the fund manager is truly nimble and can move all of the funds' holdings to a safe asset allocation in times of trouble, you will lose some money in any type of mutual fund during bad markets in any asset class. Yet over time, owning and adjusting a portfolio of well-diversified, well-managed mutual funds can be a pretty good deal for most investors. Above all, mutual funds are convenient, given the fact that as an investor, you only need to pick and monitor the fund as it pertains to your needs, goals, and financial plan. Thankfully, you don't have to manage the entire fund's portfolio.

FACT

In 2018, Fidelity Investments introduced a set of mutual funds which charge no fees to the investors. The funds are based on stock indexes and are inexpensive to operate. This is great marketing for Fidelity, as it grabs more investors who are sure to do more business with Fidelity in the future. It isn't a terrible deal for investors either as they own mutual funds with profit potential for a very low management fee: free (at least at the start of the relationship).

Is It All about the Fund Manager?

Mutual fund companies, like any other business, are always looking for ways to attract new customers. Therefore, a successful mutual fund may be marketed by associating it with a charismatic manager.

Peter Lynch, the ex-manager of the Fidelity Magellan Fund (FMAGX), became a legend in the 1980s and is considered by many to be the best mutual fund manager of all time. Under his guidance, Magellan averaged 29% yearly returns for thirteen years. Magellan delivered such heady gains for its shareholders during that period that Lynch became a media star, writing books, making talk show appearances, and retiring a wealthy man. Lynch was a big proponent of the "Buy What You Know and Know What You Buy" investment approach you learned about in Chapter 5. He remains a consultant to Fidelity Investments, but since he stopped managing Magellan directly, it simply became a decent, not an exceptional, mutual fund.

Lynch was an excellent manager. But he also had the best of times in which to ply his wares. As an investor, it's all about balance. You have to weigh the performance of the manager, but you must also temper your expectations based on market conditions because even managers like Peter Lynch can't beat a bear market.

ALERT

Beware of clever marketing by mutual funds, especially when the focus of the advertising is a star fund manager. If the manager is a celebrity, make sure that their results also measure up, especially during bad markets.

Evaluating Your Fund Manager

When reviewing a fund manager's performance:

- Look at several years of returns. If the fund has been delivering consistent returns during the manager's tenure, look at other funds that they have managed. If the performance comparison yields consistent returns, especially through good and bad markets, you've found a good manager.

- Compare the fund's performance to the market during both up and down years. See what the fund did when the stock market crashed in 2008, including how fast it rebounded and to what degree. This will tell you a lot about what you may expect in the future, as there will be other bad markets to manage through.
- Make sure that the manager is adhering to their fund's investment strategy. If you are looking for a conservative strategy and your review of the fund's latest report shows that there are mostly momentum stocks in the portfolio, you need to consider whether the fund is what you are looking for in the long run.
- Research whether the fund manager is a lone wolf or has a management team. If they are a lone wolf, the fund may suffer when they move on. They may not leave anyone at the helm that could emulate the successful strategy and deliver the kinds of returns that you may expect. If the performance of the fund is similar over time regardless of the manager, and it suits your goals, you've found a match.

Mutual Fund Families

There are many mutual fund families, which are companies that offer a variety of mutual funds to the public. Each one comes with slight differences in the amount of assets they manage. But in an industry of thousands, there are several giant firms that gobble up most of the market share: Fidelity Investments, Vanguard, PIMCO, American, Franklin Templeton, Invesco, T. Rowe Price, and BlackRock are usually near the top when you rank mutual fund companies by assets under management. These are not the only mutual fund companies, but these big companies offer a wide variety of funds in the growth, growth and income, sector-specific, hybrid, and asset allocation categories, which makes them an ideal place to start your search. They also offer plenty of options in the bond categories, ranging from Treasuries to high-yield. Some are specialists.

For example, PIMCO is primarily a bond mutual fund company, while the others offer a large variety of fund choices. Franklin Templeton specializes in international markets, while Fidelity Investments has a very large selection of mutual funds with a specialization in industry sector-specific mutual funds.

FACT

The big mutual fund companies, including Fidelity Investments, Vanguard, and T. Rowe Price, all have money market mutual funds. Get the information online or by calling their toll-free phone numbers or by visiting their websites. Review the prospectuses. Compare several money market funds and fund companies before making a final decision. Your bank may offer a money market mutual fund. Unfortunately, many banks will have higher fees and more hidden fees with worse investment returns than the mutual fund companies. Consider this if your bank starts pitching its investments to you.

There are also niche players that cater to a particular clientele, such as the Rydex and ProFunds families. These two families specialize in offering mutual funds to investors who like to switch between mutual funds on a regular basis, often on a daily basis. These two fund families also offer mutual funds that sell the markets short, or rise when the underlying assets fall in price.

When choosing a mutual fund family, consider the following:

- **Reputation:** Research whether the company has had any significant legal or enforcement actions against it in the past five years and whether there are any pending legal actions against it. If a mutual fund company turns up in the news as being investigated due to accounting problems and undergoes frequent management changes, these are red flags that should tell you to go somewhere else.
- **Primary business:** If a mutual fund company is part of a large financial conglomerate such as a retail bank, or even a big investment bank,

mutual funds may or may not be their primary focus. That may make a big difference in fees, performance, and customer service.

- **Performance:** Look at mutual fund ratings in each family during good and bad markets and review how the company's funds have fared. Consistently good results are preferable to outstanding years once in a blue moon.
- **Investment approach:** Review the overall philosophy of the fund family and how it matches your own personality and risk profile. If you are a patient, conservative investor, you may find a good fit in Vanguard, a company that does not like to service investors who like to switch in and out of mutual funds frequently. If you are someone who might enjoy mutual fund switching, you may do well with Rydex or ProFunds.

FACT

There are several great sources of information on mutual funds. First is the Investment Company Institute. The Investment Company Institute is the mutual fund industry group that chronicles the industry and keeps all the statistics and facts about mutual funds. ICI offers a great deal of information, especially regarding the state of the mutual fund industry as a whole. If you want to gather information with regard to performance of various mutual funds, you can find all you need at Morningstar.com.

Expenses, Loads, and Other Fees

Mutual funds, even the "free" ones, have expenses. Aside from trading commissions, mutual funds may pay rent for office space and may have other operational real estate and related expenses. As with any company, mutual funds also have employees who require salaries and benefits. Fund managers often travel to personally "kick the tires" of a company that they are evaluating for investment purposes. And since shareholders are the major source of income for the company, they will pay for the cost of all the things that are required to run the fund.

Load or No Load?

The first fee to consider is the load, or the fee that an advisor receives from the fund company for selling you a mutual fund. A no-load mutual fund has at least an equal chance of being as good as a load fund. Some special cases of load funds sold directly to investors are sector funds. Because these funds may have higher expenses, since they cater to investors who may not hold them for extended periods of time, mutual fund companies may charge a load for them. As a general rule, though, there is no hard-and-fast rule that says that load funds are better than no-load funds. Be careful when you buy no-load funds, though. They may have hidden fees in them that could surprise you if you didn't expect them.

ESSENTIAL

If you're looking to do sector-specific short-term trading, you're better off with an exchange-traded mutual fund (ETMF). You'll be charged a trading commission in your brokerage account but you won't likely have any penalties for getting out early.

Digging Into Fee Details

Before investing, review the expense ratio part of the prospectus. Some companies are trickier than others, although most of the large families are fairly straightforward in their language. If there is something that you don't understand in the fee structure, it makes sense to stop and look it up or have someone help you understand it. You don't want to get charged any more than necessary by a mutual fund company or any other investment situation.

Here are some typical mutual fund fees:

- **Service fees:** These are fees used to pay the salaries, commissions, and consulting fees of financial planners, analysts, and brokers who service the customers and provide support services to clients on behalf of the fund company. Unfortunately, there is nothing you can do about the fees except choose a different fund.

- **Administrative fees:** These are the fees from which the mutual fund company pays for office space, staff salaries, and office equipment and funds the general cost of running the business. These fees also include the cost of online support, check processing, auditing, record keeping, and the production and printing of brochures and shareholder reports. In some cases, the funds absorb these fees into their management fees.
- **Management fees:** This is the fee that goes to the fund manager, expressed as a percentage. Some funds have flat percentage fees, while others vary the fee based on the fund's return. As a general rule, the larger the fund, the lower the management fee percentage.
- **12b-1 fee:** This fee, which is usually between 0.25% and 1% on an annual basis, is used to pay for the fund's advertising. This fee can be seen as unnecessary, or you can agree with the fund company, whose point of view is that by advertising, it gets more clients and the overall costs of running the fund go down over time.

Total expense ratios for a mutual fund can range from 0.25% to as high as 2.5%. You have to pay attention to this as it can sap your returns. If your fund has a high expense ratio and a poor return, find a new one.

ALERT

Don't get ripped off. You don't have to pay big bucks to own a mutual fund through a financial planner or investment advisor. You can buy no-load funds with low fees directly from the fund company when you open an account. The remarkable thing is that high-load mutual funds with big expenses don't often perform any better than the no-load ones.

Making Sense of Fund Reports

Your mutual fund's annual or semiannual reports are important tools to help you measure performance. Pay special attention to the section that details the fund's holdings in order to keep tabs on the fund's manager. A manager whose style drifts from the fund's stated objectives could be a sign of trouble. If your fund's objective is small-cap growth, and you see large holdings of Apple, Netflix, and Amazon, your manager is showing signs of "style drifting."

Before deciding whether this is a positive or a negative, though, consider why the manager may be changing the objective. Is it because the market is changing? Or is it because they are chasing performance and the large-cap stocks are acting better in the current market than the small-cap growth stocks that they are supposed to be investing in? Compare this fund's performance to other small-cap growth funds. If your fund is doing better than others even with the large-cap stocks in it, it may make sense to keep it, as long as you keep an eye on it.

Here are other things to look for:

- **Familiar names:** Look for companies that fit the bill of the fund. If there aren't many that you recognize, dig deeper. Try to get in your manager's head. If your research shows that your fund manager is heavily invested in gold mining and other cyclical companies, this may be a much higher-risk mutual fund than you want.
- **Portfolio concentration:** If your fund is overweight in a particular sector, you should look into that sector and see if its fundamentals warrant that kind of exposure. If your manager is loading up on biotech or bank stocks, research those sectors carefully. Your fund manager may be onto something. Or they may be heading for trouble. At the end of the day, it's all about whether you're getting what the fund advertises and how comfortable you are with what the manager is doing.

- **Compare your fund to the right benchmark:** The annual report should list the fund's performance in comparison to the appropriate benchmark. If the report of your small-cap growth fund is comparing its performance solely to the 10-year US Treasury note, that's inaccurate and misleading. Certainly, funds often compare their performance to that of their traditional benchmark index or sector, as well as that of Treasuries. The point is that small-cap fund performance should at least be compared to a small-cap benchmark such as the Russell 2000 Index.

The report should also explain why the fund manager made the decisions reflected in their holdings, why they worked out or didn't fare well, and what the manager plans to do about it in the future. If you're scratching your head after reading the report, especially after a period of underperformance, you may need to get another fund.

Finally, even though the annual report is important, you can check your fund's performance as often as you like online, as fund companies post the fund's closing price, usually after 5:00 p.m. EST, on their websites.

Different Approaches to Mutual Fund Investing

Now that you're ready to invest, it's time to consider your mutual fund share buying and style choices. As with any other form of investing, how you go about buying and selling is dictated by your personality, your risk profile, and your time frame. No matter what you decide, the most important factor is that you make money via investing in mutual funds in a way that you don't lose sleep.

Consider mutual fund investing is a possible segue to stock investing. You buy shares in a mutual fund in hopes of selling them at a higher price or net asset value at some point in the future. If you buy shares in a fund, and it doesn't appreciate in price over a reasonable period of time, based on your time frame, personality, and needs, you simply sell the shares. Before you buy shares, review any restrictions or fees that may apply when you buy or sell shares. When selling mutual fund shares, you must also consider the effect of fees for redeeming shares in less than the allotted time, if applicable. These fees are called exit loads. Mutual funds charge these fees in order to minimize the effect of large numbers of redemptions on the fund's capital. Your fund will inform you, in its prospectus, if there are any such fees and how they apply. They also notify you on the sale ticket you have to approve before the trade goes through. No-load funds have no upfront or back-end loads. Most mutual funds, load and no-load, limit the number of times that you can sell shares per year. This number varies per fund and per fund family. On average, you can switch out of funds two to four times per year.

FACT

To open a mutual fund account directly with a company, you can visit a local investor center or apply directly online. Once you fund the account, you're all set up and you can start buying and selling shares.

Dollar Cost Averaging: Buying During Good and Bad Times

Dollar cost averaging is an investment method that is well suited for long-term mutual fund investing, especially for 401(k) and IRA plans. You do this by investing a fixed sum of money into a mutual fund periodically. Some investors opt to buy a fixed number of shares. The fixed sum of money method tends to work better, due to price fluctuations in fund shares. Many investors use the dollar cost averaging method every month or every quarter. The net effect is that, over time, you build a large number of shares in the fund. Sometimes you buy shares for lower prices and sometimes at higher prices, depending on the overall market. This method works well for IRAs, 401(k) plans, and other retirement plans.

Dollar cost averaging often makes the most sense in the beginning of your investment plan, although you can continue to invest this way as long as it suits your goals. This approach develops the habit of saving as well as offering the potential for building up your assets. It's more about discipline than the amount you put in. One good way to compromise is to have a minimum contribution and a set schedule. If you decide that you will buy $200 worth of shares in a mutual fund every month, then stick to it. If you have more in some months, it may be worth your while to put in a bit more. The key is to stick to the routine and to build assets.

Dollar cost averaging is the opposite of market timing, the style of investing that attempts to buy at specific times during market periods. For example, market timers look to buy when markets have been falling for some time and their market timing indicators are flashing signals that this may be a good moment to buy. Market timers also look to sell before a market falls. The goal of market timers is to make the most money possible when markets are trending and to sell before the trend changes. There are whole books devoted to market timing. It can be done, but it is difficult and can be a risky proposition, especially when you're just starting.

Dollar cost averaging can also be emotionally difficult, as it requires putting money into fund shares even during bear markets. If you can stomach this aspect of the technique, and you have enough time for things to work out, this is a good approach to mutual fund investing.

CHAPTER 10

The Large Universe of Mutual Funds

In a universe where you have thousands of choices, it pays to know your stuff. And the more you know about the different types of mutual funds—stocks, bonds, hybrid, and sector-specific—the better off you'll be and the better your chances of making good decisions. Each type of fund, whether it invests in stocks, bonds, or a mixture of assets, has a potential place in your portfolio. This chapter will help you make intelligent choices. But regardless of your decisions, your return will be based on the performance of the financial class in which the fund invests, whether it's stocks, bonds, or a mixture of multiple asset classes.

Index Funds

Index funds are designed to match the performance of a specific index. To do this, the funds buy the same assets or securities in identical proportions to the index. The most common and best-known index mutual funds mimic the S&P 500. Index funds are passively managed, meaning that there is little trading and asset shifting, which means lower fees for you. There are some no-fee index funds in the market via Fidelity Investments, and others may follow. Historically, the S&P 500 outperformed the large majority of all equity funds.

Index funds are attractive because they offer:

- **Ease of investing:** You know what you're getting. When you buy an index fund, you expect to earn market-style results at a low cost.
- **Variety:** There are many mutual funds that track other indexes, such as small-cap and mid-cap stocks and industry sectors. For example, if you want to own technology stocks, you can buy a mutual fund that tracks a technology index such as Vanguard Information Technology Index Fund (VITAX).
- **Diversification:** A selection of index mutual funds can help you create your own diversified fund portfolio. A good mix may be a large-cap index fund that tracks the Dow Jones Industrial Average or the S&P 500, coupled with a mid-cap mutual fund that tracks the S&P MidCap 400 Index and an index fund that tracks the Russell 2000 Index of small-cap stocks. You can add safety by adding a Treasury bond index mutual fund and a sector mutual fund that tracks a gold stock benchmark or a commodity index.

Growth Funds versus Income Funds

There are two direct ways to make money: by growing capital gains and by receiving income. A third strategy is to mix the two. Growth stocks appreciate in price while income securities pay dividends, and there are mutual funds that specialize in either approach, separately or simultaneously. There is no reason to choose between these two general categories of funds. Each type has a place in your portfolio, and an appropriate blend of both tends to make for a more stable and less volatile portfolio.

Growth Funds

Mutual funds that specialize in growth stocks are not as interested in the current price of a stock. Instead, they focus on stocks with the potential to appreciate in price. These funds will buy any stock at any price if their analysis suggests that the price will rise, even from levels that have already risen significantly. Thus, growth funds tend to gravitate toward momentum stocks that can move significantly higher for relatively long periods of time, such as months or even years. The downside is that momentum stocks eventually fall and your fund may suffer some temporary losses. These losses can be cushioned by not having all of your eggs in one basket and by periodically trimming the number of shares in a fund you own as the price rises. As long as you know this and you stay on top of things, you will not likely suffer as much as you would if you just rolled the dice and hoped for the best.

Growth stock mutual funds are interested in companies with extraordinary potential for gains, especially those with new products that are creating social trends. Think of stocks that fit the profile of Apple, Amazon, Starbucks, and Facebook and you've got the commonly held type of stocks in these mutual funds. Long-term growth funds tend to focus on more mature growth companies that still have potential, while aggressive growth funds look for the "next big deal" companies earlier in the cycle.

Capital Appreciation Funds

Capital appreciation funds are the most aggressive of all mutual funds, and when they are doing well they usually hit home runs. That's because they focus solely on high-flying momentum stocks, or stocks that have exceptional growth potential in the short run. However, when the momentum runs out, these funds can be at the bottom of the performance lists.

Income Funds

Income funds focus on stocks that pay dividends, which are passed to the fund's shareholders. Some of these funds may also hold bonds to increase their income producing potential. If you reinvest dividends, you'll build the number of shares you hold. It's a good idea to check the tax consequences of owning these funds with your CPA, as you are likely to be taxed, unless you hold them in tax-deferred accounts. These funds can be more stable in down or volatile markets. But don't let this tendency of the category lull you into a false sense of security. In the age of high-frequency trading, any stock or fund can become volatile.

Combined Growth and Income Funds

If you have a small portfolio and are looking for a one-stop shop, a combined growth and income fund may be for you. By combining growth and dividend-paying stocks, along with bonds, this type of mutual fund can deliver excellent results with less risk, although that is not guaranteed. Growth and income managers tend to be more cautious in their stock picks, and are required to balance the more aggressive picks with steady dividend payers and bonds in order to deliver steady returns in rising stock markets and decrease the potential for losses in down markets.

Value Funds

Value mutual funds invest in shares of companies that are undervalued. That means that the companies in these funds are often struggling, or are at least perceived to be struggling by the market when the value fund manager is buying their shares. But while the appeal of a value stock may be low, the reason the stock is underperforming may be as simple as the fact that its product cycle has hit a dull period or that it's undergoing a change in management. Thus, a big part of value investing is the understanding of the company, its fundamentals, and the reasons why the market does not recognize its future potential.

Value mutual funds are not necessarily market laggards. Don't be fooled. A good value manager recognizes future growth potential in an undervalued stock, then seeks to buy the stock cheap so that they can ride the stock's next up cycle when the growth managers get clued in to the story and start to buy it. Value funds aren't likely to be wallflowers during bull markets. If the fund manager did their job right, they picked good value stocks in the past that are participating in any stock market rally in the present. As the stock rises in price and the valuation rises, the manager will sell their position and put the money to work in other underperforming stocks with the goal of repeating the feat.

ESSENTIAL

At times, value funds can deliver results that are comparable to aggressive growth funds. This is usually due to both good times for this kind of investing as well as good portfolio management. Even for growth investors, it's a good idea to, at least, monitor the performance of a few value funds at any time as it may make sense to put some money in a value fund that has a hot hand.

Considering Sector Funds

Sector funds are ideal for investors who like to trade based on technical analysis and momentum, and who have variable time frames ranging from days to weeks, or weeks to months. These mutual funds buy stocks in a single sector of the market, such as health care, technology, or energy. There are even specialized funds that focus on information technology, natural gas stocks, and regional banks. Generally, the narrower the focus of a sector, the greater its tendency to be volatile and the higher the risk potential that it offers. Still, if you are a risk-taker and like momentum, sector funds are likely for you. A simple strategy is to put together a list of sector funds. An easy place to start is with the Fidelity Select funds or Vanguard sector funds. You can find them listed in the mutual fund section of *Investor's Business Daily* or *The Wall Street Journal*. Get in the habit of checking them periodically. You can chart them on *StockCharts*, see which ones are interesting, and consider whether owning shares in one or more of them makes sense.

FACT

Sector funds can deliver hefty gains. A great example was the run of Fidelity Select Health Care (FSPHX) in the eight years from January 1993 to December 2000, which delivered a nearly 300% gain to shareholders. Although this is not necessarily typical, it is not all that rare if you can find the fund that is at the center of a significant trend. This fund capitalized on what many in the health-care field call the golden age of cholesterol-reducing drugs, which produced huge earnings for pharmaceutical companies and drove their shares to incredible gains.

Balanced Funds and Built-In Asset Allocation

While growth and income funds offer some asset allocation, balanced funds and asset allocation funds put together a portfolio of stocks, bonds, and cash under one roof. Balanced funds tend to gravitate toward stocks and bonds, while asset allocation funds split the portfolio into stocks, bonds, and short-term instruments like Treasury bills and short-term bonds. These are ideal for investors who want to buy a mutual fund and worry about it as little as possible because, in this case, the manager literally does all of the worrying.

This doesn't mean that you should abandon the fund to its own devices. You should read the annual report and see what the manager is doing. And you should still monitor the fund periodically while paying attention to the fund's performance during all markets.

Here are three things to expect from a balanced or asset allocation fund:

- **Performance:** If the stock market is on a very hot streak, your balanced fund should be participating, perhaps not to the degree of an aggressive growth fund, but it should certainly be moving in the same general trend as the stock market.
- **Safety:** The goal of a balanced portfolio is to reduce risk. That means that if the stock market is falling hard, your balanced fund should be falling less due to its bond and cash components.
- **Consistency and predictability:** Although no mutual fund can have identical performance during any two different periods of time, more than growth funds, the balanced and asset allocator funds should be able to smooth out market volatility to a reasonable degree while delivering better returns than cash.

International and Global Funds

Political changes have adjusted investment opportunities in non-US markets, but these funds may still have a place in anyone's portfolio. There are some important distinctions to keep in mind when investing in these funds. Global funds may include US securities in the mix, while international funds will not. The name of the fund will describe the region(s) in which the fund invests. Consider these factors when investing in foreign-focused mutual funds:

- The risk tends to be higher in international funds, but the rewards can also be high. International funds tend to follow general market trends but they can also buck those trends depending on any regional situations, such as significant political changes. Funds that invested in South America did well in the 1990s. The early twenty-first century tended to favor Chinese investments. No matter what, the key when investing in this type of fund is to find the region of the world to where money is flowing. You can do that by making a list of different non-US funds and monitoring their share prices periodically.

- The narrower the investment focus of the fund, the greater the chance of volatility. Funds that invest in a single country are more likely to have wider price fluctuations than funds that invest in a region or a continent. For example, a fund that invests in Europe may be more stable than a fund that invests only in Bulgaria.

The global economy is not as connected as it once was after the 2016 US presidential election. That means that a change in the trend in the US economy may or may not affect foreign markets as it once did. These funds may or may not provide any added safety if you are looking to escape from a problem in the United States.

Regardless of who's in the White House, the odds favor regional and perhaps global conflicts with a higher potential for wars, which, contrary to popular belief, tend to be positive for the stock market. One of the best bull markets of all time was during World War II. The first Iraq war also spawned a major bull market in stocks. Beginning investors should use these funds only for diversification purposes and consider only using them as a small portion of their portfolio.

Small-Cap, Mid-Cap, and Large-Cap Funds

In the stock market and the world of mutual funds, the word "cap" means "capitalization," or the market value of the companies in which the fund invests. Large-cap mutual funds invest in the better-known large companies. Mid-cap funds invest in smaller—but not small—companies. Small-cap funds invest in the small companies. Micro-cap funds invest in the tiniest of the small companies.

Often, but not always, large company funds may be less volatile in bull markets, while mid-cap and small-cap funds may be more volatile while offering more opportunity for capital appreciation. As with any investment, profit potential is often linked to risk. This is because large companies are established and have a more stable earnings and income stream, while mid-cap and small companies are at different stages of development and have the potential for more bumps along the way. In order to diversify your portfolio, consider investing in all three areas while recognizing the risk/reward ratio and your own risk profile. And as with any other stock-related investment, rising trends will favor most reasonably managed mutual funds, while falling markets will hit most of them, large-cap, mid-cap, and small-cap.

ALERT

You can learn a lot from a mutual fund's name. Sometimes a mutual fund gets descriptive with its name. For example, you may run into a fund whose name and investments may be along the lines of XYZ Small-Cap Growth and Income International Asset Allocation fund. This may be a red flag that the fund invests in too small an asset class and that it may be much higher risk than the name hints at. A simple rule is that a small name often means more stock picking variety and thus may be a lower risk proposition in terms of diversification. As usual, regardless of the name, there is no substitute for doing your homework before you buy.

Bond Funds

Bond funds can lose money, especially when the Federal Reserve is raising interest rates. Still, they generally have lower risks (but also lower returns) associated with them when compared to stock funds. Their main function is to provide monthly income, via dividends. The major advantage of owning a bond fund versus individual bonds is that in a bond fund you get diversification while the fund manager does all the analysis and manages the portfolio. All you have to do is pick a good fund, keep up with how it's doing, make sure that it's meeting your expectations, and gather the income.

It's important to remember that bond fund share prices rise and fall. The longer the time frame of the bonds in your bond fund, the higher the potential for volatility. For example, if you own a bond fund which specializes in

30-year Treasury bonds, its net asset value (daily price) will be more volatile than a fund which specializes in short-term bonds that last less than two years. This is especially true during times when the Federal Reserve is raising interest rates, which usually leads to lower bond prices. Over time, short-term bond funds are a fairly safe place to use as a method for savings.

If you own bond funds, there is no guarantee that your principal won't rise and fall depending on bond market conditions and their effects on the investment portfolio of the fund. There are primarily three types of bond funds: treasury or government, municipal, and corporate, which includes funds that invest in the high-yield or junk category of bonds.

US Government Bond Funds

These are generally the lowest risk, and thus lowest potential reward, bond funds. Even though the US government runs high deficits, the risk of default remains low. So for now, and in the near future, investing in a government bond fund is still relatively safe. These funds, although not exempt from short-term periods of volatility, are excellent vehicles for stable income and for providing an antidote to the potential volatility of the stock fund portion of your portfolio.

Municipal Bond Funds

These funds invest in short-, intermediate-, or long-term municipal bonds. Cities, counties, states, and other municipal entities, including school districts, use the proceeds from these bond issuances to finance new road construction or repairs, upgrade sewer systems, or build a new high school. The incentive of most municipal bonds is that investors don't pay federal and often state taxes on the income they receive from the bonds. This extends to municipal bond funds as well. Because the income is not taxed, it tends to be lower than the income you receive from other bonds, though. Municipal bond funds can invest in national, state, or local bonds. These bond funds may be very attractive to investors in high-tax states. This advantage may only apply to bond funds that invest in the state itself, though, which is why there are many municipal bond funds that carry the state's name in their title.

Corporate Bond Funds

Corporate bond funds specialize in owning bonds primarily issued by private companies. There are multiple types of corporate bonds, with their quality being based on the kind of corporation that issues them. Generally, good-quality companies with a proven track record issue the highest-rated corporate bonds. As company fundamentals and circumstances decline, so does their credit quality, and the risk of default increases. Ratings agencies have systems to evaluate and rate corporate bonds. Corporate bond fund prospectuses detail the general quality of their holdings. The key term to look for in the prospectus and in the fund literature is "investment grade."

FACT

Socially responsible funds can sometimes be controversial since there is no set definition of the term "socially responsible." In general these funds tend to avoid products that involve animal testing, tobacco, defense companies, and companies that produce guns. Many avoid companies that may be involved with child labor. If you are interested in this kind of investing, you have to read the fund literature carefully and match it with your own criteria. It can be difficult to match socially responsible funds with profit, though, which is the driving force of investing.

Corporate bond funds offer a higher yield, but beware of funds that offer significantly higher yields, as they will almost certainly hold large quantities of high-yield or junk bonds with a much higher risk of a default happening and costing you money. Funds that hold large chunks of these bonds are very high risk and are not for everyone.

Mutual Fund Investing Checklist

This chapter has a lot of information about mutual fund investing. Use this concept summary list as a quick reference when deciding upon your mutual funds:

- Mutual funds are excellent investment vehicles for young and new investors. Think of them as vehicles through which you can invest in a variety of asset classes.
- Investing in mutual funds takes away one aspect of research, that of finding stocks, bonds, or a good mix of them to own, while reducing the work and effort that managing a portfolio of direct investments requires.
- There is a large variety of mutual funds, and that means there is a mutual fund out there that can meet your criteria and can help you get to your goals.
- Mutual funds reflect the general trends of the assets in which they invest. If you own stocks and the stock market crashes, your fund could register significant losses in the short and long term, depending on how the market reacts and how your fund manager adjusts to the situation.
- Bond funds can help cushion the volatility of a stock portfolio but have their own set of risks. Much of the risk in bonds depends on the overall trend of interest rates, the rate of inflation, and the type of bonds in the portfolio. Generally, mutual funds that invest in US government securities are safer than funds that invest in corporate bonds. Funds that invest in high-yield or junk bonds are the highest risk.
- Past performance is not a guarantee of future performance. Before buying shares in a fund, review how any fund has done in up markets and down markets. If possible, check to see what a fund has done in an environment as similar as possible to the one you are experiencing in the present. Remember that a particular fund manager in the past may have been a superstar with a vision that delivered extraordinary results and that the current fund manager may or may not be in the same category.
- You can invest in balanced or asset allocator mutual funds. Balanced funds invest in a mix of stocks and bonds. Asset allocator funds allocate their resources among different asset classes. This usually includes a mix of stocks, bonds, and cash-equivalent securities.

CHAPTER 11

Combining Funds for Performance

There is a golden rule in investing: if you can't sleep because you're worried about what you own, you shouldn't own it. Thankfully there is a counter rule: if you put together a nice mix of assets, you are likely to sleep better. But at the end of the day, your mutual fund portfolio is not just directly related to your sleep, but also your pocketbook, your retirement plan, and your income goals. This chapter considers how you can combine your risk tolerance and your goals into a mutual fund portfolio that delivers reasonable returns over time and lets you get some sleep.

Your Risk Tolerance

Chapter 1 gave your risk tolerance profile a checkup. So, by this stage of the book, you should have a good idea as to whether you are a conservative, moderate, or aggressive investor. Now it's time to put your knowledge to work in order to put together a mutual fund portfolio that fits your risk profile and your investment goals.

Once you know your risk tolerance, you can start to put together a mix of funds that, together, will deliver the kinds of returns that you are comfortable with. It is important to remember that although mutual funds do spread out the risk of owning stocks and bonds, they still reflect the risk of the assets that they own. Thus, part of putting together the right mix of funds involves considering how they will perform during difficult markets, and whether your risk tolerance will let you hold them through thick and thin.

ESSENTIAL

Look for the sweet spot. Part of knowing your risk tolerance is recognizing that being conservative will reduce your returns as well as your risk, while being aggressive will increase returns but also increase risks. The key to success is to be aware of this simple principle and to adjust your choices and expectations.

While individual stocks can make you a lot of money in the short term, mutual funds tend to maximize their returns over the long term. This is because an individual stock can respond to earnings or other positive news immediately, while a mutual fund, even if it holds a hot stock, also has other stocks, and sometimes a mixture of assets. So the hot stock is only a portion of a diversified portfolio and only has a partial effect on the net asset value, or share price of the fund.

It can be difficult and painful to hold on to mutual funds during bad markets and watch your account shrink. The most important thing is to remain patient and to know that eventually markets turn around. By reviewing the history of how any fund you invest in, whether it is a growth, growth and income, or any other category, does on the rebound after a bad period in the market, you can have an idea as to how things might develop in the future. Where fund investors make mistakes is in picking the wrong fund(s), and then becoming impatient when things get rocky.

Diversification Is Your Friend

Diversification spreads portfolio risk around. And successful diversification means owning several different types of mutual funds and allocating them in a way that your risk of a major loss is decreased. Thus, when you own three different aggressive stock funds, you are not diversifying your risk, but most likely increasing it, as you may hold not just the same types of stocks, but you may actually be repeating a fair number of stocks in the three different funds. This type of allocation means that if one of the funds gets hit, all three of your aggressive funds will get hit, and you will increase your losses.

Understanding Diversification

The concept is simple: own mutual funds that invest in different assets or asset classes and spread your risk around. These three questions will get you started:

- What is the ideal mix of mutual funds?
- How many mutual funds should you own in order to properly diversify your portfolio?
- How often should you change your asset allocation?

It is by answering these questions that you will develop a working plan to balance your goals and your risk tolerance as you develop and maintain your mutual fund portfolio.

Achieving Diversification

Diversification requires patience and an understanding of what you wish to gain with your portfolio. Here are some guidelines:

- **Be clear when setting your investment goals.** Be detailed, as this is the step that will both guide you and seed your plan. Write down your time frame, your risk tolerance, and the precise purpose of your portfolio, such as long-term growth for retirement, current income, or both.
- **Choose quality over quantity.** Pick one fund at a time. Match the fund to your goal based on whether it fits your investment strategy. If one fund takes care of your goal, then choose that one fund and wait to see how things develop. Evaluate the fund over a few months, perhaps a quarter, and see how things are working out. Consider what kind of market is unfolding and ask yourself how your fund might do if things change. The answer to that question and how it fits into your investment goal will send you in the right direction.
- **Keep it simple.** Don't make this too difficult on yourself. When you've chosen a fund that meets your criteria, don't add a similar fund to the list. For example, most growth funds will trend in a similar way, because they invest in similar stocks. Once you've chosen a fund from a particular category, go on to the next category. If the first fund doesn't work out over a couple of months or a quarter, you may want to switch it for a different fund from the same category.
- **Fewer is better.** If you find that by choosing two or three funds you've met your goals, that's great. There is no need to have more than what you need. For example, if you are a conservative investor and don't want to lose sleep, you may choose a good balanced or asset allocator fund as your only vehicle.
- **Remember to evaluate your goals and your funds' performance.** It's a good rule to look at your funds' performance on at least a weekly basis and to consider making changes to your portfolio, perhaps on a

quarterly basis, if your goals change or if the funds aren't delivering the goods.

Considering Your Choices

Once you've outlined and reconciled your investment goals with your risk profile, it's time to find some mutual funds to plug into your portfolio. And while reading a fund's prospectus is worthwhile, it makes sense to have an independent source of information. That's where a cell phone and your laptop come in handy. Check out Morningstar.com, which has both a free and a premium service. The free service is well worth your time. You can get useful information about mutual funds, including performance, fund holdings, and information about the management team. A premium subscription will give you all the free information plus detailed analysis and recommendations for mutual funds and market trends, which may help your decision-making process. If you're unsure, you can sign up for a fourteen-day free trial and see if a full subscription makes sense.

Choosing a Fund Family

Big is usually, but not always, best when it comes to choosing a fund family. That's because large, well-established fund families have money, and money tends to attract good management. It is important to understand that "best" is a relative term. Just because a fund family is large, it doesn't guarantee that their funds will outperform the market, or mutual funds from smaller fund families. The advantage of size is that the company usually has been around for a long time and therefore has a very accessible track record.

For example, Fidelity Investments, Vanguard, and American are huge fund families with gigantic mutual funds that, by and large, perform in tune with the overall market or sector that they track. In addition, in a tough market, especially one in which you want to sell shares in a fund, or even close an account, it is unlikely that you will encounter any problems in doing so with a phone call or a click of a mouse. Big fund companies usually provide better data and better security for your money online than smaller firms. For example, during the Heartbleed Bug security threat (a virus designed to steal personal data from financial websites), Fidelity's website informed its shareholders that the security vulnerability caused by the encryption software that made other websites unsafe wasn't a problem since the company used a totally different technology. The point is that big money fund families, although not invincible, may have better resources to protect clients from non-investment-related damage than smaller companies.

The Fund's Objective

Your first step is to match your goal to the fund's objective. If you want aggressive growth or capital appreciation, make sure the fund's objective states that clearly in its literature and compare the information to what you find in an independent source like *Morningstar*. If the statement in the prospectus is vague, it means that the fund manager likes to have leeway. Leeway could lead to "drift" from the advertised objective. And while drift can work in your favor, you need to decide whether you can handle it if it turns against you.

Investment Risk

The fund should state its risk profile plainly, and you should be comfortable with the level of risk in the fund if you are going to invest in it. Make sure that the fund's risk and objective match and that the combination of the two is a good match for your risk profile. If a fund is an asset allocator but the prospectus says that it's a high-risk fund, you should probably pass on it even if you are an aggressive investor. Remaining true to the fund category and how it matches your risk profile is your best bet.

Once you've made sure that the fund says what it does and actually does what it says, it's important to know how the fund performs in up markets, in down markets, in relation to the S&P 500 or its benchmark index, and how it stacks up to its competition over time. If your account is with a single mutual fund company, see if there is more than one fund in the stable that invests in the category. If there is, choose the one that has the better performance over time and that meets your risk profile and expectations.

Breakdown of Investments

The prospectus should clearly list the limits of the fund's investment breakdown. For example, it should note if the fund's maximum exposure to stocks is 60% or a different figure, as well as its maximum bond exposure. The fund should also tell you whether it uses leverage or margin, which are two terms that describe the practice of investing with borrowed money, or if it sells securities short, the practice of borrowing securities in the hope that they fall in price in order to profit from the price decline. If a fund relies on margin, leverage, derivatives, and short selling for a large portion of its activity, it is not a good bet for a beginning investor.

FACT

Leverage and margin are financial terms related to using borrowed money to invest. The goal of using leverage or margin is to own more of a security than you would own with your own capital. The downside is that if the leveraged investment falls in price, you are liable for both the loss of the investment as well as paying back the debt.

Financial History

A fund should also list its history, preferably for the life of the fund, but for no less than ten years. This information should be detailed on a per-share basis and should include year-by-year details on net asset values, dividends, and total returns so that you can gauge performance on an annual basis. This history should also include details on the fund's expenses and fees and the kind of holdings the fund has had over time.

Parsing Past Performance

The financial world's signature disclosure statement and disclaimer is: "Past performance is no guarantee of future performance." The reason is that things change and change can affect a fund's performance. Aside from the economy, interest rates, and other external factors such as politics, mutual fund performance may be affected by sector and industry trends, which can lead to one or two years of good or excellent performance followed by several years of mediocre growth or even a decline in the net asset value. More importantly, the reversal of any of these factors, which may have held performance down for the past three to four years, could be the signal of a price reversal for any mutual fund. For that reason, the best way to look at past performance is in comparison to the influences of the present with regard to all pertinent factors: interest rates, economic activity, and technology trends. Pay special attention to the fund's current holdings and how they compare to what the fund held during similar periods in the past.

Also review what the fund's category has done through any significant period of the market and compare it to the fund's performance during the same period. If a small-cap fund didn't do well when small-caps weren't doing well, such as during the decade of the 1990s, it's not the fund; it's more likely the times that held it back. By the same token, if a small-cap fund delivered stellar returns during the same period, it may be worth looking into it, as it could be a sign of superior stock picking by the manager.

Finally, when looking at long-term performance, consider the effect of fees, operating expenses, and sales charges. Have your CPA look at the tax consequences of the fund's annual payouts. This does not apply to shares held in an IRA or other retirement account. Also consider the size of the fund. The larger the fund, the harder it is for the manager to deploy their cash in the markets, given the need for very large share blocks. Pay attention to how long the current manager has been running the fund. If the fund has an excellent ten-year performance record, but the current manager started six months ago, the ten-year performance record is essentially meaningless.

FACT

When you sell shares of mutual funds within the same family, it's called an exchange. If you do it by phone, just tell the representative that you would like to exchange shares from Fund A to Fund B. If you are making the exchange online, just follow the directions on the website. The exchange will take place at the closing price at 4:00 p.m. EST on the day you make the decision, unless you make the exchange after hours. Then it will be made at the closing price on the next business day.

How Long Should You Hold Mutual Fund Shares?

Ideally, your time frame for holding a mutual fund should be one to five years. But there are some things to consider before you make your decision with regard to the holding period.

- Although there is no way to predict when a market trend will change, you should understand where you are in the market cycle before investing. Thus, if you buy a stock mutual fund late in a bull market cycle, you should expect that some kind of pullback or extended period of flat prices may develop after you buy your shares. In this case, you may want to wait until an opportunity for lower prices materializes, or to buy small numbers of shares over time as the market cycle unfolds.

Because bear markets tend to last shorter periods of time than bull markets, if stocks have been falling for the past twelve to eighteen months, the odds of some kind of rally are likely higher than normal. This might be a good time to buy some shares and see what happens.

- Know what kind of fund you are investing in. If, after looking at the market cycle, you get worried about losing money in a market correction but you still want to put some money in a fund, consider a bond fund or an asset allocator fund. These tend to move more slowly than the stock market and are more likely to produce less damage to your principal. Moreover, there is nothing wrong with putting some money in your low-risk money market fund as you wait for things to sort out in the market.

Six Fund Investment Strategies

Mutual fund investing can be confusing. But it doesn't have to be if you follow some simple rules that will keep you on the right side of things and get organized.

Start Now

Time is your best friend. The earlier you get started, the better. But don't be put off because you don't think that you have enough time to meet your goals. Even if you make your first investment in a few weeks or months, by starting the process now, you will be ready sooner than if you wait any longer. The data is clear: compounding works over time. And there is no time like now.

Go Big

Invest as much money as you possibly can as early as possible. This does not mean that you should throw your money at anything. But even if you put as sizable a quantity of money as possible in a money market fund now, it will be available for you when you find the right fund.

Information Is Salvation

The more you know about your investments, the better off you'll be and the lower your chances of taking big losses. Know as much as you can about your mutual fund and the securities, stocks, bonds, and other asset classes that it holds. As you learn, you will gain confidence and experience, which will lead to better financial decisions.

Stay Aggressive

Aggressiveness pays off in the early stages of your investing career when tempered by the knowledge that time is on your side. That means that putting money in growth-oriented mutual funds is a must in your early years. As you get closer to retirement, you can start scaling back. Being aggressive does not mean that you should be foolhardy. Always have a well-diversified portfolio, but include growth funds, especially when you are young.

Keep the Money Working

Your investment portfolio should not be your emergency piggy bank. If you take money out of your investment portfolio every time you have a financial emergency, you are taking money away from your future. So avoid the temptation of dipping into your investments to pay bills if at all possible. Before doing so, try every other way of taking care of any financial surprise.

Watch the Market

External events can hit your mutual funds hard. That means that you have to watch your own portfolio. Don't trust your portfolio manager to do anything other than what their job requires. If the market starts to look dicey, it makes sense to put any new money in the safety of your money market fund and wait to see what the market does before putting new money into your stock funds. Use the same basic strategy for your bond funds. Sometimes building up some extra cash makes sense, especially if you're looking to put it to work later at lower prices.

Tracking Your Funds' Performance

Once you become an active mutual fund shareholder, it's important to keep up with your fund's activity. Start by reviewing your mutual fund order on the confirmation slip that you will receive, either by mail or email. Make sure that your order was put in correctly. Check the amount of money you invested and verify that you got the correct number of shares. Pay special attention to any fees that were deducted when you bought the shares, especially if the fund is advertised as a no-load fund, and inquire about any discrepancies that you perceive as soon as you notice them. If you buy the fund online, you should see a confirmation page before putting the order through. If you are buying the fund on the phone, your mutual fund company representative should confirm the order to you before putting it through. Still, make it a habit to review your order confirmations as soon as possible after you receive them in the mail and compare them to your wishes.

ESSENTIAL

The most cost-effective way to buy mutual funds is through an online discount brokerage account. Even more effective is opening the account with a big mutual fund company that offers brokerage accounts as well. Then you can exchange between the funds in the broker's family or buy funds in other families, usually with no transaction costs or a lower commission than what you would get from a full-service broker.

Check your funds' performances at least on a quarterly basis. In the past, it was not unusual to check mutual funds once or twice a year. But in the age of high-frequency trading, a politically volatile world, and an economy where interest rates are on the rise after more than a decade near zero, more frequent checks are a must. Make it a habit to compare your fund to its benchmark index and to other funds in its category. Check on the fees charged by competing funds and fund families and make changes if they make sense.

When to Sell

The most difficult decision in investing is when to sell. But with a good plan, you should have decided when to sell before you buy. Generally, you should sell a fund when it no longer fits with your long-term plans. Some reasons that can contribute to this are poor performance, a change in the fund's management, market conditions, or even bad service from the fund's family. Also consider selling if your fund isn't meeting your expectations or keeping up with the market or its category. If you see that most funds in the category aren't doing well, you should consider avoiding the entire category of funds and rethink your strategy and goals.

Mostly, you should sell your fund if holding it is making you uncomfortable. Maybe it's too volatile and you're starting to get nervous. If you're reaching for the antacids, that's a sure sign that you need to look elsewhere. Your best move may be never coming back to the same fund again.

The Fund Monitoring Checklist

Here are nine tips that will keep you from losing sleep over your mutual funds:

- Inspect and carefully verify every document you receive regarding your investments. If you find errors, address them immediately and record responses and corrections in writing.
- Keep notes of all conversations with investment professionals, ranging from your CPA and financial advisor to mutual fund or brokerage company reps, with regard to your portfolio.
- Make sure that all investment-related correspondence is addressed to you. Your advisor, if you use one, should get copies. You should get the first copy.

- Keep up with your paperwork. If you make a trade and you don't get confirmation by email, text, on the fund's website, or by regular mail within a reasonable amount of time, find out why.
- If something unfamiliar or unexpected shows up in your account, contact your fund company or brokerage right away.
- Never make your investment deposit checks to an individual. Always make them to the company and list your account number. Brokerage companies and mutual fund companies always provide investment slips with critical ID information that you should include with your check.
- If you decide to use a broker, make sure you meet them in their office before putting down any money.
- Know your investments. Don't rely on someone else's research or sales pitch. Do your own homework. Get used to good independent websites like *Yahoo! Finance* where you can find great deals of information free of charge.
- When in doubt, review your portfolio. There is no reason that just because you have mutual funds, you shouldn't keep up with what's going on. *The Wall Street Journal,* Investors.com, MarketWatch.com, and CNBC.com are great sources of information that can help you put your investments in their proper perspective.

Remember, mutual funds are great investment vehicles for beginners and experienced investors. But just because the fund manager is making the buy and sell decisions doesn't mean you shouldn't still be informed and involved.

CHAPTER 12

Exchange-Traded Funds

Exchange-traded funds (ETFs) are securities that resemble mutual funds because they are composed of groups of assets, such as stocks or bonds. However, unlike mutual funds (which are priced after the market closes), ETFs trade like stocks throughout the day. They've been around since the 1990s and have revolutionized the way both individual and professional investors trade and invest. This chapter is all about how you can make ETFs work for you and how to avoid the potential errors that can cost you money.

What Are ETFs?

ETFs are hybrid securities that behave both as a stock and a mutual fund. The stock part comes from the fact that ETFs trade like stocks on an open exchange, through a brokerage account that charges a commission. The mutual fund part is that ETFs, like the traditional mutual fund, are a portfolio of securities chosen by a manager. So when you buy an ETF, you are buying shares in the portfolio, but because it trades like a stock, you don't have to wait until the market closes to buy or sell the shares. ETFs may also offer you better tax treatment and fee structures than mutual funds.

There are thousands of ETFs with trillions of dollars in assets, most of which are invested in equity-related funds with the rest in bond or other type of funds. About 1% of assets resides in hybrid funds, which hold multiple kinds of assets, much like a balanced mutual fund. And although this is a growing asset class compared to mutual funds, it's still a relatively small group. Nevertheless, ETFs are important and may make sense as part of your portfolio.

ETFs are best suited for short- to intermediate-term trading, although they can be used for long-term investing as well. And while you may not be interested in trading when you are a beginner, trading may become attractive as you gain experience. ETFs can be useful because, like with mutual funds, you are investing in an index or a sector. Thus, you don't have to pick stocks. You are picking a trend and the analysis required is less involved, but still offers you excellent profit potential if you know what you are looking for.

Moreover, there are no trading limits on ETFs. While mutual fund companies limit the number of times you can exchange in and out of a fund, you can trade ETFs like you trade stocks. And you can use margin which opens up your ability for short-term trading opportunities once you become more experienced.

In addition, some ETFs offer you the opportunity to sell the market, or specific sectors, short. Short selling is an investment method where you borrow and sell shares of a stock from your broker in hopes that they fall in price. If they do, you buy them back at the lower price and your profit is the difference between the price at which you borrowed them and the price at which you bought them back. For example, if you think XYZ is going to fall, you may decide to short it at $100. You borrow one hundred shares from your broker and sell them, gaining you $10,000. However, you still owe your broker one hundred shares of XYZ. If XYZ falls to $80, you may wish to cover your short. This means you would buy one hundred shares of the stock back at $80 per share and pocket the $20 per share profit. When you buy the stock back, it goes back to your broker since you owed them one hundred shares. If the stock price goes up instead of down, however, you could lose money and still owe your broker one hundred shares.

While this is risky and is not recommended for beginners, short selling is a useful skill when you want to hedge your risk to protect your portfolio in a falling or volatile market, or when you see a weakness in a specific area of the market. Inverse ETFs, a special category of ETFs, do the short selling for you, so all you have to do is pick the ETF. The use of inverse ETFs does require a special agreement with your broker.

ETFs offer built-in leverage. As with short selling, the use of it is dangerous even for experienced investors. Yet, as with other advanced trading techniques, the use of leverage may have a place in your strategy at some point when you become more experienced. By using leverage, some ETFs move at two or three times the rate of their underlying index. This kind of investing is to be avoided by beginners and is only designed for short-term trading.

ETFs versus Mutual Funds

There are many differences between mutual funds and ETFs. The biggest three are: since ETFs trade on an exchange like stocks, you can trade them at any time during the trading day; there is no minimum or limit in the number of ETF shares you can buy; and each and every time you buy ETF shares, you will have to pay a brokerage commission. ETF management fees tend to be lower than mutual fund fees, but that is something that you should check out before you trade any ETF shares.

Perhaps the biggest difference, and one that could make a big difference, is that ETFs don't make capital gains distributions like mutual funds. ETFs, especially ETFs that invest in bonds, do pay dividends that may be taxable. Remember, a capital gains distribution, in the context of mutual funds, is a different entity than a dividend because capital gains are incurred by mutual funds when they sell assets on which they have a profit. A dividend, in the context of a mutual fund, is a pass-through of dividend income that the fund has received. On the other hand, ETF shares will incur applicable capital gains taxes when you sell them.

Finally, ETFs update their holdings daily on their company websites. This is a better deal than what you get with mutual funds, which are only required to report their holdings twice a year. This is also important because knowing what you're buying in real time may influence your decision and could save you money in the long run as you avoid investing in something that you may not want.

What Kinds of Investments Can You Make Through ETFs?

As with mutual funds, you can find just about any category of stock or bond represented in an ETF. Historically, stock index ETFs that focused on the popular indexes, such as the S&P 500 and the Dow Jones Industrial Average, were the rage. And this is still the most popular category given their low cost and their ability to track their respective indexes. But as the market has expanded, so has the number of offerings. Now you can buy and sell ETFs that only invest in indexes that focus on aggressive growth or dividend stocks, small stocks, large-cap stocks, or blue chips.

You can also invest in municipal, government, and corporate bond ETFs that hold bonds in durations from short-term to twenty years. ETFs that specialize in real estate investment trusts and preferred stocks are easy to find. You can trade ETFs that invest in foreign currencies or the US dollar, and others offer you the opportunity to sell the bond or stock market short, and profit when prices fall. After 2014, actively managed ETFs have emerged. These funds, unlike index-based ETFs, use a portfolio manager to make changes in the portfolio based on the manager's indicators and trading philosophy.

ALERT

Actively managed mutual funds can have higher fees than index ETFs and even some mutual funds. And the return isn't guaranteed to be better since managers can have hot and cold streaks. Also, be aware of the fact that one of the reasons mutual fund companies offer these actively managed ETFs is both to broaden their investor base as well as to increase their fees. In fact, a fair portion of the time, actively managed ETFs are basically clones of their traditional mutual fund counterparts, often having the identical name. Why pay more for the same assets and sometimes worse performance?

Animal Crackers and Geometry: Spiders, Vipers, Diamonds, and Cubes

ETFs have great nicknames. But don't let the fun and games distract you, for these are all serious investments, and a wrong choice could cost you money.

- **"Spiders"** is the market's nickname for the first family of ETFs, the S&P 500 SPDR ETF (NYSE: SPY) and related funds. SPDR stands for S&P 500 Depository Receipts, which means these ETFs invest in stocks listed in the S&P 500. SPY was created by State Street Global Advisors, and spawned the Select Sector SPDRs, a series of sector-specific ETFs such as the Technology Select Sector SPDR Fund (NYSE: XLK) and the Health Care Select Sector SPDR Fund (NYSE: XLV).
- **Diamonds** *are another set of ETFs that* let you own the stocks of the Dow Jones Industrial Average, while **VIPERs** (Vanguard Index Participation Equity Receipts) are Vanguard-issued ETFs. VIPERs, depending on which one(s) you choose, offer investment opportunities in stocks, bonds, and international markets.
- PowerShares runs the **Cubes** (NYSE: QQQ), the ETF that tracks the NASDAQ-100 Index (which houses the largest capitalization shares in the NASDAQ). By investing in the Cubes, you buy into shares of companies like Alphabet, Microsoft, Apple, Netflix, Amazon, and Intel, among others. PowerShares uses a method called dynamic indexing, which allows them to focus on the best performers in the underlying index.

FACT

Terms such as "Spiders" and "Diamonds" can be confusing, but they are part of the market's jargon and are terms which you will hear. By becoming familiar with them early in your investment education, you will be better informed in the future when doing research or when market news hits the wires.

Choosing Wisely

ETFs can be used for diversification or as the sole component of a well-structured portfolio. Because of the broad choices in categories and individual funds, your portfolio can participate in a piece of just about every asset category that's available. Perhaps the largest advantage is the fact that you can do this for a lot less than what it would cost you if you bought individual stocks. For example, you could own a large-cap, a mid-cap, and a small-cap index ETF. You can add one, two, or more bond ETFs, coupled with a diversified commodity ETF, a gold ETF, and a real estate investment trust ETF. And you could further diversify your holdings by adding international equity and bond funds. You can mix actively managed mutual funds and ETFs into your portfolio as well, further diversifying your holdings.

Stick with simple strategies and asset classes. If a new strategy gains buzz and you decide to try it out, please study it and paper trade it before putting money into it. In 2018, a previously little-used strategy known as the selling short of market volatility gained popularity. This strategy was exercised via an exchange-traded note—basically an ETF with a finite life and lots of small print associated with it—known as the VelocityShares Daily VIX Short-Term ETN (VXX). When you owned shares in this ETN, you were betting on the market's volatility remaining low for the foreseeable future as based on readings of the Cboe Volatility Index, which measures the volatility of the S&P 500. Investors who bought shares in VXX were betting that the market's volatility would remain dampened in the future, as it had for the prior several years. The problem was that nothing lasts forever and on February 5, 2018, VXX lost 80% of its value in the after-hours trading session and triggered a provision in its bylaws which said if the NAV fell below a certain point, the ETN would liquidate. When it did, many investors lost most or all the money they had put into VXX in a few hours.

This example is meant to illustrate the pitfalls for any investor who fails to gauge the full risk of an investment or doesn't gather information about the worst-case scenario when investing in a particular instrument. In order to avoid this type of disaster, whether as a beginner or at any other stage, you should stick to what you understand. Sticking to the basics of using stocks, bonds, mutual funds, and ETFs that use straightforward strategies will serve you well in the long run. Furthermore, if, during your research, you find that you don't understand how something works, it's a sign that this is not an investment for you.

<table>
<tr><td>ALERT</td></tr>
<tr><td>ETFs are ideal for trading. This is because, as a more experienced investor, you will likely develop a better sense of the overall market's trend and ETFs, by design, are trend-following investment vehicles. By using ETFs you can focus on trading the trend instead of individual stocks.</td></tr>
</table>

When choosing ETFs, you should compare expenses and performances between ETFs and similar mutual funds. Index ETFs and traditional funds that invest in similar holdings should perform similarly. But if one is more expensive than the other, your overall returns, especially over the long term, could be affected. Remember that a no-load mutual fund won't charge you commission when you trade, while adding shares to an ETF will carry commission costs every time you buy. In other words, if you find a no-load mutual fund with equal or better performance compared to an ETF, choose the mutual fund. Also important is the cost per share. A mutual fund may cost less on a per-share basis than an ETF.

Competition between ETF families could save you money. For example, if Vanguard's S&P 500 ETF has lower fees than the SPDR fund, it might make sense to buy the Vanguard fund, given that it is investing in the same equities and that performance should be nearly identical.

Avoid thinly traded ETFs. Before buying shares, make sure that any ETF has enough capital invested in it and that it is actively traded. If an ETF has assets of more than $10 million and it has a robust trading volume, it makes sense to consider it. If the ETF has less than $10 million and trading volume is less than a few million shares per day, it means that it is not very liquid. And that means that you may have a difficult time when trying to sell shares.

Recognizing Special Situations

Avoid over-diversification. Many investors err by looking for such a high level of variety in their portfolio that they won't miss any kind of move in any market. The truth is that for many investors, less is more. So, before you get yourself into an unmanageable alphabet soup of ETFs and traditional mutual funds, consider your goals and think about how you can get there by keeping things as simple as possible while still giving yourself the opportunity to be flexible and profit from special opportunities.

If your goal is retirement in thirty years, and you are just getting started, there is no point in micromanaging your portfolio. Your first move is to get started. That means that by just fulfilling your asset allocation goals, based on your risk profile, your overall goal, and your time frame, you are on your way. Does this mean that you don't make changes or improve your asset allocation? Of course not; flexibility and the ability to recognize important changes in market dynamics are paramount for your long-term success as an investor.

ALERT

Sector-specific ETFs may be useful in special market situations. For example, if there is a great deal of money that is being invested in energy-related stocks, it may make sense to evaluate and consider investing in an energy specific-sector ETF.

For example, if your current core asset allocation consists of a large-cap, a mid-cap, and a small-cap equity ETF along with a diversified bond ETF and you notice that the technology stocks are on a momentum run, it might make sense to add a technology ETF to the mix. Just keep in mind that technology stocks won't go up forever. These ETFs may not be in your portfolio as long as your core holdings because you may want to sell them if they start to perform badly. In other words, consider carving out special niches inside your portfolio for special situations that can work alongside your core investments. Work this out on paper before you put your money down. Ask yourself questions and develop an analytical routine. By spending a couple of hours per week reviewing the markets and thinking about potential opportunities with a shorter-term time horizon, you may save yourself a lot of trouble later.

Buying and Selling ETFs

If you can trade stocks, you can trade ETFs. The only difference is that with an ETF you get an indexed or a diversified portfolio instead of an individual stock. Otherwise there is no change. You still need a broker. You will pay commission. And before you make the transaction, you need to do your homework and go down your strategic checklist. Consult your plan. Do your research. Consider when you will sell the shares. And understand the tax implications, if there are any. Just like with stocks, you can add conditions to your trading orders. That means you can use limit orders and sell stops. Here is the big difference, though: if you decide that you made a mistake, you can sell all the shares at any time without getting a notice from your mutual fund company because you sold your shares too soon and they don't want a "day trader" using their funds.

Market Timing with ETFs

Market timing is controversial, and it's difficult to do. And while most investment advisors will tell you it is impossible to time the markets, the fact is that the statement is simply not true. The truth is that market timing is possible, but it is hard work, very risky, and in many ways it is similar to gambling. That's why most market timers rely on systems, which are sets of rules combined with indicators that require frequent revision and analysis. Yet, because of their indexed nature and their ease of trading, ETFs are the perfect vehicle for this kind of trading, in which, based on your time frame, it is possible to profit over a few days, a few weeks, or a few months, depending on how long any market trend lasts and how good your timing strategies and attention to detail are.

It's a Risky Business

Market timing is high-risk trading. It's not investing, although it can be part of a long-term investing plan. And it is not something that should be done by investors who are just starting out. But you can learn to do it over time as long as you take the time to learn the steps required and practice via paper trading.

ETFs are great vehicles for market timing because you are focusing only on the direction of prices and not the fundamentals. The only thing that matters in trading and market timing is whether a market or a sector is primarily rising or falling. When you buy stocks, you should pay attention to valuations, company management, the company's product cycle, and a host of other parameters that are detailed in Chapters 4–6. Market timing and trading are all about putting your money into an asset based solely on the direction of prices.

ESSENTIAL

Index-specific ETFs are ideal for market timing. If you know that the largest money flows are going into the S&P 500, your best bet, as a market timer, is to invest in the S&P SPDR (SPY) or a similar ETF. This would be a trading decision that would be based on a technical assessment of the market's trend and would require a good working knowledge and a high level of experience in trend analysis and risk management.

Tools of ETF Timing

In order to make their buy and sell decisions, market timers use technical analysis, the study of price charts and trends, to pick entry and exit points for their trades. For example, when the stock market is rising, market timers often buy an index ETF such as the S&P 500 SPDR ETF. The goal of market timing is to remain in any position, such as an ETF, as long as the direction of prices remains intact.

While long-term investors have time on their side, timers are looking to make money over shorter periods of time, though not necessarily as a day trader. That means that they make buy and sell decisions more frequently, sometimes as often as every few days, although most timers are hoping to be in position for at least a few weeks, since the longer the price trend remains intact, the greater the chance for profits. By using price charts and related indicators, timers take away the emotion associated with buying and selling.

Specifically, market timers and short-term traders use indicators such as moving averages and oscillators, which help them to pick precise exit and entry points when the market is "oversold," meaning that the selling has been exhausted and it's likely prices will rise, or "overbought," meaning that the market has risen far enough that prices are likely to fall in the not too distant future. You can learn all about these useful tools at StockCharts.com.

Leveraged ETFs and Market Timing

Aggressive traders and market timers often buy a leveraged version of the ETF, which moves at two or three times the underlying price of the real S&P 500. When they use leverage, market timers can make or lose more money in shorter periods of time. Because market timers hope to turn a sizable profit in a shorter period of time than short-term investors, and because market timers tend to be experienced traders, they can afford to take the added risk of using a leveraged ETF. If a market timer concludes that the stock market is about to fall, they may buy shares in an ETF that sells the S&P 500 short. These specialized ETFs, also known as inverse ETFs, rise in price when the S&P 500 falls.

Because there are ETFs for all markets, market timers can use ETFs to time bonds and other investment classes. For example, you can use ETFs to trade commodities, including gold, oil, and agricultural commodities such as coffee, wheat, corn, and even cattle. There are specialized ETFs that offer the opportunity to trade in these areas either as part of a commodity index or as separate commodities. Market timers can also time currencies such as the euro, the Japanese yen, the British pound, the Swiss franc, the US dollar, and the Canadian and Australian currencies. And yes, there are leveraged and inverse ETFs available for timing markets beyond stocks.

ETFs As Hedging Instruments

Hedging is the practice of investing in a financial instrument that limits the risk of falling prices in another instrument. A common hedge is the use of bonds or bond funds to limit the risk in a stock portfolio. Experienced traders and investors use ETFs as hedging instruments. Aside from using bond ETFs, traders also use inverse ETFs to hedge risk. For example, let's say that the stock market has risen 10%–15% in a few weeks. History shows that this kind of an advance is not just rare, but likely unsustainable. In such a scenario, rather than selling a portfolio, an experienced trader may buy shares in an inverse S&P 500 ETF with the hopes that if the stock market corrects, the losses will be less as the inverse fund shares will rise in price. This trading technique, as with other market timing techniques, is not without risk, but could become useful as you gain experience.

Tracking Your ETFs

Tracking your ETFs is just like tracking your stocks. You can find daily prices in *The Wall Street Journal*, *Investor's Business Daily*, *Yahoo! Finance*, and many other sources, including your ETF family's web page or your online brokerage account, which will give you tick-by-tick prices if you like that kind of real-time information.

All you need to know is your trading symbols. Price tables will usually include price changes and percentage changes, as well as providing fifty-two-week price ranges. Some will provide dividend payment dates and dividend yield information. Investors.com, the website for *Investor's Business Daily*, has one of the most complete ETF sections in the market and may be worth subscribing to just for that.

CHAPTER 13

Investing with Your Conscience

If you're socially responsible or environmentally conscious, there are ways for you to invest profitably and stay true to your beliefs. And contrary to popular belief, socially conscious investing, through the right vehicles, can be just as rewarding as mainstream investments. The key to success is to find the right vehicle through which to deploy your money and to follow sound investment principles.

What Are Socially Responsible Investments?

Socially responsible investments can be a touchy subject since everyone's definition of socially aware might be slightly different. Vicky Vegan might be vehemently opposed to eating animals and might not want to invest in a restaurant chain that serves animal products, while Gary Green might not care about animal products but wants to protect the environment. Nevertheless, socially responsible investments are part of the investment landscape, but even if it sounds like a good thing to do, it's worth reviewing the ups and the downs of the approach before you jump in. Political causes and investments may not mix well. That's because investments are about making money, and political causes are about bringing about change. Socially conscious investing is no different in this regard. Still, there is a happy medium that can be profitable. That's what this chapter is about: finding the areas where social consciousness and capital gains meet.

A truly socially conscious company is one that puts its money behind helping the world and avoids business decisions in areas that are ethically wrong, or include subjectively questionable practices, especially to those who are firm believers in specific causes. A socially conscious company actively pursues helping not just their bottom line but the entire world through their actions. As a result, Wall Street and Main Street are paying closer attention to this dynamic and trying to make changes, expanding investment choices in the area. There are indexes that track socially conscious companies, along with mutual funds and ETFs that invest in these companies, making it easier for individual investors to participate. Just as important, for income investors, is the fact that municipalities and corporations are also selling bonds to finance environmentally friendly projects. Finally, as you learn more about companies through your investment research, you might find ways to change your behavior as a consumer. The key is to carefully research the general trends in the sector, and then to become acquainted with further detail as you prepare to make investment decisions.

Socially Conscious Stocks

Socially conscious stocks let you become part owner of a company whose efforts, in delivering its goods and services, are positive for the environment or other causes. This may be achieved by their use of cleaner fuels, by their development of new methods that produce less, or cleaner, waste products, or by their avoidance of doing business with known abusers of social consciousness. Sometimes these companies are donors of capital or volunteer their employees for socially responsible and environmentally positive causes.

FACT

It's best to keep it simple. You can be socially conscious by using your common sense. Starbucks (NASDAQ: SBUX) is a green company that is well integrated into the mainstream. It remains a leader in its sector while using solar power to fuel stores, buying products from local organic farmers, and by giving portions of their profits to green causes such as clean water initiatives.

It also helps to be careful. As with any kind of socially responsible investing, there is the potential for fraud. Here is a set of questions that can help you make better decisions:

- Does the corporation that you might invest in actually have products, or are things still in the development stage?
- Is there a reasonable time frame to test the products and market them?
- What is the market that the company is targeting? Is there actually a need or even a niche for the product?
- Is the company speaking in exact, real market terms? Or are they just describing generalities without any specifics?
- Does the company describe how it expects its products to evolve and how it will expand its market share over time?

- How does this corporation's ideas, technology and business models, management team, and practices compare to others who are leaders in the sector?

If you can't get good, solid answers to these questions, especially when you are looking through company-produced documents, it might be best if you look somewhere else for a place to put your hard-earned green. Generally speaking, bonds of all socially conscious companies qualify for investment by those who wish to follow this particular direction. But there are some specific categories.

Green Bonds

A green bond is a financial instrument issued by a corporation or a municipality where the proceeds will be used to finance an environmentally related project. Unlike traditional loans, where a borrower asks for money from a bank, bonds are loans that spread the risk by using money borrowed from the public, investors, and other entities, including banks. For you, as an investor, bonds let you participate in income-producing opportunities.

If the issuer is a corporation, you should consider the default risk along with your green meter, using the six questions outlined in the previous section. These bonds all operate in the same way as normal bonds, including the same ratings and risk/reward decisions as nongreen bonds.

Official green bonds (Qualified Green Building and Sustainable Design Project Bonds) are tax-exempt bonds issued both by corporations and municipalities. They earn this moniker because the federal government designates them for the purpose of developing underdeveloped, underutilized land parcels or old abandoned buildings. Often, the land where the work is to be done is polluted and contaminated, and the bond proceeds are used to clean up the environmental problems.

Green and Socially Responsible Funds

You can find traditional mutual funds or exchange-traded mutual funds (ETMFs) that specialize in green and socially responsible companies. ETMFs may be a better deal because you can look at their component stocks in real time and apply your own personal socially responsible meter to the companies in the ETMF before investing. Traditional mutual funds only publish their holdings periodically, often just once per year. Even though a fund says that it's socially responsible, all of its holdings may not measure up, so you may have to compromise or look elsewhere. Remember, when you read the prospectus, pay close attention to how much leeway the manager has to pick the fund's holdings. If the prospectus tells you that the fund may invest its money, "as much as 50%" or something along those lines, in green companies, it may not be for you.

> **ESSENTIAL**
>
> It's good to find a list where you may find a lot of socially conscious mutual funds and ETMFs to consider. You can search for this type of investment through your online brokerage or visit Morningstar.com.

Green funds are a subset of the socially conscious investing universe and come in three basic varieties: eco-friendly, alternative energy, and sustainable resource funds.

Eco-Friendly Funds

This is the broadest category of green funds, as the fund managers can invest in companies that strive to improve the environment, produce and design environmentally friendly products, or engage in activities that are aimed at reducing their negative impact on the environment.

The Calvert family of mutual funds specializes in green mutual funds and has a variety of offerings. The Calvert US Core Responsible Large-Cap Index fund may strike a good balance for you while their bond funds also offer the opportunity for diversification. The Large-Cap fund specializes in corporations that are socially responsible but have also found the sweet spot in delivering profits to their shareholders. A sampling of the stocks they hold may surprise you as they include Microsoft, Alphabet, Visa, and JPMorgan Chase.

As a general rule, beware of false claims or mushy language in fund prospectuses and other information. Look at the holdings of the fund before buying shares. If you are truly committed to socially responsible investing, you don't want to put your money in the wrong place.

Alternative Energy Funds

These funds invest in companies that develop or produce alternative or renewable energy sources, such as solar and wind power, biofuels, or hydroelectric power, and the companies that are involved in the infrastructure and manufacturing of the components used to make the final products for alternative fuel production. An example of such a fund is the First Trust ISE Global Wind Energy ETF (NYSE: FAN). According to a Morningstar.com search, in October of 2018, FAN's asset allocation was composed of 57% in utilities and 38% in industrial companies. The rest of the holdings (5%) were diversified in other relevant areas. The bottom line is that before you invest, you should dig into the details of the fund's holdings and pick the fund that most closely invests in the types of companies in which you are interested.

FACT

Dig beneath the surface in order to grow your cache of ideas and your knowledge base. Looking inside the holdings of an ETF should lead you to do research on individual companies whose stock may be worth owning, on their own or along with the ETF. For example, the largest holding of any ETF could provide you with clues as to what kind of new trends may be unfolding in any particular sector. It makes sense to jot these companies down and do more research on them later.

Sustainable Resource Funds

Sustainable resource funds invest in companies that share the double goal of maximizing profits without depleting natural resources. This is where the water funds fit. These funds invest in the entire gamut of the water industry, including water distribution, water consumption, and other subsectors of the water industry such as pipelines, storage, measuring devices, flow controls, disinfectants, and so on. The water industry is widely tracked by multiple indexes, and in turn, there are several ETFs and mutual funds that in turn track individual indexes. A diversified global water ETF is the Guggenheim S&P Global Water Index ETF (ARCX: CGW). Non–exchange-traded water funds are available, too, such as the actively managed Calvert Global Water Fund (CFWAX).

Looking Beyond the Green

Socially conscious investing is appealing. After all, you can make money while helping the planet. It sounds great, doesn't it? In reality, socially responsible investing can be just as dangerous as mainstream investing, and often for the same reasons. As with any investment, when the premise, the investment vehicle, and the execution of the management team at a company or a mutual fund are what they say they are, and everyone does what they say they will, the odds are in your favor, as long as interest rates and the economic fundamentals are in the right place. But you must stay on your guard, as scam artists are everywhere. And because socially responsible investing is a good cause, the unscrupulous are attracted to the sector like flies on waste.

Because social responsibility is partially an emotional decision, big Madison Avenue advertising firms craft socially responsible "messaging" statements and "narratives" for their clients, in order to brand companies that aren't really green or socially responsible as such in order to increase sales. The attraction of the green trend is so large and the "messaging" is so widespread that a new term, "greenwashing," is well embedded into the corporate culture. Companies, much like politicians, try to spin their products and practices to make them look green, when in fact, close scrutiny often leads to finding out that there is more effort on the spin than on the green practices advertised.

How can you see through the not-so-green fog? Use your common sense. If it seems foul, it probably is. If it seems sensible, question it anyway. Look deeply into what companies do to appear green and socially responsible. Ask tough questions. Is a biofuel company using twice the amount of oil for input in order to create clean fuels, thus negating the positive environmental effect? Do agricultural companies burn land, creating smoke pollution, in order to plant biofuel stock? Do their biofuels actually pollute the air more than gasoline as some forms of ethanol do? What happens to a riverbed and a fish population if you remove that algae to craft synthetic motor oil? The river could die, creating a waste area and a breeding ground for disease, not to mention that the water supply for a large stretch of farmland might be harmed. And if the "green" idea is so good, then why is it still in the development stage after ten years? If you look hard enough, you will find that in many cases the "green" outcome is achieved at the price of lots of environmental destruction and harm, and that the long-term implications may be worse than going to the corner gas station and filling up your SUV. Consider where a company makes its products, who their workers are, and how they are treated. Also, try to keep the searching balanced. The green and socially responsible activists are not exempt from their own spin. Think for yourself, because everyone has an agenda and is willing to craft an effective "narrative" to win.

Does this mean that socially responsible investing is bad? No way. Socially responsible investing and green initiatives have huge positive potential for the environment, and for profits. The take-home message, though, is that as an investor, you need to become an investigative reporter and dig for the best answers possible before putting your money into something that may cost you or make you regret your investment choices due to a moral commitment.

Your Socially Responsible Portfolio

Green and socially responsible investing has come a long way since the start of the twentieth century. Companies that are sincere and well managed are flourishing as they find balance between environmental consciousness and profit. And investors who used to ignore the trend are having a second look. From a price performance standpoint, big-money players are the ones that move stocks and bonds. So, when a nongreen mutual fund sees something in a green company, it is quite likely that the stock of the company is going to move higher. As an investor, you need to be aware of this dynamic, and you need to be able to act on it because as money comes into the sector, your odds of profiting also rise.

Adapt the basic tenets of investing to the socially responsible sector and you will be well served. Know your risk profile. Look for leaders in the field. Seek out top management teams that clearly state their objectives and execute their plans efficiently and successfully. Keep up with the general trends of the sector, look for news on companies that you own, and monitor how a company responds to the news. Put together a good watchlist of ETFs and mutual funds and monitor their performance. Don't be afraid to make some changes in allocation on a quarterly or semiannual basis. Remember: a quick glance at a stock or ETF chart will tell you a lot in a short period of time. And don't put all of your eggs in one basket. Maybe an index ETF is better for you, or a diversified green mutual fund is the answer.

Finally, green and socially responsible investments may be a part of your portfolio, but they should not be your entire portfolio. As with any other type of investment, there is no substitute for careful analysis, understanding your risk profile, paying attention to your financial needs, diversification, risk management, and always considering what your long-term goals are.

CHAPTER 14

Real Estate Investing: Getting Grounded and Rated

Real estate investing is all about location, lots, land, and the four rates. You might have heard it said that real estate never loses its value, especially as a hedge against inflation. But as the housing crisis in 2008 showed, nothing could be further from the truth. So do your homework before taking the plunge and consider that you will have to deal with four rates: interest rates, occupancy rates, vacancy rates, and tax rates. But, if you can handle the attack of the rates, this might be the market for you.

The Basics of the Real Estate Game

Real estate investing is a hands-on endeavor and it can be an overwhelming full-time job. To be a landlord you have to learn a whole new language, including the definition of closing costs, resale value, liquidity, inspections, and more. You will also need a good attorney in case relationships with renters, prospective buyers, business partners, and contractors sour.

Because it's harder to get out of real estate investments than to sell a stock that didn't work out, you should be well versed in the local market and the business side of things before jumping in. But if you don't mind hard work and are willing to learn about this business/investment opportunity, you may find some long-term profitable investments in this sector.

And while stocks and bonds may feel as if they are in cyberspace, real estate is tangible. You can see land and houses and trees and rocks. Moreover, as a real estate investor, your role reverses from shareholder or lender to owner. In other words, in real estate, you are selling shares in your company every time you rent or sell a property.

Using Leverage

Leverage is the use of borrowed money to invest. In stocks it's called margin. In real estate, it's a business loan that allows you to use someone else's money to take the risk of buying a property. However, leverage is a double-edged sword. When used properly it lets you own more property than you would with your own money. But even when you use leverage prudently and properly, it will still increase your risk. The fact is you have to pay back the loan as you go along and it can eat into your profits. It all comes down to having the right mix of properties and leverage and keeping your cash flow on the positive side. If you own rental property and it's empty or you have unexpected costs such as repairs or legal problems, you could be in big trouble if you are not well-financed. The bottom line is that if you use leverage, your properties have to make enough money to at least make your monthly loan payment and cover your costs. You can make real estate investing work, but it is a business, and in order to do it right, you will have to put in the time.

ALERT

Having too much leverage can cost you the whole business. Generally, the best time to use leverage is when interest rates are falling or have been low for a while.

Your Action Plan

An example of a prudent way to use leverage is when you have a set of properties producing reliable cash flow and a new property opportunity comes along that makes sense for your long-term business plan. It would make sense to use a line of credit or to apply for a loan to finance the purchase if the interest rate climate is appropriate and if the real estate market is on sound footing. An example of this type of market is when the Federal Reserve is lowering interest rates and your listings have multiple offers.

Here are a few tips to keep you out of trouble if you decide to use leverage. First, never borrow any more than you can afford to pay back. Read your loan contract carefully and make sure that there are no hidden clauses, especially if you want to restructure the loan to a lower interest rate in the future or to expand the time for repayment. Also make sure that there is no penalty for early payment of the loan. Banks like to hide little surprises into loans, especially the loans they make to young entrepreneurs. If the loan doesn't make sense, get a CPA or advisor to look at it, or just don't take it.

While you use borrowed money, invest your own money wisely. That will improve your cash flow and broaden your opportunities. Work toward finding opportunities that will create profits in short periods of time and give you predictable income, like flipping a house or getting tenants who pay their rent on time and reliably. If you make enough money in a short period of time, use some of it to pay your loan down or off altogether.

Choosing the Most Profitable Real Estate

If you've decided to take the plunge, you have to decide what kind of real estate makes the most sense based on your long-term goals, as it takes a long time for properties to develop and to provide a good return on your initial investment. The real question is whether you will hold a property for an extended period of time as a rental or whether you will try to flip it for a quick profit.

Part of the art of investing is to not only find a suitable location, but to then discern if it makes sense for your goal. A good place to look for properties is in an area that is being revitalized. A good review and a thorough analysis of the area and what's likely to happen there from a commercial and political standpoint is a must. Is this an area where people are flocking? If it is, then what's the attraction? Once you understand the dynamic, then you can tap into it in the most cost-effective manner.

Considering Commercial versus Residential Property

If you decide to invest in commercial properties, look for areas where large new attractions are being built or where large companies are moving their headquarters. Think beyond just owning a building in the area and look to the possibility of setting up a business there as a guide to what your property may offer in order to attract premium renters. Look for other businesses that are coming to the area such as a restaurant or retail establishment that could make your location attractive. You can buy an empty shell of a building and offer it as a refurbished space that can house such a business. Try to find out what no one is doing there and then fill that particular niche. Is there a dry cleaner in the area? Does it make sense to consider offering medical office space? Anything is possible if you take the time to study the needs of an up-and-coming area.

If you decide to invest in residential property, use the same principle. Families want access to shopping, good schools, restaurants, and entertainment. They also want good roads or easy access to public transportation and low crime rates. Put yourself in the renter or potential buyer's place. Would you move into this area? The key to success in both commercial and residential real estate is putting together the best possible package for your customer.

The Fix and Flip Business Model

House flipping has become a popular business model because of TV shows which feature the practice. But don't be fooled. Real estate in general, and house flipping especially, is risky with no guarantees of success even in good markets. Much depends on your ability to stay well financed and organized. Before investing, learn as much as you can about any property you may want to buy, the current state of market, interest rates, and think about how things can go wrong.

An important first step is to understand the difference between an investor and a speculator. An investor is in for the long haul, while a speculator is looking to flip a quick profit and move on to the next house. Investors are more patient and tend to look for properties that are within their means. Speculators are willing to use higher levels of borrowed money and take higher risks. As a new real estate investor, it's a good idea to invest, and learn the ropes over time. It's also prudent to find a good advisor, an experienced investor who is willing to share their wisdom or make you a partner as they teach you the basics.

FACT

Time management is a big deal in real estate. If you take a day to paint a house, you may not be saving as much money as you think. You can use that time to look for another property, especially one that is inexpensive and that you may be able to sell quickly. If you turn a $30,000 profit in 100 hours of work with the new property, you just paid yourself $300 per hour, more than enough to pay for painters.

You can start with small rental properties, such as single- or double-family homes, or even small apartment complexes with no more than four units. You can look at a fixer-upper house. Usually, the easiest properties to get started with are single-family homes due to their ease of buying and selling relative to other types of units.

The Fixer-Upper Dilemma

The flipper's dream is to buy an inexpensive older home for a small amount, then fix it up, and sell it for a lot more than you paid for it. And while this is plausible and can be done with frequency, it's not without risk and details. Consider the following factors when buying a fixer-upper:

- **Expertise.** In order to know your financial exposure and risk, you should know something about building design and construction in order to estimate the amount of work, money, and time that you'll have to put into the project. Figure out how much you can do yourself and how much you'll have to pay contractors or other experts to do things for you. Don't forget building material costs and give yourself some room for the unexpected and inevitable problems you can't see on the surface, especially hidden plumbing and electrical surprises.
- **Patience.** Real estate is not like stock trading. Even if you are looking for short-term profits, things don't always work out the way you planned them. Expect crazy things to happen once you start remodeling and develop patience and a sense of purpose. Also remember that even though you have turned a trash bin into a diamond, market pressures will affect your ability to sell a property. Be prepared to hang on to it for a while and factor in the cost for the worst-case scenario.
- **Inspection.** Don't buy a house without getting a professional home inspector to do a comprehensive inspection. Check out their references. Even the most thorough inspector won't find everything that's wrong, but they will pick out more than those who are just trying to take your money and leave.

- **Location.** Location is the most important factor in real estate. Study the neighborhood, the shopping around it, the roads, the access to highways and mass transit, the schools, and the recreational opportunities. Look into zoning issues and think about what kind of buyer you may want to attract. Good schools and easy shopping tend to attract young families, while easy highway access tends to attract good commercial buyers.

> **ESSENTIAL**
>
> In order to protect your rental property investment, you will need rental insurance and property insurance. You will need these policies aside from your homeowner's policy because your homeowner's policy won't cover any liability for alleged damages that your renters may try to blame on you or any damage done to the property by the renters.

Keep It Simple

Whether you're flipping or working with rental properties, commercial or residential, avoid unconventional or niche properties. Stick to properties in good locations, which offer a better chance of paying off over the long run. Pay special attention to any possible damages or defects in the property before you buy it. Anything that shows up after the closing will cost you money. Think about whether there will be demand for this particular type of property in five or ten years. And always keep your eyes open for special features in a property, such as a state-of-the-art kitchen, truly remarkable bathrooms, or great closet space.

Most importantly, gauge at what part of the market cycle you may be. If property prices have been rising astronomically for the past decade, as they did in the period leading to the 2008 crash and again in 2017 and 2018 before the Federal Reserve interest rate hikes began to bite, it may make sense to look for bargain properties or to wait until the market changes. If things get bad enough, you may be able to buy premium properties on the cheap in a few months.

Common Sense Is Key

When flipping or investing in rental property, use your common sense and your gift of observation. If you bought a house in what seemed to be a vibrant area and over the next few weeks you learn that the largest employer in the community is leaving and the house next door to your property is empty, expect that your property is going to be difficult to rent and will be difficult to sell unless you move quickly. It's better for you to research this kind of situation before you buy. No matter how attractive any property is, its future sale value will only be as good as its location and the local economy.

Building Wealth Through Rental Properties

When deciding about your real estate investment future, you may ask: To buy or not to buy? But that is not the only question. What should you buy and how do you go about buying it? The answers have to do with deciding between commercial and residential property and determining which makes better sense for you at the beginning of your real estate investing process. No matter what your decision is, several things will be consistent. For example, you need to figure out how much money you will need up front, and whether that money will come from your savings or a loan. Much of what happens will depend on your financial situation and whether your bank considers you a good loan risk. And equally important, if you're loan-worthy, is what the terms of the loan will be and whether it makes sense to go into the venture with a partner or partners.

Of course, it may not be wise to borrow money to invest in real estate. That's because that loan payment could squeeze your cash flow. Things will get worse if you're not able to get tenants, or if you lose any tenants you may have. Remember that real estate is not like stocks and bonds. You need a lot more money to get started and to keep things rolling. It also takes time to buy, sell, and rent properties. And during the entire time that you own the property, whether it's making money or not, you'll still have to pay the bills.

Do Your Homework

Beware of what you don't know. If a seller is giving you a great deal on what seems to be a premium property, something may be up. It could be anything, such as a bad economic event that is not quite known yet or something more closely related to the property, like a new freeway overpass that is going to be built across the street from your potential rental place. In order to avoid being duped, always consider the following:

- Is this a prime location? When in doubt, in real estate think about the property's location: past, present, and future.
- Has this property been rented before? Try and get as much detail as possible, including the length of any rental engagement and any particular circumstances.
- How old is the property? The older the property is, the more likely that it will require a thorough inspection and a substantial repair budget.
- Is your property up to code? This is where an inspector comes in handy—to find out if your plumbing, electricity, foundation, and roof meet local ordinance requirements.
- How much repair work is required? Based on your inspection results you'll have an idea as to how much work the property will need. Consider what it will cost to remodel the interior for business or rental purposes. Think in as much detail as possible and plan to spend twice as much or more than the highest estimate as your worst-case scenario. For instance, older homes and office spaces may not be wired for high-speed Internet and multiple phone lines. Any landscaping, painting, and repair work will also cost you money and time.
- Are there other maintenance costs to consider? If you go commercial, who will pay for the janitor service and alarm and security costs?
- Are there specific zoning laws in the area? If you plan to rent the property as office space, make sure that the city has designated your area as commercial. If you are thinking of owning the property as your

own business, make sure that you can run that type of business in that area.

- How accessible is the property? Review how easy it is to get to your property and reconcile it with your goals. A business property needs to be well located, easy to access, and visible, while a summer cottage will be better if it's well hidden and private.
- What's coming in the future? If a new mall is coming, how will it affect your business property? Do you want to own a rental property just as they're starting a year-long construction project across the street?
- How much will the insurance cost? Compare costs from several agents and figure them into the overall costs of your property and its future maintenance.
- What will the effect of property taxes be on your costs? How will they affect your profit margin or your ability to pay back a property loan? How much of the property taxes may be a personal or corporate tax deduction?

If you are still game after reviewing the previous checklist, you may be cut out to be a real estate rental investor. If suddenly you're not all that interested, there may still be a way for you to invest through a real estate investment trust, which will be covered later in this chapter.

The Management Challenge

You've survived the buyer's stage of real estate investment. Now it's time to consider what it takes to manage your properties for maximum efficiency and income. That means brushing up on your management skills and having an eye for detail for the specific requirements of property management.

Think of it like this. Once you own rental property, you are the landlord. Just think of being on the other side of the renter's experience. Remember that a good landlord tends to keep tenants, while a not-so-good one has trouble renting the house and can lose money. As a landlord, you're not protecting your own home. You are managing a source of income. That means that you have to be aware of what it takes to keep the place going. Think about the time and money that it requires and measure that against your return. Contrast the time you spend on the property to how much time you spend on your mutual funds.

Maintenance

If you are handy, you can do some of the maintenance, although it may make more sense to hire someone so you can handle other things required by the property. If you hire someone, you have to factor in the costs of the contractor(s) and how reliable and experienced they actually are. As a rule, contractors tend to have multiple jobs at any one time. That can make them hard to pin down with regard to when they will actually show up to do the job. You may have to manage angry tenants or wait with an empty house during times when repairs are pending. And unlike with owning stocks, you are the one who will be getting the complaint calls.

Landlord-Tenant Communication

Of course, being a good landlord is doable and can be profitable. Much of being a good landlord is in how you communicate with your tenants. Tenants should be aware of your expectations, your rules, and your regulations in advance. Don't sign a lease unless these points are addressed and agreed upon by the tenants. Any changes in the terms should be communicated in a timely fashion in writing, and you should have proof that the tenant actually received the information and agrees to the changes.

Other Important Considerations

It will take some time from the moment you buy the rental property to the time you will find tenants. If you don't have the time to manage the property, hiring a professional management firm may make sense. And even though these firms take care of landscaping, maintenance, and other important issues, they charge fees, which means that you have to calculate this into your expenses and pass the costs on to your tenants.

Real Estate Investment Trusts

If you're not quite ready to become a flipper or a landlord, you can still invest in real estate via real estate investment trusts (REITs, pronounced "reets"). A REIT is an investment company, in many ways similar to an exchange-traded mutual fund (ETF), which allows you to participate in real estate without being on the front lines. You can buy REIT shares on a stock exchange, or you can buy a mutual fund or an ETF that invests in REITs.

REITs have been around for decades and are a convenient and fairly safe way to invest in real estate. You make money in a REIT as you do with stocks, by collecting dividends and when the share price rises. Because of the legal structure of a REIT, the business is not taxed but the shareholder is. This is what is known as a pass-through security.

What's in a REIT?

Unlike mutual funds, REITs don't buy stock in companies. Instead they buy real estate investments, usually in the form of properties or mortgages. The income from property REITs comes from the cash generated by the property. Mortgage REITs invest in mortgages used to finance the purchase of properties. In the case of mortgage REITs, the income flows from the money generated by the mortgages. Hybrid REITs invest in a little of both. Mortgage REITs lend money to real estate investors and tend to pay a higher dividend than property REITs, but they can have a higher risk of losses because they only make money as long as the investors pay back the loans.

Why should you care about all of this? Because REITs can be attractive investments and can provide income and capital gains without the potential hassle of owning rental or commercial properties. You can get a great deal of information about REITs through the National Association of Real Estate Investment

Trusts, also referred to as Nareit (*www.reit.com* or via their toll-free number, 1-800-3NAREIT). REITs often have their own websites, and discount brokers have access to REIT information, although since REITs are an area of special expertise, it makes sense to use a broker with experience in this particular area.

Comparing REITs

Picking the right REIT depends on many factors:

- **Dividend yield.** Compare the dividend yield of the average REIT to that of US Treasury bonds. For example, in October 2018, the average REIT, according to Nareit, had a yield of 4.6% while the US 10-year Treasury note was yielding 3.13%. At first glance, a yield of 4.6% is pretty attractive compared to that of T-bonds. More important, however, is the fact that REITs as a total investment class were down nearly 5.5% for the year while T-bonds were even for the year. This is because during 2018, the Federal Reserve raised interest rates aggressively and REITS tend to do worse than T-bonds during periods of rising interest rates. The flip side is that during good times REITs pay better dividends than stocks.
- **Earnings growth.** To understand how much money your REIT is making, look to the funds from operations (FFO). The trend in this number tells you how well things are going. It is the net income, excluding gains or losses from property sales and debt restructuring, and including real estate depreciation.
- **What your REIT's holdings are.** Know what kinds of properties the REIT holds. It can be anything from shopping centers to office or apartment buildings, resorts, health-care facilities, or other forms of real estate such as farmland or empty land awaiting development.
- **Geographic locations.** Make sure you know where your REIT invests: regionally, nationally, or internationally.
- **Diversification.** In order to spread your risk, consider a diversified REIT that owns different kinds of properties in different locations. You can do the same thing if you buy several different kinds of REITs.

- **Management.** The management company of your REIT is as important as with a mutual fund or a company CEO and their team. The more experienced and the better the track record of management, the more likely you are to make money over time.

REIT Mutual Funds and ETFs

You can also own REITs through traditional mutual funds and exchange-traded mutual funds. Morningstar.com has great data on REIT funds, and most of the major mutual fund companies offer mutual funds dedicated to REITs. Many of them are no-load funds and most pay quarterly dividends, which makes them attractive as income-producing vehicles. Nareit also has great data on funds and offers a list on their website. There you will find up-to-date news on the industry, a directory of REITs, a list of REIT ETFs, and a portfolio optimizer tool to test the risk/reward profile of a mix of REITs.

Tracking Your REITs

REIT prices are quoted online and through any website or app that offers online quotes. REITs have symbols like stocks, so just type the letters in the quote as you would with a stock. REIT mutual funds and ETFs are like other similar securities, and you can keep up with their price online as well.

All in all, real estate investment is not for everyone, but it can be a profitable endeavor. REITs can offer a simpler, less time-consuming, and less labor-intensive way to participate in this investment area.

CHAPTER 15

Taking More Risks

Risky investments are not for everyone because they offer both the possibility of making big gains and suffering equally major losses. And while most investors are more than happy to make big bucks, especially over short periods of time, no one enjoys watching their money evaporate. This chapter is all about the ins and outs, the good and the bad, of risky investments and risky investment techniques and how they may or may not be something that makes sense for your portfolio.

The Two Faces of Risk

Risk is the balance between winning and losing. Some investors are willing to avoid risk, while others embrace it for a chance at a big gain, along with the potential for losing large amounts of money. Indeed, risk-taking behavior is influenced by the notion that you can make a lot of money in a hurry by taking big chances.

There are two ways to increase your risk. One is by using alternative or derivative securities, such as options, and the other is by using risky maneuvers, usually involving leverage. When the two are combined, the risk/reward ratio can reach high levels of unpredictability. Alternative securities can be an acquired taste, but can include securities such as initial public offerings (IPOs), commodities, options, futures, leveraged ETFs, and cryptocurrencies. Riskier strategies include the use of margin, short selling, and hedging. By combining alternative securities and techniques, you are likely to increase your portfolio's volatility and you may lose money rapidly. Because investing should not be like a trip to Vegas, this chapter is about developing an understanding of higher-risk investments, how to use them appropriately, and when it's best to avoid them altogether.

Selling Short and Using Margin

Short selling is the opposite of going long. "Going long" is Wall Street jargon for buying stocks, bonds, or other assets. Long investors are hoping that their assets rise in price. "Going short," or short selling, is the opposite. Short sellers are hoping that prices drop.

Selling Short

Short sellers borrow stock, usually from their brokers, and sell it. If the stock drops in price, the short seller buys it back at the lower price, profiting from the difference in the price at which they borrowed it and the price at which they bought it back. Short selling is not for new investors.

Here is an example of how it might work. Jane has been watching Amazon and thinks that it's about to start a meaningful decline due to a bad earnings report. So Jane borrows and sells one hundred shares of Amazon stock at $1,700. Jane just gained $170,000 but owes her broker one hundred shares of Amazon. Amazon does indeed have a catastrophic earnings report and shares drop $200. Jane buys one hundred shares for $1,500 each and pockets $20,000 (one hundred shares × the $200 price drop). The broker then sends the shares back to the original owner.

If Amazon's price didn't move up or down, Jane might have gotten cold feet and gotten out close to even. But if Amazon had beaten its earnings expectations and the stock had rallied, say up $200 to $1,900, Jane would have lost $20,000 plus the purchase price of the stock, totaling $190,000. If Jane got stubborn, hoping that Amazon would eventually fall, but the stock kept gaining, Jane's losses could be even worse.

Here is something else to remember: Jane has to pay commission on any trade, whether the trade goes her way or not. Also, if Amazon had paid a dividend during the time that Jane was short, Jane would have passed that dividend to the broker or the original owner of the stock.

Margin Trading

Margin involves borrowing money from your broker to buy stocks or to sell them short. It requires a margin account, which is an account where you can trade with leverage or margin. It usually requires you to sign an agreement with your broker, and they'll vet your finances and your trading experience. Think of a margin account as one in which you can buy more assets by borrowing some money from your broker than you could with your own money. Usually, the money in the account is about a 50-50 split between your own and your broker's. Thus, margin buying lets you buy more stock with less of your own money. The shares you buy count as collateral for your loan.

And while this may sound like a good deal, it can be tricky, because margin is a form of leverage. If your stock goes up, you're okay. If the price drops, you've got some problems because your margin account needs to have at least

25% of the value of the stock you borrowed by federal law. Your broker may have a higher margin requirement as well, which is why you should read your margin agreement carefully before signing it. When your balance drops below the maintenance margin set by your broker, you will get a "margin call," which is Wall Street lingo for "you need to put up more money." You can do that by writing a check or by selling the stock at a loss and hoping that it covers your debt.

FACT

Experienced traders with short-term strategies, such as hedge fund managers and day traders who use sophisticated and often technical analysis–based techniques, often use margin. Even these traders can get into trouble, though, as short-term volatility and big drops in the stock market are often attributed to hedge fund bets that went wrong and triggered margin calls.

Here is an example. Jane, that big risk-taker, wants to buy one hundred shares of ABC stock because she thinks it's the next great social media wonder. ABC is selling at $50 per share but she only has $2,500 so she borrows $2,500 from her broker in her margin account. Jane now has one hundred shares of ABC—$2,500 worth of equity in the stock plus a $2,500 debt to her broker. Unfortunately the price of ABC drops to $34, so the total value of the one hundred shares is now $3,400. But because it is owned on margin, her equity drops to $900 because she still owes the broker $2,500 plus the interest accrued on the margin loan. Jane's choice is to put up another $1,600 or sell her shares at a loss and pay off the loan.

Initial Public Offerings

Another risky strategy is buying initial public offerings, or IPOs. An IPO is what happens on the day when a company first goes public and the stock makes its debut on the stock exchange. On that first day, the gains on the price can be extreme, and so can the losses. By selling stock to the public through an IPO, a company raises money without taking on debt. It's also an opportunity, in many cases, for early investors to cash in some of their shares and be rewarded for their initial risk. New investors, impressed with the company's performance, buy into the company at this stage in hopes of participating in the company's good fortunes.

Investment banks, such as Goldman Sachs, are the underwriters of the IPO. That means that they are the ones that handle the details of bringing the company's shares to market and collect fees for doing the work. The potential stumbling block for an IPO, if there is one, is whether the SEC allows it to happen, based on whether the process has met the criteria established in the Securities Act of 1933. Because investment banks are thorough and because their reputation often depends on the success of an IPO, it's very rare for this process to go awry.

Should You Get In on IPOs?

The lure of making big bucks in a short period of time is significant. But the downside to IPOs is worth considering. For one thing, small investors don't have much of a chance to get shares at the initial offering price, which is often significantly lower than where the shares can trade in a few minutes' time after the stock goes public. That's because professional investors, who buy large blocks of stock, tend to swoop up the initial supply at the lower prices and then flip them in a few minutes to pocket the quick profit produced when the stock pops. As a small investor, even if you have an experienced broker handling your IPO transactions, you don't have much of a chance against the deep-pocket professional. Thus, although getting in right away may sound attractive, it makes sense to add IPO stocks to your watchlist and see how things go with them for a while before you take the plunge.

FACT

Companies sometimes sell stock after their initial public offering. This process is called a secondary offering, and it's done to raise money for some purpose, such as buying back debt or financing an acquisition. Secondary offerings sometimes will issue a special class of nonvoting stock and are usually not as big a news item as is an IPO.

Domo's IPO: When Things Go Wrong

A perfect example of an IPO debacle was what happened with Domo, a Utah-based software analytics company. Before the IPO, it had a private value of over $1 billion. But when the company went public with the IPO, it disclosed that there was little cash on hand, had a negative cash flow, and was likely to lose money for the foreseeable future. It began at $23.80 in early 2018 but by the end of the year, the price had dropped to nearly $15 per share and was still losing money. The stock was hyped by its underwriters but turned into a bust in its first year of trading. The bottom line is that IPOs are a risky proposition for all investors, but especially small investors and those who are just getting started.

Sector Investing

When you invest in a single sector of the stock market, usually through an ETF specializing in a single area of the market, you can make outsized profits or you can take big losses, depending on the general trend of the market you are investing in. In fact, sector investing is best approached via the use of technical analysis. You can put together an ETF list in your favorite app and review the movement of their prices and all of their charts for any particular ETF you own or are looking to own. Use chart analysis including indicators such as moving averages to help you spot changes in trends and set entry and exit points accordingly.

Social Media Investing

Social media stocks such as *Facebook* and *Twitter* were popular in the early 2000s due to their groundbreaking impact on society. Unfortunately, both companies became involved, willingly or otherwise, in politics. They may have also used questionable practices to harvest financial gain from selling their users' information, both of which negatively affected their stock prices. That said, social media is not likely to go away and may still provide viable investment alternatives. There will be an emerging social media company in the future that may be the next *Facebook* or *Twitter*. But don't be fooled by the glitter. When investing in social media, it's still important to apply the general principles of investing. Ask all the questions you would ask of any individual company. Dig into the fundamentals of the company. Get to know management. And always consider the technical aspects of the stock.

FACT

Sector trends often last for several years. For example, in the 2010s, social media and information technology were the best sectors in the market. But this is likely to change in the next decade, given the controversies surrounding Facebook's privacy practices and the general behavior of the markets. You should consider and monitor other sectors of the market, such as health care, biotech, and other areas of technology such as artificial intelligence and robotics.

Commodities and Precious Metals

Commodities are the raw materials that are used to manufacture products ranging from food to high-tech gadgets. The major factor influencing commodity prices is supply, or the ease of availability of the product. Even the fear of a decrease in supply, such as the inkling of a trade war, can send commodity prices higher. The trick when investing in commodities is to have a good handle on the supply, and then be aware of when there might be a spike in demand. Commodities, even when owned indirectly through a mutual fund or ETF, are an important component of a diversified portfolio.

Commodities

Investing in commodities requires a fair amount of homework and a good understanding of technical analysis. Aside from investing directly in commodities, keeping up with the price activity in this area of the markets may provide useful information about other commodities as well as the industrial and market sectors where any individual commodity plays a vital role. Here are examples of everyday commodities worth considering for investment:

- **Lumber** is used in home building and furniture. Generally speaking, a housing boom is bullish for lumber prices.
- **Oil** is a centerpiece of the global economy. Aside from being a commodity in and of itself, it is also an influence on gasoline, heating oil, and natural gas prices. Oil is a major contributor to the price of chemicals, which gives it significant influence on other commodities and industrial sectors.
- **Cotton** remains a major global player, as it is used in clothing and other lesser-known products such as coffee filters.
- **Wheat** is a key commodity given its central role in food around the world.
- **Corn** is the most widely traded grain in the world, with uses in food, animal feed, biofuels, and building materials. Soybeans are also an important agricultural commodity.
- **Gold, silver, and platinum** are perhaps the most popular commodities given their use in jewelry. Silver is an important industrial metal, while platinum is central to the automobile industry given its use as a major engine component in catalytic converters.
- **Coffee, cocoa, and sugar** are known collectively as "the softs." Anyone who needs a morning cup of java or enjoys a candy bar can appreciate these three commodities.

The best way for nonprofessional investors, at any stage of experience but especially in the early stage of investing, to participate in these markets is through a mutual fund or an ETF. An ETF may be superior because of the ease of trading throughout the day. This is particularly important when commodity prices are going through a volatile period.

ESSENTIAL

If you are interested in commodity ETFs, the Invesco DB Commodity Tracking Fund (NYSE Arca: DBC) is a broad index of commodities and offers diversification. Holdings include oil and gold, as well as a batch of agricultural commodities. It's a good idea to track this ETF's price and general behavior for a few months or longer before considering investing in it, as it can be volatile.

Gold

Gold is a different type of animal. While it may make sense to invest in other commodities via paper through mutual funds or ETFs, gold gives you a more practical set of choices. You can choose to invest in gold indirectly through paper assets, but you can actually own physical gold, via jewelry, gold bars, or bullion coins, fairly easily.

Gold bullion is the pure, raw form of gold before it is shaped into bars. This may be the most difficult way to own gold as an individual investor. Gold bars must be made of at least 99.5% gold bullion and weigh a uniform 400 troy ounces (the standard weight measure of gold). Gold bullion coins are legal tender, although they are not used as currency very often anymore. Their worth is usually more than their face value, although that depends on their weight and the market price of gold at any one time. Gold coins tend to be popular investments, especially among collectors.

Trading Currencies

For new investors, it can be difficult to see how you can make money by trading money. But currencies, although not the best market for a newbie, can still be lucrative. The simplest currency trade is what anyone does when they visit a foreign exchange booth while traveling abroad. In fact, currency trading, known as FX for foreign exchange, is a huge market, with over $2 trillion exchanging hands on a daily basis.

Most of the trading involves the major global currencies, such as:

- The US Dollar (also known as the Greenback)
- The UK Pound Sterling
- The Japanese Yen
- The Euro
- The Canadian Dollar (a.k.a. the Loonie and the Canuck Buck)
- The Swiss Franc (sometimes called the Swissie)

- The Australian Dollar (also called the Aussie)
- The New Zealand Dollar (referred to as the Kiwi)

Currencies trade in pairs. For example the USD/Yen pairing refers to the exchange rate between the US dollar and the Japanese yen. The value of this pairing will be different from other pairings, such as the Euro/Yen, because currency pairings are only based on the relative value of one currency versus another.

FACT

Currency traders are known to be eccentric and their trading terminology bears this out. For example, the unit of price movement in a currency is called a "pip." Thus, a three-pip move in a currency means that it has moved three basic trading units. In comparison, when a stock or a bond changes in price, it is considered a "tick." Another unique nickname is the one given to the pairing between the US dollar and the UK pound sterling. This pairing is referred to as "the cable." So if you read an article about the price change in "the cable," you'll know it's in reference to the US dollar and the UK pound sterling.

The Unique World of Currency Trading

Currency traders have their own language, and the currency markets are significantly different than the stock, bond, and commodity markets, where there is usually an exchange, a regulatory agency, and a set of verifiable rules. Currencies trade "over the counter." That means that every trade is between two private parties through a trading platform provided by a dealer, usually a bank, that operates only as an intermediary in the sense of providing quotes and housing the account.

And although that may sound frightening, the currency markets work because they are self-regulating. Because large corporations and big trading houses participate in them, they have a vested interest in self-policing. Just to be clear, though, this is not a market for inexperienced investors. If you must consider it, make sure that your currency dealer is registered with the National Futures Association; they are likely to participate in binding arbitration should you have a problem. Also, don't open a foreign currency trading account without reading the agreement first.

> **FACT**
>
> Currency trading may be useful to you if you are a night owl since it goes on twenty-four hours per day, starting at 5:00 p.m. on Sunday and going on continuously all week until 4:00 p.m. on Friday.

Think Interest Rates When Trading Currencies

Aside from the lack of an exchange, the nuts and bolts of currency trading is a bit different than with stocks, bonds, and mutual funds. When you buy and sell currencies, there is an interest rate component. Currency buyers earn interest, while sellers pay interest.

It sounds a bit on the goofy side, but it does work. First you sell a currency. Then you use the proceeds to buy another. In reality, the transactions occur simultaneously. If you are the seller, you pay interest to the buyer. If you are the buyer, you get interest and own the currency.

Each currency has a particular interest rate associated with it, which is calculated in increments of $\frac{1}{100}$ of a percent, also known as a basis point. This works out as follows: if you sold a currency with a rate of 500 points and bought a currency with a rate of 700 points, your net return is 200 basis points (2%).

> **ALERT**
>
> Currency trading is not for the uninitiated. Most online currency trading platforms let you do paper trading without using real money. It's a good idea to use this technology in order to work out the kinks of your strategy before you actually plunge into this kind of trading.

Derivatives and Options

Derivatives are investments that derive their value from another investment. Without the underlying asset—as the related investment is called—a derivative is worthless.

All derivatives are contractual agreements between two parties. Commonly used derivatives are options, futures, swaps, and forward contracts. Derivatives can be written on stocks, stock indexes, bonds, currencies, and commodities, as well as weather data, the size of crops, or even more esoteric things, such as the derivatives that nearly crashed the world economy in 2008. Those derivatives were written as bets on whether people would actually make their mortgage payments.

The most commonly traded derivatives are options based on stocks. An option gives the holder the right, but not the obligation, to buy or sell the underlying security at a specific price by a specific date. In other words, the option trader is betting that the price of a security will move in both the direction and the amount they expect. The key to options trading is to make a bet on the direction of the move and the magnitude before the option expires. Stock options are the most common of options, so this section will focus on them the most.

FACT

The largest options exchange in the United States is the Chicago Board Options Exchange (www.cboe.com). Their website has a huge wealth of information, including options symbols and other data that can be helpful in analyzing the stock and bond market.

Stock Options

Options trading has a language all of its own. Here are basic facts and terms:

- **Call option.** This option lets you buy one hundred shares of XYZ stock at the specified price.

- **Put option.** Put options let you sell one hundred shares of XYZ stock at the specified price.
- **Expiration date.** This is the date on which the option becomes worthless.
- **Strike price.** This is the specified price of the stock on which the option is based.

Option buyers are *buyers*. Option sellers are known as *writers*. When you write an option, you sell the buyer the opportunity to buy or sell the underlying security at the underlying price.

For example: if you bought an October (of the current year) 35 Call option on XYZ stock, you would have the option of buying one hundred shares of XYZ stock at $35 on or before the expiration date of the option, usually the third Friday of the month. If you buy the 35 Call option when the stock is at $35 and it rises to $55, you could exercise the option and buy a stock that is selling at $55 for only $35. You could then turn around and sell it for $55, pocketing the nice profit. If the stock falls below the strike price, you would let the option expire worthless. A call option has unlimited upside potential, while your risk is only what you paid for the option if it expires worthless. A put option, however, can be a risky proposition if the stock rises in price.

> **FACT**
>
> Options allow you to participate in the price trend of the underlying asset for a fraction of the price which you would pay for owning the asset. For example, a call option on a $50 stock may be purchased for $2. Thus options trading can provide huge percentage returns on your initial investment while limiting your losses at less than if you own the underlying asset.

The value of an option is influenced by four different factors: the underlying price of the stock, the strike price, the cost of holding a position in the underlying stock, and an estimate of the future volatility of the stock.

Selling Options

Selling (writing) options is a better technique to develop than buying options and it is a technique that you should work on. This is because when you write an option, you get paid a premium. You can sell an option without owning the stock (naked write) or you can own a stock and sell an option (covered write). You can learn a lot more about selling options at JoeDuarteintheMoneyOptions.com.

LEAPS

LEAPS (Long-Term Equity Anticipation Securities) are long-term options. If you wanted to bet on the direction of a stock over the next several years, you would buy LEAPS, which don't usually expire for two to three years and sometimes last for five to ten years. Beyond that distinction, LEAPS are similar to regular options, except that they are fewer in number. You can usually find LEAPS for the most heavily traded stocks.

Employee Stock Options

Employee stock options differ from publicly traded options because unlike listed options, there is no third party involved. Instead, employee stock options are a direct contract between the employer and the employee. Here are a few important facts:

- Employers use them as incentives and rewards for employees.
- There may be some tax advantages associated with these options. For example, they may be used as sources of deferred income. You can discuss more specific advantages with your CPA if applicable.
- Employee options have mandatory holding periods before the employee can exercise them and can be as long as one to ten years.

Employee options are often used by startup companies or companies that are in the midst of rapid periods of growth. Often these companies have plans for going public at some point in the future and use these options to both entice, recruit, and retain good workers in order to keep the growth momentum moving forward. The downside is that if the company goes bust or underperforms, it could be difficult to cash these options in.

Trading Futures

A futures contract, unlike an options contract, is an obligation to buy or sell an asset at the expiration of the contract. Most futures contracts are based on commodities, such as wheat, corn, oil, or cattle. The reason for this is that futures were designed for farmers in expectation of delivery of their crops. But the markets have expanded beyond commodities to include stock indexes, bonds, metals, and currencies. Even more interesting are the futures contracts that deal with housing prices and weather.

Trading futures is a risky business. Prices move rapidly and tend to be volatile. Because of the pricing structure of the contracts, one tick (basic unit of price in any contract) can mean that you gain or lose a fair amount of money in a very short period of time.

Here is an example. A West Texas Intermediate crude oil futures contract contains 1,000 barrels of crude oil. The minimum tick is $0.01, or one cent, for one barrel of crude oil. Each tick is worth $10 per contract. That means a $1 move in the price of crude oil (one hundred ticks) means a $1,000 change per contract, up or down. If you are a big trader and you are holding one hundred contracts, a $1 move is worth $100,000.

The Strange World of Cryptocurrencies

A cryptocurrency is composed of computer code—called a blockchain—which creates a cryptocoin such as Bitcoin or Ethereum. These instruments are then traded on various exchanges all over the world. You can trade options on *Cryptos* on the Cboe and there is at least one crypto-based ETF—the Bitcoin Investment Trust (GBTC).

It's too early to pass judgment on cryptos because even though they've been around for a few years, they've only been prominent since maybe 2016. There have been several high-profile fraud cases involving cryptos, and there are still regulatory hurdles to cross. Furthermore it's hard to buy food or anything tangible with a Bitcoin, just as it is difficult to buy food with stocks and bonds. But because of the newness of the cryptocurrencies, it may be more difficult to turn them into a conventional currency whereas stocks, bonds, and traditional assets are more accessible and liquid. This is a highly complicated and fluid market so become aware of these instruments but learn how to invest in mutual funds, trade stocks, and save your money before diving into this area.

That said, it seems as if cryptos are not going away anytime soon. For one thing, major financial firms such as Fidelity Investments and ICE, which owns several major stock exchanges, are increasingly involved in trying to improve the trading conditions and the liquidity of cryptocurrencies. More than anything, at this stage of the game, cryptocurrencies are going through growing pains. But they are indeed growing and over time, it is likely that cryptocurrencies will have a more secure place in the financial world.

FACT

Cryptocurrencies are heavily tied to the Internet and there are many great websites to help you learn more. Two of the best are Investing.com and CCN.com. *Investing* has real-time cryptocurrency quotes and *CCN* covers the crypto universe news in-depth on a daily basis.

In conclusion, alternative investments are not for the novice investor. Over time, as you gain experience, you may slowly move into these areas. Most professionals, though, will tell you that these types of investments are for trading, not for long-term buy and hold strategies. This, of course, could change over the next few years or sooner.

CHAPTER 16

Working with a Financial Advisor

If you're wondering why a book about self-directed investing has a chapter on financial advisors, consider that every child needs a bit of parenting. If you are a serious investor, and you apply yourself, you will likely succeed over time. But in the early stages, an advisor can be a mentor. Even if an advisor does not make your investment decisions and is not holding your hand, an experienced second opinion can come in handy. This chapter is about finding out what kind of advisor makes sense for you and how you may make the best use of such a potentially useful tool.

What Kind of Advice Do You Need?

If you are an independent person, you may wonder if an advisor is a good idea. But think about it: you are about to put real money on the line. Even if you are naturally cut out to be an investor, having a little help in the early stages may be a good idea. Much depends on how much sense the concepts involved in market analysis and asset allocation make to you. If you are comfortable with these aspects of investing, you probably don't need an advisor. But if you can't decide whether you want to own growth stocks or whether bonds make sense, you may need an advisor.

The Personal Survey

A good way to decide on whether or not to use a financial advisor is by taking a personal financial survey. Consider the following: Does the thought of managing your own portfolio make you uncomfortable? Are you always second-guessing your decisions? Would you be able to buy stocks in a down market or when there is short- or longer-term decline in the markets? Are you willing to put in the time to analyze market trends, to look for the best-performing sectors, and to crunch numbers to evaluate individual securities, such as mutual funds, stocks, or exchange-traded mutual funds? Perhaps the most important question: How strong is your resilience after a failure? Is your favorite TV channel CNBC? Is your first morning read *The Wall Street Journal, Investor's Business Daily,* or *Yahoo! Finance*? If you answered yes to many of these questions, it's likely that you are cut out to be a self-directed individual investor. If you are a real enthusiast about investing, you may even want to consider a career as an investment advisor. There is a good market for this type of professional these days, especially an able one.

If, however, you find yourself agonizing over which mutual fund to own, you hate reading the financial press, or you just don't have the time, you may be someone who needs to consider hiring a professional.

The Time Trade

A significant factor when deciding on whether you will use a financial advisor is time. Because it takes a long time to be a serious investor, a financial advisor may be a good trade-off due to time constraints and what you are getting in return: time with family or work.

Another time-related issue is that at the beginning, you will, and you should, take longer to make even the simplest of decisions. Having someone who can assist you in speeding things up while providing sound advice makes sense. Finally, if you eventually want to make your own decisions, you could only use an advisor for the first few months or the first year in order to expand your own knowledge base. Your advisor may be an excellent source of learning materials, such as books or websites that you can begin to use to gain insight and experience before slowly weaning yourself away and doing your own portfolio management.

> **ESSENTIAL**
>
> A good financial advisor should be a true consultant, working with you on developing a long-term investment plan and asset allocation strategies to help you achieve your goals. Your advisor may also help you with budgeting, tax, and estate planning and guide you in setting up college savings plans. Without an advisor, you have to do all these things on your own.

What Can You Expect from a Financial Advisor?

Because different kinds of advisors provide different services, you should understand the key differences before choosing an advisor who fits your own knowledge, risk profile, and personality. Look to find an advisor who helps you gain confidence and insight and who helps you to make sound financial decisions.

Here are some of the different kinds of advisors:

- A money manager is someone to whom you delegate the decisions after a thorough consultation about the style and purpose of your investing. Some money managers will only do a certain kind of investing, such as aggressive or income-related securities. Once you choose your money manager, you will leave all the decisions to this person and check the progress on statements or when you have conferences.
- Financial planners help you map out your long-term strategies and offer investment advice. The difference between planners and money managers is that you make the final call about pulling the trigger.
- Analysts and advisors focus on giving you information but are not involved in planning. They simply give you advice but you do everything else on your own.

Financial professionals, regardless of the type you choose, will send you at least quarterly reports with details about the status of your accounts. It's a good idea to meet with them more often than quarterly if possible and to discuss the results in person. This helps you both develop your relationship and may also give you an opportunity to learn a few things. You can be as active as you want to or can be, but it's a good idea to keep close tabs on what's going on. Remember: your financial professional has other clients, and it's not always easy to keep up with everything. What this means is that you should work with a good professional who is available and willing to spend time discussing your account with you. If you can't get face time with your advisor or they never return your calls on time, move on. Look at it this way: even if you have a small account, you are still paying a fee for their services. That means that you should have a reasonable amount of personal access.

The Advisor's Roles

Your advisor should monitor your portfolio and review and discuss any changes in allocation or investment choices that might make sense. They should also monitor the markets and let you know of any potential concerns or significant events that will affect your account's balance and performance. Most of all, your advisor should keep you from becoming emotional if the markets turn volatile. Their job is to keep you focused on your long-term goals and provide the tools to get you there.

Where a good advisor comes in handy is in a down market. During these periods, the advisor's job is to keep you from losing big amounts of money and to preserve your wealth. The best advisors are the ones who minimize your losses and manage your emotions. A good portfolio manager, whether they manage a billion-dollar mutual fund or your more modest account, should have a sense of timing and should be able to make changes in your asset allocation if allowed to do so and it's needed. This might be a simple thing, such as not investing your newly deposited cash as they wait for a better opportunity, or advising you that maybe you should take some profits after a mutual fund has had a good run for the past few months. More importantly, the advisor should be able to communicate these strategies and changes to you and make sure that you are comfortable with what they did and why.

Shopping for the Right Financial Advisor

Once you decide that you would like to use an advisor, it's equally important to find the one who makes sense for you. An easy trap is to hire one with a long-term track record without considering other aspects of the job. Consider whether this person who will be managing your money in one form or another is someone you can get along with. Look at their firm or whether they are self-employed. Get details about the services provided. Look at samples of monthly or quarterly statements and make sure that you will understand what they say. If they work for a big company, make sure that they aren't or haven't been under investigation for fraudulent practices. Check into their customer service. Ask detailed questions about how well insured the company is against fraud and whether the advisor goes to periodic continuing education courses.

Most of all, ask them about their successes and failures and what they tend to do in down markets. Ask to see some results if possible.

There is what seems to be an alphabet soup in the certifications of financial professionals. Think of it this way: you wouldn't want a radiology technician to take out your appendix. That is the job of a medical doctor trained as a surgeon. The same thing applies to your money. You want the right person for the right job. If you want a high-level, aggressive stock trader for your advisor, you may not be well served by the same person who handles your car insurance. So while this letter jumble can be confusing, it's worth your while to do some research on what each of these certifications mean before making a decision about whether to employ this person.

Certified Financial Planner (CFP)

An advisor who has earned the CFP certification has put in their time and has experience in virtually every area of financial planning, from the study of the stock market and individual stocks to the intricacies of estate planning. A CFP gains certification through a rigorous program involving a standardized curriculum that requires passing a certification examination, work experience that meets certification requirements, and passing the CFP board's fitness standards for conduct, a stringent set of ethics guidelines. The criteria and the requirements for certification are created, monitored, and enforced by the Certified Financial Planner Board of Standards (www.cfp.net). CFPs specialize in creating long-term financial plans and providing the strategies required to meet goals.

Chartered Life Underwriter (CLU)

These are insurance professionals, certified by The American College, who pass through rigorous training and licensure programs aimed at the insurance field. They have to pass eight courses, meet minimum experience standards, and follow a strict code of ethics in order to become licensed. They are also required to undergo high-level continuing education.

A CLU's expertise goes beyond your life insurance and includes training in estate and retirement planning. But while a CLU may make sense for your longer-term strategies, another financial professional may better serve you when it comes to stocks, bonds, mutual funds, and real estate investment trusts.

Chartered Financial Consultant (ChFC)

These professionals are also accredited by The American College and are often CLUs as well, but with added benefits. In order to earn the extra letters, they delve into every area of financial planning from the client's perspective. Their goal is to customize a plan based on your financial know-how, position, and goals; put the plan in motion; and keep it on track. After they complete the program, they must pass the requisite exams and have three years of experience in the industry before they can call themselves ChFCs. These professionals can become a one-stop shop for you, as they are well versed in tax planning, investments, insurance, retirement, and estate planning.

Personal Financial Specialist (PFS)

A certified public accountant (CPA) with additional financial planning qualifications is known as a personal financial specialist. This type of professional may be worth looking for, given their intricate and intimate knowledge of the tax code. This particular aspect of financial planning could be useful when you are looking to minimize the tax burden of your investment portfolio.

Keeping both the CPA and PFS designations requires continuing education and adherence to strict ethical guidelines. A PFS can be very helpful in determining your net worth and your retirement needs and can help you formulate the right strategies for your long-term goals. The tax planning expertise is also an added bonus.

Registered Investment Advisor (RIA)

This is the certification that most advisors who are primarily money managers receive. To become an RIA, you have to pass a state certification test. Some RIAs are also brokers. Others are CFPs or CPAs. The reason for becoming an RIA is solely to manage active client accounts. Basically, anyone who passes the test, follows the continuing education and ethical directives of their state, and runs a clean shop can become an RIA. The state securities board or the Securities and Exchange Commission regulates RIAs. The Securities and Exchange Commission usually regulates those who manage more than $25 million in accounts, although there are several exemptions both to who must register as an advisor and who must regulate them.

How Much Will It Cost?

Much of your cost depends on what type of advisor you choose. As a general rule, though, financial advice is not cheap. At the same time, advisors are required to give you their costs up front along with a detailed list of what your money will be buying. There isn't one single payment arrangement for advisors. That's why you need to get the facts up front from each advisor before you make your decision. At the end of your interview process, you should have a good idea as to what you are paying for and whether it is worth it.

The three most common fee structures are commissions, flat fees, and fees based on a percentage of your assets under management. There may also be some transaction fees, below-minimum-balance fees, and account maintenance fees. Some advisors, especially money managers, charge a combination of fees, such as a flat fee for office and materials expenses and a separate fee based on a percentage of assets under management. The one constant expense, in addition to the advisory fee, that you will incur will be trading commission fees.

Commissions

Advisors who get paid via commissions, separate from trading commissions, make money by selling you something, like a mutual fund or an annuity in the case of a banker or an insurance agent, or by trading your account in the case of stockbrokers. Much of the time, commission-based advisors are ethical and scrupulous. Unfortunately some prey on novice investors, so it may make better sense for you to use a fee-based advisor.

Flat Fees

Fee-only advisors get paid an annual fee. You are their source of income, and their fee is not based on your assets or how well your account does. Sometimes, these advisors get fees from mutual fund companies and brokerage houses for having certain kinds of securities in your portfolio. They need to tell you that they do this. If they don't and you find out later, you should fire them. Period.

Percent of Assets

This is the way money managers get paid. A money manager, or an RIA, usually charges 1% to 3% of your total assets under management annually to manage your account. You usually pay the fee on a quarterly basis (0.25% to 0.75%) whether the advisor makes money or loses money for you during the quarter. Smaller accounts are sometimes charged larger fees, which fall if the account grows. Money managers tend to focus on larger accounts and are often active traders. As with anything else in investing, getting all the information you can up front will help you make a better decision.

What's Best for You?

More than anything else, you need to be realistic. If you have a small account but you need advice, a consulting arrangement may make sense. You can use a financial planner to help you put together a plan and consider a quarterly or biannual conference with them, or just make contact when you have a question. For estate planning, a CLU may make sense. If you come into a large sum of money from an inheritance, bonus, or a promotion, you may want to talk to an RIA and retain a good PFS. Above all things, make sure you know what you are paying for, keep up with your portfolio, participate in the decision-making process, ask questions if something doesn't seem right, and don't hesitate to move your money if you're not getting the service that you're being charged for.

How to Find an Advisor

Finding an advisor may take a while since a big part of the process is finding someone who is both qualified and a good communicator. It makes sense to take your time and to get it right early in the game. Try to get a good referral from someone you trust, a friend or a family member. You may not keep that particular advisor, but at least you'll get started with someone with a track record and a good reputation. If that doesn't deliver the goods, you can get good recommendations from the National Association of Personal Financial Advisors, the American Institute of Certified Public Accountants, the Society of Financial Service Professionals, and the International Association of Registered Financial Consultants. Take your time. You don't want to get this wrong.

CHAPTER 17

Doing It Yourself

Investing is a personal thing—there are no two people who put their money to work in the markets in the same way. If you are an independent, thoughtful, patient, and adventurous person, this—the golden age of DIY investing—could be your perfect time. Because of online trading, the wealth of information available on the Internet, and the rise of investing apps, there is almost no reason why you can't be your own money manager. This chapter is all about helping you make the decision to do it yourself and setting you on the right path.

How Much Work Are You Willing to Do?

To manage or not to manage your own money? That is the proverbial, if not altogether Shakespearean, question. Maybe more to the point is asking yourself how hard you are willing to work to grow your nest egg. Sure, anyone can pick stocks and mutual funds. But it's not that easy to manage a portfolio. Much of the work involved in managing money includes study, analysis, and monitoring of your overall return.

The development of a routine that starts with your morning coffee and a review of the action in the overnight markets may not be appealing. But if you are managing your own portfolio, you are a money manager, even if you don't work for Fidelity Investments or Vanguard. And money managers spend a lot of time reviewing their portfolio and making sure that things are headed in the right direction. This kind of routine doesn't develop overnight. But it is something worth working toward if you are serious about managing your own portfolio.

Online Investing

The greatest advance in the history of the financial markets for the individual investor was the widespread growth and the rapid improvement of the online world. Because of this, you have access to a world of real-time information and the ability to manage your investments yourself with instant feedback. Learn to use it and make it your money management home.

FACT

You're only as good as your "trading rig" (jargon for your computer setup used in online investing). Make sure you're using the latest operating system for your PC or laptop. Also, don't scrimp on security and on good programs that keep your computer clean of malware and viruses. Your financial accounts can (and likely will) be hacked if you don't protect your computer. You can find excellent reviews and links to trial versions of great computer security programs at www.cnet.com.

The Ups and the Downs of Online Investing

The biggest advantages of online investing for DIY investors are control of their own accounts, vast access to excellent and timely information, and the ability to make decisions and change asset allocation or strategies rapidly. When you add the convenience of 24-7 access to your financial information, the efficiency of having your data in front of you instantly, and the low prices of commissions for online accounts, you have a great tool at your disposal. The downside is that you are on your own when it comes to making decisions about what to invest in and how to go about it. The good thing is that because of the way online investing is set up, you can learn to manage the potential negative aspects of the dynamic by being disciplined, thinking things through, and preparing yourself for a very rewarding experience if you take the time to get it right.

As you become more sophisticated in your investing, you may want to get into pro-style chart analysis. Make sure that your home computer and your smartphone can handle the big data associated with stock charts. Slow downloads can kill a good buying or selling opportunity. The bottom line is that, as with anything else, online investing requires a thorough understanding of what you're doing and its potential pitfalls. Here are some practices that will keep you from being sorry that you became a DIY online investor:

Are You Well Connected?

Internet access is a basic necessity if you are to develop an online investing presence. If you don't have a good connection at home, at work, or through your smartphone, you will be in trouble. Be aware of the fact that if you are not well connected and a negative event in the markets happens, you may find yourself in the uncomfortable position of not knowing what your accounts are doing.

Setting Up Your Online Account

Make sure that you choose the right type of online trading account. With some online brokers, you will set up a mutual fund account that only allows you to make exchanges between their own funds. If that's all you want to do, that's fine. If you want to trade stocks, ETFs, or mutual funds from different fund families, you will need a brokerage account. If you are interested in short selling and trading options, you will need a margin account.

As a novice investor, it may make sense to set up your brokerage account after you've gained some experience with mutual fund switching and investing. Margin is best reserved for more experienced investors. Options trading should be left for well-financed and very experienced traders. You can work your way to that as you gain experience. But because of the risk, it's not the place for a novice investor to get their feet wet in the early days of what should be a lifetime endeavor.

Preparing Before Trading

Before you become a mutual fund switching or stock trading maven, put your money in the broker's money market account linked to your trading account. Think of the money market account as a place where you store your investing capital. Always deposit or wire transfer your new contributions to this account too. There is no hurry to start allocating money into the markets.

If you must put some money to work right away, use small amounts and see how things go before making bigger bets. Do your homework and find the mutual funds or stocks that best match your long-term plans before allocating. Read the prospectus and online information at *Morningstar* and *Yahoo! Finance*. Don't be afraid to call the fund family or the broker and ask their phone reps questions. Don't make a move until you're sure that this is what you want to do.

Checking the Market

As a DIY investor, you have to put in the time to manage your own money. Get into the habit of checking the general trends of interest rates, the stock market, and the general financial and economic themes of the moment on a frequent basis. Pros do this daily. You may want to do it at least once or twice per week. Instead of checking your *Facebook*, *Twitter*, or *Instagram* with your morning coffee, go to *CNBC*, *MarketWatch*, or *Yahoo! Finance* and make sure that there is nothing ridiculous going on in the world that will have a negative impact on your portfolio that day.

What Moves Your Money?

If you check the market, you should know what events mean to your portfolio. That means that you have to figure out how your mutual funds and stocks respond to what the market is doing. To get a feel for which index or market sector influences the price of your mutual funds, check the closing price of the index on a regular basis and compare the price change in your mutual fund to the activity in the index.

Most growth funds tend to rise and fall in tandem with the NASDAQ Composite Index (NASDAQ). If your growth fund does the opposite, meaning that it falls when NASDAQ rises, it may not be a good growth fund. Do this for all your funds. The more you perform these tasks, the better off you will be as an investor.

Develop Contingency Plans Before Problems Arise

Aside from deciding how much money you will put into the markets and how often, you should think about what will make you take money out of your stocks or mutual funds. Thus, before you get started or as you go along, you should develop a plan that will allow you to act decisively if markets become volatile or prices start to drop aggressively.

Assume the Worst

What will you do if the Federal Reserve raises interest rates? What will you do if the economy starts to shrink? Will you change your asset allocation? How will you change what financial assets you own? Will you set limits on your losses? If so, how much are you willing to lose before you cash in your chips? Will you buy more shares of your aggressive mutual fund when stocks fall and they take the fund's share price down with them? If so, how often will you buy these dips? What will you do if your Internet connection goes down and you know that the market is going to be volatile?

Develop contingency and emergency plans with your financial planner or consultant. You can also read blogs and articles online about these themes. The important thing is to be prepared for difficult times.

ALERT

Beware the talking heads on TV and online. There are many so-called "experts" on financial television and online blogs. Some are there only to hawk their products while others may actually be helpful. Over time, develop a good feel for who knows what they're doing. And don't let the fancy credentials or the big brokerage association influence you. Check out what they say and find out for yourself whether they are trustworthy or not.

The Dangers of Online Investing

There are two basic problems with online investing. One is that it's so easy that you can spend all your time monitoring your portfolio. Even worse, especially when you are inexperienced, is that because of the amount of data you may receive, you may become impatient and make mistakes that will cost you money. You may end up making too many trades, many of which may not work out because of inexperience or market conditions.

Indeed, too much data can lead to indecision, which can lead to anxiety and trading failures. You can start to second-guess yourself and, as doubt creeps in, you may miss excellent trading opportunities or just plain burn out. Be patient and sort out which sources and methods are consistently accurate and fit with your personality while honing your own analysis of market and company fundamentals, technical analysis, and risk management skills. Everyone's trading develops along different lines. You may be excellent at short-term trading based on moving averages and other technical approaches. Others may be more patient and rely on specific indicators, such as momentum measures. The best way to learn what you're good at is to paper trade using different methods and see which ones work best for you.

Another problem for beginning investors is the potential for scams. Unfortunately, as you look for investment ideas, you may stumble upon websites that are dishonest and are just interested in taking your money. Some of these websites may actually be criminal and only interested in stealing your identity and getting access to your financial information for personal gain. This is known as phishing.

Even if these websites are not criminal, they may be interested in selling you access to information, which will not make you any money. This is especially true of websites that promise you wealth through penny stocks. This shady practice is known as a "pump and dump" scheme. The scammers are stuck with owning losing stocks and "pump" them up to gullible investors in order to "dump" the loser shares into their account. The bottom line is that if it sounds too good to be true, it is. Avoid the easy-money lures and always do your homework.

Avoiding the Scammers

A great way to avoid scammers is to visit the SEC's website (www.sec .gov). Under the "Latest News" section you'll find the agency's latest actions against scammers. There you will read about how criminals try to manipulate the system unscrupulously for their personal gain, and your losses. The website's enforcement link has a wealth of information about companies that are in violation of their required reporting to the SEC but are still being actively traded. These companies, in many cases, are actively promoted by so-called "market makers," who may in fact be stock promoters. Stock promoters get paid by a third party to help them get rid of bad stocks. They try to trick investors into buying shares of stocks that are still listed but have no businesses or earnings, and haven't filed any kind of notice with the SEC to document the status of their current business.

What to Do If You Get Caught

Even if you read this book and are a cautious person, you may still get caught in a fraudulent scheme. If you get caught, or in the course of your research stumble onto a website that looks suspicious, you should contact your state's securities board or go to the SEC website's EDGAR section to see if the security is currently registered. You can also ask your state securities board if a person that has contacted you has a valid securities license in your state and whether there are any open complaints against them. Of course, not every website is fraudulent, but it pays to be aware that fraud is out there and that caution is always the best policy.

Investing with Apps

Apps are great tools to keep tabs on your stocks. Two great free apps for stock investing are associated with CNBC.com and Investing.com but function separately from the web sites. Both offer information on all markets but CNBC's app is best for stocks while Investing.com's app is more about the futures and currency markets, and even has a great section with real-time quotes for currencies and an excellent 24-7 real-time quote section which lets you review overnight futures trading in stock indexes as well as stock exchanges around the world.

With the CNBC.com app you also get top-notch CNBC financial news and updates to your phone as events happen. You can sign up for CNBC PRO as well for a subscription premium. The best feature on the CNBC app is the watchlists you can set up for your stocks and exchange-traded mutual funds.

Both the Investing.com and CNBC.com apps offer basic stock charting and alert services to your phone. You may want to start with the CNBC app as the charts are simpler to view but still useful when trying to make buy or sell decisions on an alert, while you can work your way up to use the more complex charts on Investing.com's app as you gain more experience or if you are focusing on trading currencies and futures.

Apps to Manage Your Portfolio

There are other apps available to help you invest, such as Stash, which combines personal finance and trading. It allows you to select ETFs and individual stocks while offering investment advice and access to retirement accounts. However, it isn't free. Stash is basically a registered investment advisor app that charges a fee based on the amount of money in your account. For example, the charge for an account with $5,000 or less is $1 per month and you can open an account for as little as $5.

Wealthsimple is also a registered investment advisory firm app. It offers automated investments and deploys your money into ETFs based on your risk tolerance. You can choose a conservative, balanced, or growth mix of portfolio alternatives and the app also has human advisors available for questions and consultation.

One last app to consider is Acorns, which is also a registered investment advisory firm app. It combines investment advice, brokerage service, and personal finance. You can earn rewards that can be converted into investments by shopping at stores affiliated with the app.

The upside to all of these apps is their convenience and low fees. The downside is that they do collect and often sell your data as part of their business models. But at least they tell you that they are doing it in plain language via their privacy policies.

Online Investing versus Apps

You don't have to choose between online investing and phone apps. Online brokers offer excellent apps which let you view your account balances; do research; and trade stocks, ETFs, and mutual funds on any mobile device or PC if you have an account with them.

Two very popular broker apps are thinkorswim from TD Ameritrade and the Fidelity Investments mobile app. Fidelity also offers Active Trader Pro, a more sophisticated trading platform for PCs. These apps offer fully operational, professional-grade trading suites that are free of charge if your trading volume is high enough, although the features may be slightly different on different mobile platforms. Both apps feature high-grade charting; research; access to pro-trader-level news and analysis services for stocks, bonds, ETFs, and options; and high-speed trading execution. Perhaps the best feature of broker apps is the high level of support when things don't function.

What to Look for in an Investment Website

If you're going to be an online investor, it's a good idea to find good sources of information, ranging from those that provide actionable recommendations about what to buy and sell or how to allocate your portfolio to those that provide good, sound educational information that will make you a better investor. There are three basic types of websites that cater to investors: big portals like MarketWatch.com; brokerage websites that house your accounts; and subscription websites that provide detailed analysis, such as charts and editorial commentary, as well as buy and sell recommendations. Of course, no one website will be appealing to everyone. Yet the good ones, no matter what attracts you, should meet a basic set of criteria.

The Big Portals and Subscription Websites

Here are some important characteristics to look for in an information website:

- **Easy to use and access.** If it's not easy to navigate, you won't use it, no matter how good the information is.
- **News you can use and commentary that makes you think.** If a website is all about personalities and celebrities, it won't help you make money. Look for information that attracts you and that, if possible, makes something in your life or your investments more efficient, useful, and profitable, whether in time, money, or both.
- **Free real-time quotes and access to fundamental data for big portals.** If you're going to spend time reading an article, the site should

have access to real-time quotes and access to basic financial data for the securities that it's discussing. That way, if you find an interesting recommendation, you can start researching it immediately.

- **Good, insightful analysis and easy-to-understand buy and sell recommendations for subscriber websites.** If the site provides recommendations and model portfolios, make sure that they list their results. If you have to pay a subscription fee, you should be getting good information for your money.

Your Account Website

Your broker's website should have some basic but very important features. They include:

- **Security.** An easy-to-access, password-activated, hacker-proof site with high-level security.
- **Ease of use.** It should require a trading screen that's easy to move through and that warns you when your order has errors.
- **Real-time quotes.** You don't trade stocks without the latest prices. Last hour's quotes may look good but are useless when you are ready to pull the trigger.
- **Versatility.** You should be able to trade stocks, mutual funds, ETFs, and bonds on the same website.
- **Immediate confirmations. You** should always be able to confirm your trades before purchasing.
- **Real-time updates for your accounts.** You should know how much money you have every time you click that icon to refresh the page.
- **Customer service.** Access to 24-7 instant customer service, online, by chat, by phone, or all of the above, is a must.
- **Low minimum balance requirement.** This is a must for someone who is just getting started.
- **Access to specific buy and sell orders,** such as limit orders and sell stops, should be standard on your standard trading menu.

- **An automatic daily sweep** of any money that you don't have invested in the markets into a money market fund is essential.

Useful Investment Websites

There are hundreds of investment websites. But there are only a few that offer something special that makes them stand out from the rest. Here is a list of very useful sites and what makes them different from the rest of the pack. This is not a ranking list, but it is meant to provide a cross section of sites and to give you a variety of ideas as to what is out there.

MarketWatch.com (www.marketwatch.com). This is one of the original portals of online investing. Thus, it has stood the test of time. Aside from providing access to great information, such as company financials and real-time quotes, the editorial content, especially the analysis, opinion, and news reporting, is top-notch.

Investors.com (www.investors.com). This website is the online presence of *Investor's Business Weekly*. This site is all about trading and investing. You get a wealth of information about the stock market, individual stocks, futures, options, ETFs, and mutual funds. "The Big Picture" column is as good a daily market recap as there is. The site has free content but may be worth a subscription.

Investing.com (www.investing.com). This is a great website if you become interested in foreign currency trading. It has great access to global economic reports as they happen, although it focuses mostly on trading.

Yahoo! Finance (https://finance.yahoo.com). This is a big portal similar to *MarketWatch*. The major difference is that much of the editorial content is linked from outside sources, although these are high-level sources. Real-time quotes, great financial research on companies, and general news are also available.

CNBC.com (www.cnbc.com). Although CNBC has changed its format over the years, it's still the leader in business TV. Its website has interesting editorial content, which is more topic-focused and newsy than other financial websites. It also features commentary and reviews of important data from credible analysts with a proven track record.

The Motley Fool (www.fool.com). The "Fool" specializes in making financial analysis and recommendations easy to understand. It's a good place to get comfortable with analysis and the markets overall.

Morningstar (www.morningstar.com). This is a premier financial information site with special emphasis on mutual fund ratings and performance data. It's a great place to do your homework.

Crunchbase (www.crunchbase.com) is all about startups that are making their way to IPOs. This site features analysis on companies with cutting-edge technologies and new products on the market.

TradingView (www.tradingview.com) is an online trading community where traders exchange ideas and discuss trading topics.

Millennial Money (https://millennialmoney.com) is a blog which helps people learn how to reach financial independence at a young age.

CHAPTER 18

Investment Taxes

Everyone has heard the line about taxes and death being inevitable. It's true, and investments are no exception. It's important to know that, unlike other forms of taxation, investment taxes can be managed with some flexibility. That means that before you invest, you should find a good CPA or tax expert to help you make the best possible choices in this area. And while no one likes to pay taxes, the other side of the coin is that in investing, if you pay taxes, it's a sign that you are making money.

General Changes in the 2018 Tax Law

Before diving into investment taxes, it's important to recognize that the 2018 tax changes may affect all of your taxable income, and thus affect your ability to invest. Of course, everyone is different, so you should check with your CPA as to how the changes affect you specifically.

Generally speaking, the tax law expanded the tax brackets along with many of the rules for individual and corporate deductions. Some of the major changes include an increase in the standard reduction, an elimination of the personal deduction, and limited tax reduction for many individuals and married couples. The 3.8% investment tax associated with the Affordable Care Act remained but the penalty for not having health insurance was removed. Unfortunately, unless an extension is given, the current changes are set to expire in 2025. You can get all the details at the IRS website.

How Taxes Affect Your Portfolio

When you become an investor, you will join the ranks of those who toil on one side or the other of a long-standing tug-of-war between Wall Street and the US government. Wall Street fights hard to keep taxes on investments as low as possible. Uncle Sam wants a big chunk of it. So while your political preferences may lean one way or the other, the reality of it is that if you invest in a non-retirement account, you will pay taxes now. If you do most of your investing in an IRA, a 401(k) plan, or a similar retirement vehicle, you will pay taxes later.

There is no point in fighting taxes. Instead, it's better to focus your efforts on learning about investment taxes and to figure out how to legally pay the least amount possible. It makes sense to become familiar with the two ways the IRS will take their share from you: capital gains taxes and investment income taxes. Once you understand these concepts, you should go talk to your accountant and see how you can make the best of the situation.

Although any investment may be taxed at some point, most often you will have to deal with taxes on your American stocks, bonds, and mutual funds, as well as the effect of your tax-deferred strategies, such as your IRA, 401(k), and other retirement plans.

> **FACT**
>
> The tax changes which went into effect in 2018 reduced capital gains and dividend taxes based on whether you file jointly or as an individual as well as your income bracket.

Types of Investment Taxes

There are three general ways in which the government taxes investments: through capital gains, investment interest, and dividends. Company profits are, at least partially, passed through to shareholders, who choose to receive them either as a dividend payment or decide to have them reinvested in company shares through a dividend reinvestment plan (DRIP).

Capital Gains

A capital gain is what you receive when you sell a security, stock, bond, or other asset for a profit. Capital gains taxes differ based on your investment income, your tax bracket, and how long you held a security outside of a retirement account. Both short-term capital gains, which are applied to investments held less than a year, and long-term capital gains, those assessed on investments held more than a year, are based on your tax bracket. Thus, based on the 2018 tax law, individuals pay no capital gains taxes if their filing income is below $36,800. Joint filers pay no capital gains up to a filing income of $77,200. Single filers with long-term capital gains with income between $36,801 and $425,800 and joint filers between $77,201 and $479,000 pay a 15% tax while those with income above either $425,800 for single filers or $479,000 for joint filers pay 20%.

Interest and Dividend Income

Interest income, which you receive from your bank account, bond holdings, or money market fund, is taxed at your ordinary income tax rate. If you own municipal bonds, this may vary, so you should double-check this with your accountant.

Mortgage deductions are capped at $750,000 until 2025. Margin interest, which is the interest you pay on loans from your broker to buy stock, is still deductible on Schedule A, a special section of your tax return. Check with your CPA for more details.

Dividend income is taxed based on how long you own a stock and whether the dividend is "qualified" or "ordinary," based on the IRS definition of both terms, which is complicated and beyond the scope of this book. However, in general, the longer you hold the stock, the more likely you will pay a lower tax rate on dividends.

Specifically, the tax rate you will pay on ordinary dividends will be the same as your ordinary income rate and the rate you will pay on qualified dividends will be your capital gains rate. You can get the full details at the IRS website (www.irs.gov).

Crafting Your Investment Tax Strategy

The two major goals of a sound strategy are to keep as much money as possible in your pocket as you can, and to do it legally. In other words, avoiding taxes within legal means is acceptable; evading taxes is illegal and can lead to major headaches and even bigger penalties if it is discovered. Your best chance of achieving success comes from thorough discussion of the topic with your tax and investment advisors.

FACT

The 2018 tax cuts are temporary and are set to expire by 2025 unless Congress adjusts the law.

You may want to explore legal tax shelters, although the IRS and Congress are closing more of them as they look for more tax revenue and seek to reduce illegal tax reduction strategies and money laundering. Unfortunately, there is nothing anyone can do when Congress makes these changes except write their senator or representative. Fortunately, in many cases, some tax shelters which have been in place for some time may be exempt or phased out over time. Enforcement action is increasing, especially when it comes to offshore accounts and similar vehicles. Consider your mortgage and business expenses, and if you're feeling a bit more sophisticated, you may want to look at oil and gas limited partnerships.

How to Measure Gains and Losses

If you had a tough year investing, the only positive is that it is likely that you will reduce your tax bill. On the other hand, if you had big gains, get ready to pay a fairly good-sized tax bill, unless you've done some planning ahead of time. Start your tax planning in October. If you have some losing stock or mutual fund investments, you may wish to sell them to reduce your taxes.

By the same token, if you've had a big loss, consider selling some of your winners. This may sound counterintuitive, but you are actually locking in more of your big gains, as the losses essentially hide your gain from Uncle Sam. The net effect is that your losses, by offsetting your gains, reduce the amount of taxes you would pay for the winners.

The key to success in tax planning is being measured and thorough. Moreover, remember that taxes are an integral part of your investing plan. Knowing how you can reduce their effect on your portfolio's long-term growth, and doing all the legal things that you can to minimize their effect on your net profit, you will go further. Finally, remember that your first goal is investing for profit and long-term growth, not tax planning. Indeed, your best tax plan won't do you a bit of good without good investments that actually make you money.

Know Your Holding Period

The holding period, how long you actually hold an investment, is what decides how much of a capital gains tax you will pay once you sell it. It's not complicated, a rarity in the tax code. If you hold an investment for more than one year before you sell it, you will incur a long-term capital gains tax, which is a lower tax rate and is based on your tax bracket. If you hold an investment for one year or less, your holding period is considered short-term and you will have a short-term capital gains bill on it, which will be based on your tax bracket for ordinary income. If you bought XYZ mutual fund on March 1, 2017, and sold it on March 1, 2018, it's a short-term holding period. If you sell it on March 2, 2018, or later, it's a long-term holding period, which means you lower your tax bill by being patient.

Make the Most of Your Deductions

Many expenses related to your investment portfolio can be tax deductible. These can include phone calls to your broker or advisor, or any other expenses related to communication and fees. Here is a list of some of them:

- Trading account management fees
- Books, magazines, subscriptions to websites, apps, investment newsletters, or investment courses that you read or participate in to improve your financial management skills
- Travel expenses to meet your financial advisor or for an investment course
- Fees related to record keeping of your investments, account setup fees for your IRA, or custodial fees

Methods for Reducing Your Tax Liability

Okay, there is no avoiding the paying of taxes on your investments. If you make money, the government makes money. But you can pay the least amount possible if you make plans before you invest. The key is to understand the ups and downs of your tax strategy and to relate them to the particular circumstances of any investment while coordinating the effect of the investments on your overall taxes. The following section provides some excellent guidelines to get you on the right side of the dreaded tax issue.

Stocks

In order to make sure that your tax liability is correct, you must keep the confirmation slips of your stock trades, especially if you've bought shares of the same company at different times. When you sell the stock, determine whether you have a gain or a loss by subtracting the cost basis of your stock (the amount you paid plus commission) from the sale price. You must also note the holding period, or the length of time you held the stock, in order to determine whether you will apply the long-term or the short-term capital gains rate to the sale.

Here is an example:

Let's say you bought one hundred shares of the fictitious Walla-Walla Corporation (WW) for $1,000 in January 2016, including the commission costs. Your basis is $10 per share.

In March 2016, you bought another hundred shares of WW worth $2,000, including commission costs. This time your basis is $20 per share.

You like Walla-Walla, and it continues to shine, so in February 2017, you buy another hundred shares for $3,000, including commission. Your basis for this one is $30 per share.

Walla-Walla continues to do well, but in October 2018, it hits $50 and you think it's time to take some money off the table. So you have your broker sell one hundred shares.

Without further instructions, your broker will follow the IRS guidelines of selling the first-in, first-out shares. Thus, your shares from February 2017 will go. If you want to sell a particular set of shares with a better tax advantage, your broker will do that. No matter which shares you sell, you will receive $5,000.

The difference of your profit margin and your tax rate would come from the holding period. If you sell the January 2016 shares, your tax rate would be less since you held them for over two years (January 2016 to October 2018). That would give you a $4,000 long-term gain. The March 2016 shares would have a $3,000 long-term gain, while the February 2017 shares would bring you a $2,000 short-term gain.

Remember, your tax decisions should be based on your current needs if possible. If you have some short-term losses, you can use the short-term gains to offset them. If you don't have any transactions to offset, you can just use the long-term shares in order to pay the smallest amount of tax on this profitable trade. The key is to have this strategy thought out before you trade and to keep good records.

Mutual Funds

Mutual funds are a bit more complicated, as they have three different potential tax implications: dividend distributions, capital gains distributions, and gains or losses from selling of shares. Gains and losses from selling is the easiest to understand. If you sell shares for more than you paid for them, you will get a tax bill. If you lose money at the sale, you can use the loss, as you would with any other, to potentially offset a gain. Time factors for short-term or long-term holding periods are applicable as normal. You figure out the basis for your calculation as we did for stocks in the previous section.

Dividend distributions and capital gains distributions are a bit different. At some point during the year, often in the May-June and/or the November-December time frame for stock funds and sometimes monthly or quarterly for bond funds, your mutual fund will pass on capital gains and dividend distributions. Dividend distributions, per share, result from the dividends that the mutual fund collects on its holdings. Capital gains distributions are the proceeds from the funds' profitable asset sales. As these are passed on to you, you have to report them on your tax bill even if you receive the distribution in more shares of your fund holdings rather than cash.

FACT

The dividends from a municipal tax bond fund are usually not taxable. Also consider that if you are holding mutual funds, stocks, or any other investment that pays dividends or offers any other kind of distribution, these are tax-deferred, meaning that you don't pay taxes at the current rates. In that case, the distributions are best taken as shares of the mutual fund to increase your fund holdings.

Municipal Bonds

The interest income earned from municipal bonds, because states and municipalities issue them, is exempt from federal income taxes, just as the interest from federal securities is exempt from local and state taxation. As a result, municipal bonds pay lower interest rates than bonds that are fully taxable, such as corporate bonds.

Unfortunately, municipal bonds are not 100% tax-free securities. That's because even though the interest is lower, any capital gains or losses that you receive when you sell them are taxed based on the same rules for other assets, including your tax bracket and the holding period. That means that if you sell munis for more than you paid for them, you will pay taxes. On the other hand, if you sell them for less, you will have a reportable tax loss and can use that to your advantage.

Life Insurance

Although term life insurance is a good thing to have, it has little benefit other than in death. However, there are other special types of life insurance policies that may be useful as investment and tax advantage vehicles for you. That's because by choosing a whole life, universal life, or single premium policy:

- You can save for retirement. Instead of paying only for insurance, part of your premium builds cash value. The IRS does not tax these investment premiums.
- You can borrow from your policy. Once your policy builds cash value, you can borrow from it, and you don't have to pay it back. If there are loans outstanding at the time of death, they are deducted from the insurance payoff to your beneficiaries. Interest due on the loan may also be paid via the policy's investment income.
- Although this is not advisable for routine expenses, if you have a financial emergency, it is possible to use the cash value of your insurance policy to cover it. If you are faced with this kind of significant choice, check with your insurance professional and your financial advisor before making this type of decision. The bottom line is that this may be a good alternative to have in your arsenal.

Annuities

Annuities are another popular insurance-investment hybrid with big tax advantages. Annuities are structured so that your heirs will inherit the amount of money that you have put into the policy, even if it's lost money. What makes annuities even more attractive is that, similar to IRAs and 401(k) plans, they allow you to save tax-deferred until you withdraw funds.

Think of an annuity as a tax-deferred mutual fund or CD. It rises in value, but you don't pay the taxes until you retire. At that time, you can take out a lump sum or receive payments periodically. An important point to remember is that while you can deduct your contributions into an IRA or other retirement plan, you can't deduct money you put into an annuity. The other thing to remember is that annuities are usually expensive to buy and have large surrender fees. They also have expense and mortality risks (risk based on your risk profile, age, health, and so on). There are also annual maintenance fees that tend to be higher than those charged by mutual funds.

ALERT

Beware the penalties. If you cash out your annuity before retirement age, you are likely to run into steep penalties, also known as surrender charges. The best way to avoid this is to look into the details before you buy. All annuities are not created equally, and even some in the same categories will have different charges and structures depending on the company that issues them. Furthermore, if you withdraw from the annuity before age 59½, the IRS will tack on a 10% penalty.

Understanding Legal Tax Shelters

Technically speaking, all the actions that you take to reduce your taxes, whether offsetting gains with losses or making maximal contributions to your IRA, among other things, are considered tax shelters. In order to shelter your income from the tax collector, you can either defer the tax bill by contributing to your retirement fund or avoid paying taxes completely via tax shelters. You can shelter taxable income in many vehicles, including investments and special investment accounts, and by using planning strategies that lower your current taxable income or offer favorable tax treatments.

A very useful tax shelter often overlooked by novice investors is real estate. But it's a great tax shelter for one reason: the depreciation deduction you get on investment properties, especially rental properties. Depreciation is a calculation on paper that determines the loss of value in assets, such as real estate due to wear and tear. This allows the business to write off the cost of an expense over time, which means that instead of a one-time write-off, you can write off the cost over a longer period of time. This deduction increases your net income by spreading out the tax deduction over the life of the property.

Use your imagination and consider oil and gas investments, such as limited partnerships. They offer big deductions for drilling and exploration costs. The downside is that if the partnership does not find oil or gas, you will likely take some losses. This could leave you with some deductions but no income to offset them. Similar shelters include equipment leasing– and cattle breeding–related partnerships. You will have to go through a specialist investment advisor to find these in most cases.

The easiest ways to shelter your money from taxes are to:

- Hold on to your investments for longer than one year to reduce the capital gains tax rate.
- Put as much money as possible in tax-deferred investments, such as IRAs, 401(k) plans, and college savings accounts.
- Maximize your itemized deductions by including your investment-related expenses.
- Above all, work closely with your tax professional to shelter the maximum without breaking the law.

By being aware of the tax consequences of your investments, by keeping good records, and by knowing the rules ahead of time, you can craft an excellent set of strategies that will keep more money in your pocket, legally.

CHAPTER 19

Investing for Education

High education prices, from elementary school through college, will be around for the foreseeable future. Therefore it's never too early to start saving so that your kids will have a chance at a good higher education. Fortunately, there are several investment options that will help you to save for this important event without sacrificing your retirement. You can invest in state-sponsored 529 plans or set up your own plan similar to an IRA. You can even do both. The most important thing is to look at all your options and get started as early as possible, especially with all the advantageous changes found in the 2018 tax law.

Start Planning for Tuition Now

You can't go wrong by saving for your kids' school tuitions now. Even if you don't have children, start saving for their college tuition when you start thinking about having them, because your savings will have a chance to grow through the power of compounding. Consider that college costs can run from $10,000 per year to over $50,000. K–12 costs at private schools are also pricey.

Sure, this sounds daunting, especially if you have very young children or are in the planning stages. However, there are some great tools that can help you get a handle on this and to organize your planning.

Tax-Sheltered Education Savings Plans

Until 2009, the tax collector took a bite of any investments that you made to save for college. That changed with the American Opportunity Tax Credit program that lets you deduct a portion of your college costs under certain circumstances. The program was originally designed to grow college savings in a tax-deferred format and, in some cases, even without a tax bill. Because the 2018 tax law made some changes in parts of this act, consult your CPA for details as early as possible in the process, as these programs can be changed by Congress as time passes.

With these plans, you can grow your college nest egg in a tax-deferred format, save more, and have better choices when it's time to spend the money. Think of this as a similar process to saving for retirement, except the need for the money may come sooner and the money may be spent faster. By using this tax-deferred format, you can keep more of your money for your intended use: your child's college tuition.

You have to do your homework because not all college savings programs offer significant tax advantages. However, the ones that do are tailored so that one or more of these factors will apply. First, college savings accounts are not tax deductible. Second, the earnings on your investment grow tax-free. Third, the money is also tax-free when you withdraw it to pay for approved college expenses. You can get the details for what's specifically covered at the IRS website.

The 529 Plans

Qualified tuition plans, known as 529 plans, offer significant tax advantages. These state-sponsored plans revolutionized the college savings landscape. In 2018, the government expanded the scope of these plans so that the money housed in them can be used to pay tuition at elementary, secondary, private, or religious schools. There are two categories: savings plans, the most popular and commonly used type, and prepaid tuition plans.

> **ALERT**
>
> The tax laws limit the amount of money from a 529 plan that can be used for elementary, middle, or high school expenses to $10,000. There is no limit for college expenses.

The account holder, usually a parent or grandparent, sets up the account on behalf of the future student, also known as the beneficiary, and makes the investment decisions for the plan. These include investment choices, asset allocation, and risk management. There may be some limits on one or more of these functions depending on the particular state laws. When the need arises, you can use the money you've saved over the years to pay for education-related expenses, including fees, books, and other needs that meet the criteria in the state and conform with federal tax laws. The best aspect of 529 plans is that as long as you follow the rules and spend the money on what the plan allows, you won't have to pay federal income taxes. In most cases you won't have to pay state taxes either.

Review the limit of how much you may be able to contribute in your state. There are usually no income limitations, which means that if you are in an upper income bracket, you can still take advantage of these plans. The 529 plans are not federally tax deductible but you won't have to pay taxes on the earnings since they grow tax-free. Some states may give you breaks. In 2018 you could deposit up to $15,000 per year as an individual and $30,000 per year as a couple and claim the federal gift tax exemption. You can get more details at www.savingforcollege.com.

ALERT

Pay attention to what you spend your college savings plan money on. If you use it for expenses that don't qualify, you could receive a tax penalty on top of any other taxes you may have to pay. Read the fine print because there may be some key exceptions as to what's allowed.

There are some limitations to consider. For one, investment choices in 529 plans may be limited and the lifetime contribution limits range from $235,000 to $520,000. Some states may offer only one or two mutual funds, while others may offer as many as thirty choices. Also, you can only switch investment choices once per year. Finally, the fact that you have a 529 plan reduces the amounts that you can qualify for in other forms of financial aid.

Coverdell Education Savings Accounts

Coverdell Education Savings Accounts (ESA) offer tax advantages and flexibility, as the money can be used for any education-related expenses, including primary, secondary, and college educations. The contributions are not tax deductible, but the earnings on the account are tax-free when you use them for allowable expenses.

If an ESA makes sense, though, you would open the account at your local bank, brokerage, or other financial institution for each individual child. One child can have more than one ESA to their name, such as when different family members wish to contribute separately. Again, if you have any questions, the IRS website has all the answers.

Contributions are limited to $2,000 per child total. That means that if your child has three accounts, the $2,000 annual contribution must be split between the three accounts. Excesses, even if more than one party contributes them, will get you a tax penalty on any amount over the $2,000. You can't contribute to ESAs after the child turns eighteen, with the one exception being that you can contribute in the same year if you use the funds to pay for tuition.

The downside to ESAs is that they can severely limit or completely eliminate the amount of financial aid that your child can be eligible for. This is because an ESA account is considered your child's asset. This type of item on a financial aid evaluation goes to the minus column with regard to what your child might need.

Of course, there are other limitations. Your contributions are limited based on your income. As of the 2018 tax year, individuals who make less than $110,000 or couples with $220,000 adjusted gross incomes could make the full $2,000 contribution per child. Finally, the benefits must be completely used by the time the beneficiary turns thirty years of age.

Although ESAs have their limitations, the advantages make them worth considering. Here are the three major ones:

- You can use the proceeds for any level of education: primary, secondary, or college.
- You can open the account anywhere you want; invest the ESA in any type of investment, stocks, or mutual funds; and control it in any way you wish.
- You can contribute to both 529 plans and ESAs as long as you understand the rules, keep good records, and plan for the tax consequences.

Prepaid Tuition Plans: Are They Worth It?

If you're one of those people who likes to lock in future possibilities now, you may consider paying for your child's tuition ahead of time. You can do this through a prepaid tuition plan, which lets you pay now for tuition payments that you will get later. All states have different quirks and nuances with this type of plan, which is covered under the 529 umbrella.

The money you put in the plan today buys college tuition at today's public college rates and guarantees that price when it's time for the child to go to college, no matter what the cost is at that time. Some states offer a transfer value that allows you to pay some private college costs depending on whether the private colleges have agreements with the state. In order to have the guaranteed price, you sign up by the yearly deadline set by the state and then buy however many tuition units you want. For example, if your state charges $100 per tuition unit and you buy twenty units, you have purchased $2,000 worth of tuition in the future at today's prices. Before you open one of these accounts, you should check your college institution options, including both private and public. If you don't end up using the money, you can transfer it to another relative, or save it for grandchildren. In some cases you can get a full or partial refund. The downside is that these plans reduce your child's eligibility for financial aid, dollar for dollar. That means that if your child decides to go to a more expensive private school, you probably won't qualify for financial aid.

Plans vary widely from state to state, and while all states offer full prepaid four-year college tuition plans, many states let you pay for room and board costs through the same plan. Always check the individual state plan rules. You may be able to choose a plan from another state if it is better at meeting your needs. So which is the plan that is best for your family? Consider choosing a prepaid tuition college savings plan if:

- You don't like uncertainty.
- You lose sleep worrying about the future.
- Your tax bracket and circumstances will disqualify your family from financial aid.
- The school your child wants to attend is covered by a prepaid plan.

Finally, remember that if your prepaid plan doesn't cover all your costs, you can also set up an ESA. Between these two plans, you might put yourself in a better situation. Just because you have the two plans doesn't mean you will be upsetting any tax planning.

Education Bonds and CDs

Mutual fund–based 529 plans have had huge appeal during times in which the stock market has delivered high returns. But educational CDs and bonds will have a place, especially if you are a risk-averse saver or in periods of uncertainty. Always consider these vehicles as they offer you the opportunity for safety and portfolio diversification.

Education Bonds

Education bonds are issued by the US Treasury and are similar to savings bonds. Specifically, education bonds must be issued after 1989 and are series EE or I bonds. These bonds are different in their tax treatment from regular savings bonds, as your interest earnings will usually be completely exempt from federal income tax. Here are the rules:

- You must use the bond proceeds, interest, and principal to pay for the qualified educational expenses in the same year that you redeem the bond.
- You can't buy these bonds unless you are at least twenty-four years of age.
- You have to register the bonds in your name if you plan on using them for your own educational expenses.
- If you plan on using them for your children's education, you must register them in your name or your spouse's name.
- If you're married, you won't get the tax benefit unless you file a joint return.
- Your child can only be registered as a beneficiary, not as a co-owner of the bond.

Always check with your CPA or check online to see if there have been any changes in the rules. The US Treasury website (www.treasurydirect.gov) is also a good place to look for the latest information.

College Certificates of Deposits

A certificate of deposit is a long-term bank deposit that pays you interest over its life. Once you buy the CD, you can't withdraw it early without a penalty and you give up the interest payments that remain over the life of the deposit. In the case of a college certificate of deposit, the idea is similar, with some wrinkles. You still deposit a lump sum of money for a specified period of time. There is still a penalty for early withdrawal. The difference is that the interest rate paid is a college-oriented rate based on the Independent College 500 Index (IC 500), an index created by the College Board, the same people who put the SAT together.

This is the big picture. The IC 500 rate is considered the benchmark for the inflation rate of college expenses. Banks then link the return on the education certificates of deposit to reflect the annual figure of the IC 500. Although there are some standards to govern these instruments, you should always check before you sign on the dotted line to make sure you understand how your bank "links" the rate of return on the CD to the IC 500. The good thing is that the IC 500 rate is the lowest rate that an educational CD will pay. The rate could be higher.

FACT

The Independent College 500 Index is compiled from the costs of full-time tuition, room and board, and fees from the nation's most expensive not-for-profit colleges. The index is published once per year and is a measure of the change in costs on a year-over-year basis with information compiled from the schools that comprise the index. It's not a bad idea to check this out on a yearly basis at https://professionals .collegeboard.org.

The actual method of using these CDs is pretty simple. Once you've made sure you read the fine print and have all the details ironed out, you buy units. Each unit is the cost of one year's education. The minimum account to fund a unit is $500. You can buy the whole year at once or build it up over time, such as by using an automatic monthly savings plan. The beauty of the CD is that the money you deposit will grow at the same rate, or better, than the IC 500's year-over-year rate of change.

CHAPTER 20

Retirement Planning

It's never too early, or too late, to plan for retirement, but early is better. The longer you save and invest, the more time your money has to grow based on its own gains. The reality is that the traditional blend of social security, company pension plans, and job security standards no longer apply. This chapter is all about helping you hone your retirement planning skills and get ready to fund a big part of your own retirement through 401(k) plans and IRAs.

The Genius of Tax-Deferred Investing

Tax-deferred investing is so ingenious that it's hard to believe that Congress or the government had anything to do with it. In fact, it is nearly the complete opposite of everyday investing, where every dollar of profit made is fractured by taxes that must be paid to the government. Look at it this way: if you have a savings account that pays interest, at the end of every year, you give the government some of the interest as part of your tax bill. With a tax-deferred account, you still pay taxes. But you do so at a later predetermined time. The net effect is that your money builds up faster in the present, and you don't pay taxes on it until you withdraw it from the tax-deferred account.

FACT

A tax-deferred account is different from a tax-exempt account. The latter is an account in which you never pay taxes. A good example of a tax-exempt investment is the interest on a municipal bond. Remember that even tax-exempt investments may be taxable. If you sell a municipal bond for a profit, you still pay taxes on the capital gains.

The IRS will most likely tax the income and capital gains generated by your investments outside of tax-deferred accounts in the present. This general principle applies to stocks, bonds, mutual funds, and real estate. Even businesses and niche investments, such as collectibles, will generally have a date with the tax collector.

Thus, the allure of tax-deferred investments is that you can delay paying taxes, as long as you don't withdraw the money from the account. Even better is the fact that contributions to tax-deferred investments in most cases are tax deductible, either partially or completely. Of course, there are some notable exceptions, such as Roth IRAs or deductions that are phased out for higher-income taxpayers.

The downside is that early withdrawal from these accounts sets you up to pay some hefty penalties that really eat into the amount of money that you withdraw. In fact, most experts worth their salt will tell you that it's just not worth it to withdraw from a tax-deferred account until you reach retirement age, which may change in the future as life spans increase and government budget deficits make Social Security shrink.

ALERT

Beware of neglecting your retirement accounts. Too many people put money into their IRA or 401(k) plans and don't bother to look at what's happening to their nest egg. Just because it's a long time from the present to the time when you will need the money, and even though stocks tend to rise over long periods of time, you should apply the traditional principles of investing to your retirement plan. Always pay attention to your asset allocation, monitoring your returns with regard to how the markets are acting, and making sure that the accounting and the fees are correct and fair.

Finally, the money you put into tax-deferred accounts, such as 401(k) plans and non-Roth IRAs, is pretax money. That means that the money is deducted from your taxable income, so not only do you not pay taxes on the money you put into the account, your overall taxable income is reduced as well. To get more information on your marginal income tax rate and your maximal contribution to tax-deferred accounts, check out the IRS website.

It's Never Too Early to Start

This is not a deeply scientific or philosophical statement: the earlier you start investing, the more time you will have to maximize the amount available when it's time to retire. It's really a simple concept; you want to give your money the most time possible to become as large a sum as possible. Think about all the uncertainty that can happen in a lifetime. There will be economic booms and busts. There will be periods of dramatic changes in technology. And there will be wars, climate events, and periods of personal difficulties. The bottom line is that starting early gives your money more time to ride the ups and downs, and to recover from any significant surprises.

Let's say that you have two twenty-five-year-olds in similar jobs with similar earnings and similar access to a 401(k) plan. Ellie decides that she is going to start out right away, so she socks $2,000 per year into her plan for ten years, until she's thirty-five, and then never invests again. Rory waits until he's thirty-four before he gets started. He puts $2,000 in his plan for thirty years, and saves three times as much as Ellie. If they both earn 10% per year on average until they retire, Ellie ends up with $556,197 while Rory ends up with $328,988. That's because Ellie started earlier and let the markets compound her way to a better retirement fund.

They both did a nice job of saving. And they both ended up in better shape than many. But the numbers speak for themselves. The moral of the story is that by starting out early, you can end up in a much better place. To get an idea as to how compounding may work for you, visit www.investor.gov and search for the investment compounding calculator.

The 401(k) Plan

These hybrid DIY retirement plans have been around long enough now to have stood the test of time; 401(k) plans are set up by employers, and have largely replaced traditional pension plans, essentially shifting the burden of retirement, at least partially, to employees. If you use them correctly by investing in them early and staying connected to their progress, you can do quite well and have a tidy little, or big, nest egg by the time you call it quits from your job. Your company will give you a list of options where you can invest, and the money is pooled and invested into stocks, mutual funds, bonds, or other investments.

Here are some significant reasons not to miss an opportunity to start contributing to your 401(k):

- The money you save in the plan is earmarked for your retirement and is deducted from your pretax dollars.
- You get a tax deduction, and you don't pay taxes on the money in the plan until you take it out in the future.
- Employers usually match your contribution partially, as much as 10%, 25%, or even 50% of what you contribute. That means that just by the act of making your contribution, you trigger some free money into your account. The bottom line is that your employer's matching contribution is helping the growth rate of your investment at no charge to you.
- Because the money is in a retirement account, you won't get at it easily before it's time, and neither will the IRS. That means that it will have the best chance to grow and be there when you need it.

There is, as always, a downside. If you take the money out before a set date, usually age $59\frac{1}{2}$, the IRS will whack you with a hefty penalty. And as always, it's very important to know where the money is being invested and to keep tabs on what kind of return the plan is delivering.

Your 401(k) Investing Strategy

Retirement investing is all about the long term. That means that it's not as important to worry about weekly or monthly changes in the stock or bond market as it is to put money into the plan's money market fund from which you can make allocation decisions later. Nevertheless, there is no excuse for neglecting your nest egg and avoiding important decisions as they arise. The most important thing is to keep adding money to your account in regular intervals. The investment approach known as dollar cost averaging, where you put the same amount of money into some of the mutual funds in the plan in regular intervals, usually either monthly or quarterly, is ideal for 401(k)s. But it is also important to adhere to your risk profile and to follow good investment discipline as you would in any other investment.

That means that you should make sure that you know how each of the investment choices in the plan is working at any one time. And don't be afraid to make changes from one class of investment to another over time in order to get better returns or reduce risk, depending on the long-term trends of the markets. In other words, a 401(k) is no different than other investments when it comes to your responsibilities.

Especially dangerous may be the investment option available to some 401(k) investors, where the employing company's own stock is the major investment vehicle for the plan. If this is the case, the plan is only as good as the company's stock at any one time. If your company is faring well, your retirement is likely to do well during the period. But if things are not going well, such as if your company is in danger of bankruptcy or is having legal trouble, your retirement may be in jeopardy. It's not necessarily a bad thing to have some company stock in your 401(k), especially if that's how your employer contributes its portion to your plan. Think of that as free money. Just make sure that company stock is not the major portion of your investment or the only asset in your 401(k).

You Can Take It with You

You can't take your money when you die. But you can, and should, take your 401(k) plan with you when you change companies or become self-employed. If your new employer has a 401(k), you can have your current plan transferred or rolled over to a new account. Rolling it over, or having it directly transferred from one trustee to another, will save you 20% that would be levied on the money if you take possession of the money in the plan yourself. If you take possession of the money but don't reestablish it as a retirement plan with your new employer, you'll get hit with more taxes and penalties. Another negative is the fact that if you take possession and then restart the 401(k) elsewhere, you need to come up with the 20% that your old employer took out from your own pocket. If you become self-employed, then turn your 401(k) into an IRA.

No matter what you do, make sure that you avoid taking possession of the money yourself, and that you make all the rollovers, transfers, and establishing of new accounts within sixty days of starting the process.

Taking Money Out of a 401(k) Plan

This is tricky. Because 401(k) plans allow you to borrow from them, it's tempting to use them as piggy banks to fund down payments for a new home, or maybe to buy a sports car. Still, in most cases, you're just asking for trouble when you take out money tagged for retirement for short-term uses. Of course, if you are facing a life-or-death situation, such as your house is near foreclosure or you're hit with some unforeseen medical expenses, and you have no other means of getting through, your 401(k) is fair game, but not without cost. Early withdrawals are expensive, as you will have to pay the full tax bill on the money you take out, and a 10% penalty.

There is one loophole that could save you a big tax and penalty hit. If you borrow from your 401(k) plan under certain circumstances, you may not incur penalties or tax consequences as long as you follow the rules. However, there is a catch. You have to pay back the loan in full before you stop working for the employer who maintains the plan.

Here are the rules of engagement under normal circumstances: you can take distributions (withdraw money) from your plan without penalties starting at age 59½, whether you are retired or not. By the time you turn 70½, you have to take out the minimum required distribution.

Individual Retirement Accounts (IRAs)

IRAs are immensely popular because they allow you to save for retirement while deferring taxes, are very flexible in what you can use for investment vehicles, and come in two basic types: traditional and Roth. An even nicer touch is that in 2005, the Supreme Court ruled that IRAs are fully protected from creditors if you need to file for personal bankruptcy.

Traditional IRAs

The good thing about IRAs is that Congress, in its quest to make the Social Security fund last longer, periodically changes the rules to make it more advantageous to save for retirement through IRAs. For example, in 2008 your maximum contribution was $5,000. In the 1990s, the maximum that you could put in a traditional IRA was $2,000. As of 2018, you could contribute $5,500, or $6,500 if you were above age fifty, to your IRA. Married spouses can contribute to individual IRAs if they file jointly, even if only one spouse works. Contributions may be tax deductible depending on the situation and the current state of the rules, which do change from time to time. Your contribution can't exceed your taxable compensation for the year. You can find easy-to-use IRA contribution information at IRS.gov by searching for IRA information.

QUESTION

Can I save for retirement if I work part-time?
According to the IRS, anyone who works part-time can contribute as much as their total earnings, up to $3,500 per year, to an IRA.

As with 401(k) plans, you can start withdrawing your money at age 59½, and you must start withdrawing the minimum out of the account by the time you reach 70½. You will pay taxes at the current tax rate when you make your withdrawal, but only on the amount that you withdraw. And here is a bonus: your income level, even if you work part-time, is likely to drop when you retire. That will likely put you into a lower tax bracket.

You can start your IRA through a bank, a brokerage house, or a mutual fund family. Because there is stiff competition for your business, you should look for a no-fee IRA. Those are easy to find through the big mutual fund families and brokerages. Banks tend to offer fewer options, and may have higher fees. And with a mutual fund or brokerage firm, you will have a greater opportunity to tweak your asset allocation and to manage your portfolio according to market conditions and your risk profile. Don't be too passive with this money. Consider taking some risks if it suits your risk profile. But always be aware that with unmanaged risk you could incur big losses. As a general rule, keeping an eye on your IRA on a weekly, monthly, or quarterly basis makes more sense than minding the store every five years. There is no substitute for knowing what you need to know when you need to know it.

Roth IRAs

These IRAs have been around since 1998, and they offer a different approach to retirement savings. Because you pay the taxes on the contributions as you add the money to the account, you don't pay taxes when you make withdrawals. Your contributions are also not tax deductible as with traditional IRAs. The benefits of the Roth accounts are simple:

- You don't have to pay taxes when you withdraw the money.
- There is no minimum distribution requirement.
- If you are a young part-time worker or a college student, the Roth may make the most sense since your tax bracket will only go up as you get older. With a Roth you can sock more away with less worry about paying taxes later.
- If you don't withdraw the money, you can pass the account to your heirs tax-free when you die.

Generally, the contribution limits are similar to those for traditional IRAs. However, they are subject to income levels, and they are subject to change. It's a good idea to get advice from your CPA or visit the IRS website for the latest information.

You can roll over money from a traditional IRA to a Roth account, but you should check with your tax advisor and make sure that it's a good idea to do so based on your current financial situation. If you can't deduct your current contributions but still have money available to save for retirement, you may want to use the Roth option, if you are eligible. Roth IRAs also make sense if you expect higher tax rates upon your retirement or if you think you might need that money before you retire. If you are uncertain about the future of tax rates, or the unknown keeps you from getting sleep, a Roth IRA may make sense for you.

If you decide to make the switch to a Roth, you can start by asking your current IRA custodian about your next step. They will provide you with a good analysis of your situation and send you the correct forms. Your CPA will also help. Make sure that you are well informed and comfortable before making the switch.

To Roth or Not to Roth: Which Makes the Most Sense?

The answer to the proverbial Roth IRA question depends on whether paying taxes now or later makes the most sense for you. And, as with everything else financial, what you do depends on your individual financial situation and expectations for the future. You can calculate your heart away. And you can research this until you are blue in the face or have carpal tunnel syndrome from punching your smartphone, tablet, or PC keyboard looking for answers. Your CPA is also likely to generate some fees based on your query, while likely making the most sense as a source of assistance.

But here is the real answer: no one knows what lies ahead over the next thirty years. Politics, your health, and the general chaotic nature of the universe will influence what happens, no matter what you do. So keep it simple: whether you choose a traditional or a Roth IRA, you are making a good decision because you have decided to save for your retirement. So do your homework, talk to your accountant, and jump.

Health Savings Accounts (HSAs)

The Affordable Care Act changed everything with regard to health care. Even if the law is modified in the future, it is likely that higher deductibles and out-of-pocket expenses will remain, along with higher health-care costs. You should also consider the fact that Medicare benefits, disability requirements, and other forms of assistance, such as Medicaid, are also likely to change, probably toward the side of being less generous. That's why it makes sense to consider a health savings account. Here are the basic facts:

- With an HSA you can save money for your health expenses, much as you would save for retirement via an IRA or a 401(k) plan.
- You must have a high deductible health-care plan, with no other health coverage.
- Generally, the higher the deductible, the more you can save in an HSA.
- You can manage your HSA in a similar fashion to your IRA, and the money and the compounded earnings that you don't use will be there until your death.
- You must not be enrolled in Medicare. That means that you can no longer contribute to your HSA once you enroll in Medicare.
- If you die, your beneficiary receives the money in your HSA. If the beneficiary is your spouse, the HSA becomes your spouse's HSA. If your beneficiary is someone else, that person will pay taxes on the money in the HSA for the current tax year.
- You must not be listed as a dependent on someone else's tax return.

There are some different rules for employers, employees, and the self-employed with regard to HSAs. And there are likely to be some changes to these general requirements in the future as the health-care system dynamics change. You can get the most current details by reviewing Publication 969 from the IRS. There is also useful general information at the US Treasury's website.

Time and Focus Are Your Best Allies

There is an old saying that goes: "Youth is wasted on the young." Nonsense. That's just sour grapes from old people who have wasted their time. Youth, especially when it comes to retirement planning, is a blessing and an opportunity. That's because time is on your side and because, if you stay focused, you can learn from your mistakes and have the time to show that you have learned from them.

Here are some things that you can do and that will serve you well over time. Take advantage of all your tax-deferred opportunities. If you can invest in an IRA and a 401(k) simultaneously, do it. Even if you can't deduct both of your contributions, they will still grow tax-deferred. Plan for the worst-case scenario. Plan your retirement as if Social Security will not exist when you turn sixty-five. It will probably still be there. But if you've planned for the worst, you will make a better effort and be in a better position. Sometimes it pays to worry and plan ahead. This is one of those times.

Online and Discount Brokers

Included are the largest, most accessible discount and online brokers in the United States. The list is meant to help you get started quickly in your DIY investing. The list is purposely tilted toward the largest brokers because they tend to have the best online platforms, 24-7 support, easy-to-read tutorials, and well-trained reps who can help you get started or answer questions as you progress.

Charles Schwab
- www.schwab.com
- 800-435-4000

High volume and low prices from one of the biggest of the brokerage houses. Local branches located throughout the United States.

E*TRADE Financial
- https://us.etrade.com/home
- 800-387-2331

High volume, very popular site with low prices. Walk-in branches in several states.

Fidelity Investments
- www.fidelity.com
- 800-343-3548 or 800-972-2155

Fidelity Investments is an excellent hub for financial services. It manages nearly a trillion dollars in assets and offers brokerage services, mutual funds, annuities, retirement planning and advisory services. It has top-notch customer service and even offers weekend phone reps to answer questions and manage issues. Many investor centers located throughout the United States.

TD Ameritrade
- www.tdameritrade.com
- 800-669-3900

TD Ameritrade offers the thinkorswim trading app, which is a full suite of analytical and order execution services for active traders, including pro-level stock charts and access to wire services and news such as Bloomberg and CNBC. It has more than one hundred local branch offices nationwide.

USAA
- www.usaa.com
- 800-531-8722

A full slate of financial services including insurance, mutual funds, and retirement programs, is offered to current and former military personnel and their families.

Vanguard Brokerage Services
- https://investor.vanguard.com
- 800-349-5814

Vanguard Brokerage Services, unlike Vanguard mutual funds, doesn't mind if you trade in and out of securities. Otherwise they are a standard discount broker offering a wide variety of services.

Investment Publications

The Internet is full of websites that will provide you with excellent information, while others will waste your time and money. Some will give you big ideas, while others will help you to make investment decisions. As always, when choosing sources of information, consider your risk profile, your long-term goals, and your willingness to spend time tending to your investing program before you make any buy or sell decisions. This group of websites is a very good set of places to get started. And most of them have apps, mobile sites with excellent execution, or both.

Some of the sites listed are by subscription but are worth the money if you are really going to put in the time and effort. To help you decide which publications are the most useful to you before you shell out the money for a long-term subscription, you should check out the free sections of the websites or take advantage of the free trials. Among other resources, you can gain valuable insight about investing from the following:

The Wall Street Journal

The Wall Street Journal is the leading global newspaper with a focus on business. Founded in 1889, the newspaper has grown to a worldwide daily circulation of more than two million readers. In 1994, Dow Jones introduced *The Wall Street Journal Special Editions*, special sections written in local languages that are featured in more than thirty leading national newspapers worldwide. *The Wall Street Journal Americas*, published in Spanish and Portuguese, is included in approximately twenty leading Latin American newspapers. *The Wall Street Journal* offers digital-only subscriptions for less than $30 per month. You may be able to get student discounts and other lower prices.

▶ www.wsj.com

Barron's

Barron's is also known as the *Dow Jones Business* and *Financial Weekly*. With its first edition published in 1921, *Barron's* offers its readers news reports and analyses on financial markets worldwide. Investors will also find a wealth of tips regarding investment techniques and in-depth information here. *Barron's* may cost you $100 per year or more and is not the best place to start, but it is worth considering as you gain experience.

▶ www.barrons.com

Investor's Business Daily

Founded in 1984, *Investor's Business Daily* is a newspaper focusing on business, financial, economic, and national news. The publication places a strong emphasis on offering its readers timely information on the stock market and stock market–related issues. The online edition offers annual subscriptions for less than $300 per year or monthly subscriptions for less than $30 per month. It also has specialized publications which emphasize trading and investment styles which can be useful as you gain experience. The IBD app features real-time stock charts and news, similar in format to the website.

▶ www.investors.com

MarketWatch

MarketWatch offers news, financial market analysis, and personal finance information via well-written, easy-to-understand articles, blogs, and alerts. If it has to do with money, it will get covered here. They even discuss mortgages and the housing market, interest rates, travel deals, seasonal shopping guides, credit card finances, retirement planning, and automobile ratings. There is also a mobile app with comparable content.

▶ www.marketwatch.com

Yahoo! Finance

Yahoo! Finance is a data-driven site with articles covering daily stock market activity, in-depth stock and mutual fund quotes, and information on listed options and commodities. It also covers more traditional financial topics via articles and blogs. *Yahoo! Finance* has an app which is similar in content to the website.

▶ https://finance.yahoo.com

CNBC

CNBC.com is the traditional home of financial news. The website is the complement to the 24-7 cable television channel. It has ongoing news coverage and discussions along with after-market stock market discussion and trading shows such as *Mad Money* hosted by Jim Cramer and *SmartMoney*. You can get a quick overview of the markets here, and their programs will often have thoughtful analysis on key stocks and earnings reports.

The CNBC app is very useful, offering similar coverage to the channel via articles and blogs as well as market graphics for stocks, bonds, commodities, and currencies. Perhaps its best feature is the watchlist feature which lets you follow individual stocks and ETFs.

▶ www.cnbc.com

Value Line

This website offers in-depth ratings, reports, opinions, and analysis on stocks and specific sectors of the stock market, based on the activity in the Value Line Composite Index. The Value Line Composite Index is an index of 1,700 stocks compiled by Value Line, which is considered a reliable and broad index of the market. The Value Line Composite Index offers a look at a very broad selection of stocks and can be useful in gauging the health of the market beyond the S&P 500. This service is pricey, with a cost in the range of hundreds of dollars per year, and may not be suited for those on a budget, but it does offer professional-level data and research as well as mobile access, both of which may be useful as you gain experience and a bigger budget.

▶ www.valueline.com

CCN

This website is all about cryptocurrencies and blockchain. It includes quotes as well as news and blogs about this emerging financial sector. It updates frequently and should be a bookmark for crypto fans. Perhaps its best feature is the in-depth articles about the insider activities such as emerging platforms, the interaction between different factions of the crypto world, and the moves governments make as they adapt to cryptos.

▶ www.ccn.com

Crunchbase

This is a great place to go when you are looking to investigate small tech companies and startups. The site offers podcasts, news and analysis of IPOs, and information about private companies as they move toward IPOs. The premium service has features such as its search engine, which lets you explore *Crunchbase's* entire database of information. Once you find what you want, you can tag it in order to get alerts about the companies or topics.

▶ www.crunchbase.com

Glossary of Terms

Investing has a language all its own, but it doesn't have to be intimidating. The average investor only needs to know the basics, so if you have an understanding of the terms in this glossary, you're off to a good start.

annuity

A contractual financial agreement between you and an issuing company. You give the issuing company a certain amount of money, and in turn the company promises to invest your money and repay you according to the option or payment method that you choose.

arbitrage

The practice of taking advantage of the difference in price of the same security traded on two different markets. For instance, if Nortel Networks were trading at $100 (US) on the Toronto exchange and $99 on the NYSE, an arbitrageur would buy shares on the NYSE and sell them on the Toronto exchange.

asset

Anything you own that has monetary value, including cash, stocks, bonds, mutual funds, cars, real estate, and other items.

asset allocation

The specific distribution of funds among a number of different asset classes within an investment portfolio. Investment funds may be split among a number of different asset classes, such as stocks, bonds, and cash funds, each of which has unique risk and return characteristics. Determining just how to allocate funds depends on the financial plans of the individual investor.

average daily volume

The average number of shares traded per day over a specified period.

bankruptcy

A legal process where a party acknowledges that they are unable to pay their debts, and makes arrangements for those debts to be legally (if not financially) settled. The party declaring bankruptcy either allows their assets to be sold to repay creditors to the extent possible (liquidation bankruptcy), or works with the court to set up a plan to pay all or some of their debt over a period of several years (reorganization bankruptcy).

bear market

A market in which a group of assets (normally securities) falls in price or loses value over a period of time. A prolonged bear market may result in a decrease of 20% or more in market prices. A bear market in stocks may be due to investors' expectations of economic trends; in bonds, a bear market results from rising interest rates.

beneficiary

A person (or other entity, like a charitable foundation) who is named in a legal document (like a will or a trust agreement) to receive specific assets or to have the right to use specific assets.

bid price

The price a prospective buyer is ready to pay for a security. The term is commonly used by traders who stand ready to buy or sell security units at publicly quoted prices.

blockchain

Computer code used to describe and quantify data. It is commonly used to record transactions and as the basis for cryptocurrencies.

blue chip

A term used to describe companies that have established themselves as reliably successful over time, often by demonstrating sound management and creating quality products and services. Such companies have shown the capability to function in both good and bad economic times, and usually pay dividends to investors even during lean years. Most blue chips are large-cap, *Fortune* 500–type stocks like IBM or General Electric.

bonds

Loans from investors to corporations and governments given in exchange for interest payments and timely repayment of the debt. Interest rates are usually fixed.

budget

A detailed listing of income and expenses by category, usually prepared with an eye toward the future. Used by households and businesses alike to gain a tighter control over incoming and outgoing cash.

bull market

An extended period of rising securities prices. Bull markets generally involve heavy trading, and are marked by a general upward trend in the market, independent of daily fluctuations.

capital gain

The appreciation in the value of an asset that occurs when its selling price is greater than the original price for which the asset was bought. The tax rate on capital gains depends on how long the asset was held, and is often lower than the rate on ordinary income.

capital gains distributions

Payments to the shareholders of a mutual fund based on profits earned from selling securities in the fund's portfolio. Capital gains distributions are usually paid once a year.

cash flow

Financial term referring to the amount of cash left over after all current expenses, excluding long-term debt and taxes, are covered.

certificate of deposit (CD)

Money deposited with banks for a fixed period of time, usually between one month and five years, in exchange for compound interest, usually at a fixed rate. At the end of this term, on the maturity date, the principal may either be repaid to the depositor or rolled over into another CD. Any money deposited into a CD is insured by the bank (up to FDIC limits), making these very low-risk investments. Most banks set heavy penalties for early withdrawal of monies from a CD.

commission

A fee charged by a stockbroker (and, in some cases, a financial advisor) who executes securities trade transactions for an investor. This fee is generally a percentage based on either the number of shares bought or sold or the value of the shares bought or sold.

compound interest

Interest earned on the original investment (or deposit) amount plus any previously earned interest; effectively new interest is paid on already-earned interest. This helps the investment grow more quickly than it would with simple interest, which is applied only to the original investment amount.

cost basis

The total original purchase price of an asset, which may include items other than just the asset price, such as sales tax, commissions, and delivery and installation fees. This total amount is subtracted from the sale price of the asset to compute the capital gain or loss when that asset is eventually sold.

creditor

Any person (or entity) to whom you owe money.

credit risk

The risk that the principal you've invested through debt securities (like bonds) will not be repaid at all or on time. If the issuer of a debt security fails to repay the principal, the issuer is deemed to be in default.

cryptocurrency

An emerging currency category based on blockchain. Common versions include Bitcoin and Ethereum.

cyclical

When applied to the duration of markets, cyclical means a bull or bear market that lasts a short period of time, usually less than twelve months. An example of a cyclical bear market is the bear market which started in October 1990 and ended in January 1991.

default

To fail to repay principal or make timely payments on a bond or other debt investment security as promised. More likely to happen with high-yield corporate bonds (a.k.a. junk bonds) than other types of bonds.

discount broker

Brokerage firms that offer cut-rate fees for buying and selling securities, usually online or over an automated teleservice, although some also offer fax trade order options. Among the most prominent are Charles Schwab and TD Ameritrade.

diversification

The process of optimizing an investment portfolio by allocating funds to a number of different assets. Diversification minimizes risks while maximizing returns by spreading out risk across a number of investments. Different types of assets, such as stocks, bonds, and cash funds, carry different types of risk. For an optimal portfolio, it is important to diversify among assets with dissimilar risk levels. Investing in a number of assets allows for unexpected negative performances to balance out with or be superseded by positive performances.

dividend

A payment made by a corporation to its shareholders that represents a portion of the profits of the company. The amount to be paid is determined by the board of directors, and dividends may be paid even during a time when the company is not performing profitably. Dividends are paid on a set schedule, such as quarterly, semiannually, or annually. Dividends may be paid directly to the investor or reinvested into more shares of the company's stock. Even if dividends are reinvested, the individual is responsible for paying taxes on the dividends earned. Mutual funds also pay dividends, from the income earned on the underlying investments of the fund portfolio. Dividends usually are not guaranteed (except with certain types of preferred stock) and may vary each time they are paid.

dividend reinvestment plan (DRIP)

A plan allowing investors to automatically reinvest their dividends in the company's stock rather than receive them in cash. Many companies waive the sales charges for stock purchased under the DRIP.

dividend yield

The current or estimated annual dividend divided by the market price per share of a security. Used to compare dividend-paying shares of different corporations.

Dow Jones Industrial Average (DJIA)

An index to which the performance of individual stocks or mutual funds can be compared. It is a means of measuring the change in stock prices. This index is a composite of thirty blue chip companies. These thirty companies represent not just the United States; rather, they are involved with commerce on a global scale. The DJIA is computed by adding the prices of these thirty stocks and dividing by an adjusted number that takes into account stock splits and other divisions that would interfere with the average. Stocks represented on the Dow Jones Industrial Average make up 15%–20% of the total market.

due diligence

An in-depth examination of a company's business prospects. Used by investors to analyze prospective investments.

earnings growth

A pattern of increasing rate of growth in earnings per share from one period to another, which usually causes a stock's price to rise.

equity

Equity is the total ownership or partial ownership of an asset minus any debts that are owed in relation to that asset (like a home with a mortgage). Equity also refers to the amount of interest shareholders hold in a company as a part of their rights of partial ownership. Equity is considered synonymous with ownership, a share of ownership, or the rights of ownership.

exchange-traded mutual fund (ETMF)

An investment pool, similar to a mutual fund, whose shares trade over an exchange much like shares of stock. Most ETFs mirror a benchmark index, holding the securities tracked by that index.

financial advisor

A financial planning professional (typically licensed and accredited) who helps people manage their wealth. Functions may include preparing a retirement savings plan, devising tax strategies, and preparing an estate planning strategy, among other financial services.

foreclosure

A legal process that terminates an owner's right to a property, usually because the borrower defaults on payments. Home foreclosures usually result in a forced sale of the property to pay off the mortgage.

foreign currency exchange markets

Market where trading activity determines the value of a currency in relationship to other currencies. One unit of exchange is known as a pair. An example of a commonly traded currency pair is the value of the US Dollar/ Japanese Yen.

fundamental analysis

An analysis of a company's current and past balance sheets and income statements used to forecast its future stock price movements. Fundamental analysts consider past records of assets, earnings, sales, products, management, and markets in predicting future trends of a company's success or failure. By appraising a company's prospects, these analysts assess whether a particular stock or group of stocks is undervalued or overvalued at its current market price.

going public

When a company that has previously been wholly privately owned offers its stock to the general public for the first time.

good until canceled

Buy or sell limit order that remains active until canceled.

growth investing

An investment style that emphasizes companies with strong earnings growth, which typically leads to stock price increases. Growth investing is generally considered more aggressive than "value" investing.

hedge

Hedging is a strategy of reducing risk by offsetting investments with investments of opposite risks. Risks must be negatively correlated in order to hedge each other—for example, pairing an investment with high inflation risk and low immediate returns with investments with low inflation risk and high immediate returns. Long hedges protect against a short-term position, and short hedges protect against a long-term position. Hedging is not the same as diversification; it aims to protect against risk by counterbalancing that specific area of risk.

individual retirement account (IRA)

A retirement account that anyone who has earned income can contribute to. Amounts contributed to traditional IRAs are usually tax-deferred. Amounts contributed to Roth IRAs are not currently deductible but taxes are never levied on the earnings.

inflation

A general increase in prices coinciding with a fall in the real value of money, as measured by the Consumer Price Index.

inflation risk

The risk that rising prices of goods and services over time will decrease the value of the return on investments. Inflation risk is also known as purchasing-power risk because it refers to increased prices of goods and services and a decreased value of cash.

junk bond

A high-yield bond that comes with a high risk of default. Junk bonds are generally low-rated bonds and are usually bought on speculation. Investors hope for the yield rather than the default. An investor with high risk tolerance may choose to invest in junk bonds.

leverage

The practice of using borrowed money to invest or trade. Common forms of leverage include margin loans and lines of credit.

liability

An amount owed to creditors or others. Common personal liabilities include mortgages, car payments, student loans, and credit card debt.

liquidity

The ease with which an asset can be converted to cash at its present market value. High liquidity is associated with a high number of buyers and sellers trading investments at a high volume.

load

A sales charge or commission paid to a broker or other third-party when mutual funds are bought or sold. Front-end loads are incurred when an investor purchases the shares, and back-end loads are incurred when investors sell the shares.

margin

Trading financial assets with money borrowed from the broker who performs the transaction. Margin trading requires a special agreement between the investor and the broker and is regulated by the Federal Reserve. Brokers charge interest for margin trades.

market capitalization

The current market price of a company's shares multiplied by the number of shares outstanding, commonly referred to as "market cap." Large-cap corporations generally have over $10 billion in market capitalization, mid-cap companies between $2 billion and $10 billion, and small-cap companies less than $2 billion. These capitalization figures may vary depending upon the index being used or the guidelines used by the portfolio manager.

market risk

The risk that investments will lose money based on the daily fluctuations of the overall market. Bond market risk results from fluctuations in prevailing interest rates. Stock market risk is influenced by a wide range of factors, such as the state of the economy, political news, and events of national importance. Though time is a stabilizing element in the markets, as returns tend to outweigh risks over long periods of time, market risk cannot be systematically diversified away.

market value

The value of an asset if it were to be immediately sold, or the current price of a security being sold on the market.

mutual fund

An investment that allows thousands of investors to pool their money to collectively invest in stocks, bonds, or other types of assets, depending on the objectives of the fund. Mutual funds are convenient, particularly for small investors, because they diversify an individual's portfolio among a large number of investments, more unique securities than an individual could normally purchase on their own. Investors share in the profits of a mutual fund, and mutual fund shares can be sold back to the company on any business day at the net asset value price.

National Association of Securities Dealers Automatic Quotation (NASDAQ)

A global automated computer system that provides up-to-the-minute information on approximately 5,500 over-the-counter stocks. Whereas on the New York Stock Exchange (NYSE) securities are bought and sold on the trading floor, securities on the NASDAQ are traded via computer.

net worth

The value of all of a person's assets (anything owned that has a monetary value) minus all of the person's liabilities (amounts owed to others).

New York Stock Exchange (NYSE)

The largest securities exchange in the United States, where securities are traded by brokers and dealers for customers on the trading floor at 11 Wall Street in New York City.

price/earnings (P/E) ratio

A measure of how much buyers are willing to pay for each dollar of a company's earnings, calculated by dividing the current share price by the stock's earnings per share. This ratio is a useful way of comparing the value of stocks and helps to indicate expectations for the company's growth in earnings, most useful when comparing companies within similar industries. The P/E ratio is sometimes also called the "multiple."

price-to-book ratio

Current market price of a stock divided by its book value, or net asset value. Sometimes used to assess companies with a high proportion of fixed assets or heavy equipment.

quotation

The current price of a security, be it either the highest bid price for that security or the lowest ask price. Sometimes also called a "quote."

reinvestment

The use of capital gains, interest, and dividends to buy more of the same investment. For example, the dividends received from stock shares may be reinvested by buying more shares of the same stock.

risk tolerance

An investor's ability to tolerate fluctuations (including sharp downturns) in the value of an investment in the expectation of receiving a higher return.

rollover

Immediate reinvestment of a distribution from a qualified retirement plan into an IRA or another qualified plan in order to retain its tax-deferred status and avoid taxes and penalties for early withdrawal.

secular

Term which refers to the length of a bull or bear market. A secular bull market is one which lasts several years. An example of such a market was the bull market in stocks which started in 2009 and was still in place in 2018.

Securities and Exchange Commission (SEC)

A federal government agency that was established to protect individual investors from fraud and malpractice in the marketplace. The commission oversees and regulates the activities of registered investment advisors, stock and bond markets, broker/dealers, and mutual funds.

security

Any investment purchased with the expectation of making a profit. Securities include total or partial ownership of an asset, rights to ownership of an asset, and certificates of debt from an institution. Examples of securities include stocks, bonds, certificates of deposit, and options.

socially responsible investing

Investing in companies that meet an ethical standard by using a carefully employed screening process before purchasing any securities.

split

When a corporation increases its number of shares outstanding. The total shareholders' equity does not change; instead, the number of shares increases while the value of each share decreases proportionally. For example, in a two-for-one split, a shareholder with one hundred shares prior to the split would now own two hundred shares. The price of the shares, however, would be cut in half; shares that cost $40 before the split would be worth $20 after the split.

Standard & Poor's (S&P) 500 Index

A market index of five hundred of the top-performing US corporations. This index, a more comprehensive measure of the domestic market than the Dow Jones Industrial Average, indicates broad market changes.

stock

An ownership share in a corporation, entitling the investor to a pro rata share of the corporation's earnings and assets.

technical analysis

The use of charts and statistics to predict movements in securities prices. Technical analysis uses manual charts and computer programs to identify and project price trends in a market, security, mutual fund, or futures contract.

total return

The change in value of an investment over a specific time period, typically expressed as a percentage. Total return calculations assume all earnings are reinvested in additional shares of the investment.

underwriter

A person (or company) who distributes securities as an intermediary between the issuer and the buyer of the securities. For example, an underwriter may be the agent selling insurance policies or the person distributing shares of a mutual fund to broker/dealers or investors. Generally, the underwriter agrees to purchase the remaining units of the security, such as remaining shares of stocks or bonds, from the issuer if the public does not buy all specified units. An underwriter may also be a company that backs the issue of a contract by agreeing to accept responsibility for fulfilling the contract in return for a premium.

value investing

An investment approach that focuses on companies that may be temporarily out of favor despite strong success potential or whose earnings or assets are not fully reflected in their stock prices. Value stocks will tend to have a lower price-to-earnings ratio than growth stocks, and are considered to be currently undervalued, making them good investment "deals."

volatility

An indicator of expected risk, categorized by the range of price movement of a security. It demonstrates the degree to which the market price of an asset, rate, or index fluctuates from its average. Volatility is calculated by finding the standard deviation from the mean, or average, return.

yield

The return, or earnings, on an investment. Yield refers to the interest earned on a bond, or the dividend earnings on an equity investment. Yield does not include capital gains.

Index